# Transatlantic Spectacles of Race

# Transatlantic Spectacles of Race

## The Tragic Mulatta and the Tragic Muse

KIMBERLY SNYDER MANGANELLI

Rutgers University Press

NEW BRUNSWICK, NEW JERSEY, AND LONDON

Visit our Web site: http://rutgerspress.rutgers.edu

Manufactured in the United States of America

LIBRARY OF CONGRESS CATALOGING-IN-PUBLICATION DATA

Manganelli, Kimberly Snyder.

Transatlantic spectacles of race : the tragic mulatta and the tragic muse / Kimberly Snyder Manganelli.

p. cm. — (American literatures initiative)

Includes bibliographical references and index.

ISBN 978-0-8135-4987-3 (hardcover : alk. paper)

ISBN 978-0-8135-4988-0 (pbk. : alk. paper)

ISBN 978-0-8135-4991-0 (e-book)

1. Racially mixed women in literature. 2. Tragic, The, in literature. 3. Race in literature. I. Title.

PN56.W6M35 2012

809'.933522—dc23

2011023487

A British Cataloging-in-Publication record for this book is available from the British Library.

THE AMERICAN LITERATURES INITIATIVE

A book in the American Literatures Initiative (ALI), a collaborative publishing project of NYU Press, Fordham University Press, Rutgers University Press, Temple University Press, and the University of Virginia Press. The Initiative is supported by The Andrew W. Mellon Foundation. For more information, please visit www.americanliteratures.org.

*To Joe,*
*for showing me the ocean*

# Contents

# Acknowledgments

Tracing the textual genealogies of the Tragic Mulatta and Tragic Muse has taken me from archives in Charleston and New Orleans to libraries in London and Paris. It would have been impossible to study the transatlantic circulation of textual bodies explored in this book without the generous support of Cornell University's English Department and Clemson University's English Department and College of Architecture, Arts, and Humanities. The research travel grants provided by these institutions allowed me to visit the Historic New Orleans Collection's Williams Research Center, Howard-Tilton Memorial Library's Special Collections Division at Tulane University, the Louisiana Division of the New Orleans Public Library, the South Carolina Historical Society, the Schomburg Center for Research in Black Culture, the British Library, and La Bibliothèque Nationale de France in Paris.

This book, which began as a dissertation at Cornell University, was shaped by my advisors, James Eli Adams, Shirley Samuels, and Laura Brown, whose encouragement and expertise made the research and writing of this project such a pleasurable pursuit. I am especially grateful to Jim Adams for providing detailed comments on multiple drafts of the dissertation chapters. The project also benefited from conversations with Trevor Hope, Dorothy Mermin, Molly Hite, and Hortense Spillers. While I was an undergraduate and master's student at Auburn University, Paula Backscheider and Alicia Carroll provided the foundation in research and writing that prepared me for my studies at Cornell. I am also indebted to Jim McKelly, whose undergraduate class on the American novel introduced me to the beautiful complexities of

William Faulkner's *Absalom, Absalom!*, a work that continues to haunt and inspire me. These acknowledgments would be incomplete without also thanking Mary Ann Rygiel, my first teacher of Victorian literature, whose dynamic classes on Jane Austen, the Brontës, and Thomas Hardy inspired me to become a professor of English so I could share the works of these authors with my own students.

While in graduate school, both my life and research were enriched by the friendship of Shea Stuart, Sharyn Pulling, Joanne Campbell Tidwell, and Jessica Van Slooten at Auburn University, and Derek Matson, Zubair Amir, Katherine Terrell, Mimi Yiu, Ed Goode, Hilary Emmett, Mike Garcia, Jen Dunnaway, Akin Adesokan, Wyatt Bonikowski, Andy Rehn, Robin Sowards, Danielle St. Hilare, Jade Ferguson, Kate Hames, Ogaga Ifowodo, Susan Hall, Meghan Freeman, Dwight Codr, Shirleen Robinson, Anita Nicholson, and Janice Ho, at Cornell University. I am especially grateful to Sarah Heidt, Amber Baird-Baidinger, Alice Te Punga Somerville, Nadine Attewell, and Hyowon Kim for making my time at Cornell the experience of a lifetime.

At Clemson University, I have had the good fortune to join an English Department that has been a congenial, supportive, and intellectually invigorating environment for research and writing. In short, I thank all of my fabulous colleagues for making the English Department such a fun place to work. I owe special thanks to Sean Williams, my department chair, for providing funds for the reproduction of images in this book, Lee Morrissey, whose counsel and resourcefulness during his tenure as department chair were instrumental in shaping my career at Clemson, as well as Jonathan Beecher Field for always taking time to share articles and other materials related to my project. I am also grateful to Susanna Ashton, Catherine Paul, Martin Jacobi, Steve Katz, Clifton "Chip" Egan, Barton Palmer, Michelle Martin, Lisa Dykstra, Amy Monaghan, Aga Skrodzka, and Jillian Weise for encouraging and supporting me in innumerable ways. In addition to their well-timed pep talks, enthusiasm, and unwavering support, Rhondda Thomas, Dominic Mastroianni, Brian McGrath, Mike LeMahieu, Elizabeth Rivlin, Will Stockton, Erin Goss, and David Coombs took time to bring law and order to early drafts of the chapters that follow. I also thank my students, who read several of the books examined in this project, especially Deanna Dixon, whose directed study helped me reenvision the book's conclusion, and the students in my course on the English novel, who read *Daniel Deronda* with me each spring. In addition, I thank Aglaia Kargiatlis and Ashley Crider for providing summer research assistance, and James Funk for helping me in the final stages.

Leslie Mitchner, Katie Keeran, the editorial and production staff at Rutgers University Press, Susan Murray, and Tim Roberts at the American Literatures Initiative seamlessly guided this project through the publication process. I owe special thanks to Rachel Friedman for acquiring the manuscript, as well as the Andrew W. Mellon Foundation for their support of the American Literatures Initiative. In addition, I am grateful to Amanda Claybaugh and Cherene Sherrard-Johnson, the once anonymous readers of this project, for taking the time to offer invaluable detailed comments that helped me move the book in a new direction. I also thank *Victorian Literature and Culture* for publishing portions of chapter 5, and John Barton and Jennifer Phegley, editors of *Transatlantic Sensations*, for publishing chapter 3, and for granting me permission to reprint the material here.

Words cannot adequately convey the gratitude I feel toward my family. I thank Eppie, Charles, Lauren, Lindsey, and Erica Manganelli for welcoming me into their family and for their encouragement and support. I will be forever grateful to my parents, Barbara C. and R. J. Snyder Jr., for their love and support, and for always making education the highest priority. My mother, who was my first teacher and editor, gave me the most important gift a parent can give a child—a library card. Through our many trips to the Mobile Public Library, I fell in love with books. My father, whose work ethic I both admire and have tried to emulate, schooled me in common sense, while my sisters, Ashley and Tracey Snyder, make it impossible for me to take myself too seriously. I thank Ashley for keeping me company during my first research trip to New Orleans and Tracey for providing many of the treats I've enjoyed during the course of writing this book.

I must also thank the patron saints of this project. Nick Davis, master of analogy, provided the soundtrack for this journey. I thank him for always knowing when I most needed a phone call, a metaphor for the writing process, a half hour of laughter, or advice from his wonderful friend and mentor, Susie Phillips. I am enormously grateful to Cameron Bushnell and Angela Naimou for sharing their Friday afternoons, words, and wisdom with me, and for their willingness to talk through ideas and read drafts in their roughest forms. Their friendship has truly been a gift. Finally, I dedicate this book to Joe Manganelli, my co-conspirator in life, who has lived with this project for as long as I have. I thank him for taking this journey with me, for helping me move my seemingly infinite collection of books from the South to the North and back down south again, for telling me to take that first trip to Paris, and for the love and support that makes this and so much more possible.

Transatlantic Spectacles of Race

# Introduction: "I Thought That to Seem Was to Be": Spectacles of Race in the Nineteenth-Century Transatlantic Imaginary

*"My heritage!" It is to live within*
*The marts of Pleasure and of Gain, yet be*
*No willing worshiper at either shrine;*
*To think, and speak, and act, not for my pleasure,*
*But others'. The veriest slave of time*
*And circumstances. Fortune's toy!*
*To hear of fraud, injustice, and oppression,*
*And feel who is the unshielded victim.*

—ADAH ISAACS MENKEN, "MY HERITAGE" (1860)

In early July 1862, the American actress and poet Adah Isaacs Menken had just completed a successful run at the Bowery Theater in New York City, where she captivated audiences in a range of productions, including *The Three Fast Women, or the Female Robinson Crusoes*, *The French Spy*, *Joan of Arc*, *Lola Montez*, and the play adaptation of Byron's *Mazeppa*.[1] As the Tartar prince in *Mazeppa*, the role that would make her an international sensation, she cross-dressed, performed death-defying stunts on the trick horse Zofloie, and at the play's climax was stripped down to a nude bodysuit by enemy soldiers (fig. 1). With the press and public clamoring to know more about the young woman whose performance in *Mazeppa* shocked theatergoers and whose recent divorce from the boxer John Heenan made headlines, Menken decided to begin writing notes for her autobiography. Before heading to Boston for a two-month engagement at the Howard Athenaeum Theatre, she mailed the first installment of "Some Notes of Her Life in Her Own Hand" to Gus Daly, a friend and playwright living in New York, whom she asked to edit the notes into a book. As Daly explains in his introduction to the "Notes," which he published in the *New York Times* shortly after her death in 1868: "Everybody was asking, 'Who were you before?' The reckless girl was not averse to paying the penalty and gratifying this curiosity, but

FIGURE 1. A. Liebert, photograph of Adah Isaacs Menken. (R. Sheeley Collection.)

with a shrewd sense of justice, she was determined the public should pay for this knowledge which it sought."[2]

As several of her poems from the early 1860s show, the woman who would soon be christened "La Menken" by the American and European press was acutely aware of her commodification on the public stage. Her posthumous collection, *Infelicia* (1868), the title of which means unhappy or unfortunate, includes several poems, such as "Myself," "Gold," and "Sale of Souls," that reveal the unfortunate life of a woman on the stage. In "My Heritage," which was first published in the *Sunday Mercury* in June 1860, Menken responds to the following letter from J. W. Overall, a poet and critic for the *New Orleans Sunday Delta* and *Daily Delta*: "'Why are your letters so sad? Forget the world—laugh at poverty. Be glad and happy with your heritage of genius.'"[3] For La Menken, her heritage is not one of genius but one of commodification "within / The marts of Pleasure and of Gain." She portrays the actress as a victim of the public market, selling her emotions for the pleasure of those who attend her performances. In each of these poems, she emphasizes the commercial aspects of fame, lamenting in "Reply to Dora Shaw," a poem written for a fellow actress and poet:

> What though I frequent Folly's Fair,
> Where hands and hearts are often sold?
> What if my smile be the lightest there?
> When nearly viewed 'tis something cold.[4]

In "Myself," she also depicts the division between the actress's private and public selves when she writes: "I trim my white bosom with crimson roses; for none shall see the thorns. / I bind my aching brow with a jeweled crown, that none shall see the iron one beneath." These poems show not only her awareness of her body's market value, but also that "La Menken" is merely a mask. Although the poems in *Infelicia* seem to reveal the private self behind that mask, biographers from the nineteenth century to the present day have discovered that Adah Isaacs Menken was comprised of a multitude of mysterious selves.[5] As she muses in "Myself," "After all, living is but to play a part."[6] No truer words could be used to describe Menken's varied, adventurous life, in which she acted many parts for her public admirers and critics. In fact, Menken played so many parts that her biographers are still struggling to determine who she really was. Was she of Jewish ancestry or a free woman of color? Was she a tragic victim of the corruptive influences of stage life or a femme fatale? Although she describes herself in "My Heritage" as "Fortune's toy," an "unshielded victim" enslaved to "time and circumstances," the "Notes" that she sent to Daly, as well as the accounts of her life she provided in other essays and interviews, gave her the power to constantly refashion her identity.

Biographers have had difficulty uncovering the truth about Menken's past in part because she often fictionalized the details of her biography, playing on tropes of adventure tales and sensation fiction in accounts of her childhood and private life. In a biographical sketch published in *New York Illustrated News* in March 1860, Menken tells eager readers that she left her hometown of New Orleans to become a dancer "at the Tacon Theatre in Havana, before a 'respectable and wealthy old Cuban offered her his fatherly protection.'" She "became his adopted child," and upon his death, she inherited his "large estates in Texas."[7] Her biography then transitions into a captivity narrative in which she is "a white maiden seek[ing] protection" after she is kidnapped by "'Indians' on the Texas frontier . . . who are intent on making her the concubine of Chief Eagle Eye." The "white beauty" is rescued by Laulerack, an Indian maiden who "guides her to safety before falling victim to a gunshot wound inflicted by a group of traveling white men."[8] Two years later, Menken invented a new heritage for herself in the "Notes" she sent to Daly. Blending elements of the fairy tale and adventure fiction, her narrative opens in France, where her mother's "lineage could be traced to kings and princes." Her mother had a twin sister, but even though they "bore the same names . . . they could not be confounded by even the most casual observer. One a delicate blond[e], the other a Spanish-looking brunette. Both the same form, the same features, voice, gesture, expression, and yet so unlike." After the "dark" sister drowned in a boating accident, Menken's mother, the "delicate blond[e]," settled in New Orleans, where she married an American student whose father was a Revolutionary war hero.[9] As in her story of Laulerack, Menken displaces her own dark hair and eyes onto a figure of otherness who is then eradicated from the text. "Pairing herself with a woman of color," Daphne Brooks asserts, "became for Menken a way of undoing her own 'whiteness' while also producing it."[10] Although her body was subject to systems of racial and gender categorization, appropriating the popular genres of her day allowed Menken to "textualize" herself, and thereby redefine how her body circulated in the public market. As Daly observes, La Menken became the "eccentric heroine of her own life."[11]

Most of her biographers agree that she was born Adelaide McCord in 1835 in Milneburg, a town near New Orleans. However, attempts to verify her parents' background and racial heritage have produced a variety of answers. Was she the daughter of Auguste Théodore, a free man of color? Or was her father Creole and her mother of Jewish-Irish descent?[12] Menken claimed Jewish ancestry after moving to Cincinnati, Ohio, with her second husband, Alexander Isaac Menken, telling her husband's family that her father had been Jewish. However, one of her earliest biographers, the American sensation writer George Lippard Barclay, reveals that in 1863 Menken declared to "'a group of abolitionists' that her father had been a 'free man of color.' . . . There may be some substance to the claim, for she told Newell that 'I cannot, as the daughter of an octoroon, sympathize with the cause of the Confederacy.'"[13] However, there is also evidence that Menken publicly supported the Confederacy, even being arrested as a Confederate spy during her tour in Baltimore, Maryland. Other evidence that Menken may have been of African ancestry is her transformation of "Isaac" into "Isaacs," one of the few details that remains consistent throughout her history. Renée Sentilles explains that Menken's respelling of her name links her to New Orleans's *gens de couleur libres* and *plaçage* since "adopting a man's name with an added 's' or 'e' was a strategy practiced by the quadroon mistresses of white Creoles in New Orleans."[14] Was Menken really an octoroon passing as a Jewish actress, or was she merely signifying that her marriage to Alexander Menken was not legal since she had not divorced her first husband, W. H. Kneass? Although Menken wrote poems such as "Judith" and "To the Sons of Israel," and plagiarized the poems of Penina Moïse, a Jewish poet in Charleston, her efforts to convert to Judaism were rejected by the rabbi of the Menken family's synagogue. Although she was denied conversion, Menken continued to claim Jewish ancestry throughout her life, even "refusing to perform on Jewish holidays . . . and requesting a Jewish burial."[15]

In addition to her own self-fashioning, Menken's racial heritage has also proven difficult to determine because she lived during a time when mixed-race African American and Jewish identities, particularly as they related to femininity and national identity, were the subjects of debate in legal, scientific, and literary discourse. By midcentury, for example, Parliament emancipated Jews in England, scientists such as Josiah C. Nott published treatises arguing that miscegenation would lead to the "extermination" of both whites and blacks, and juries in New Orleans courtrooms were asked to determine the racial identities of such women as Sally Miller and Anastasie Desarzant.[16] In literature, however, the Tragic Mulatta and the Tragic Muse defied such categorization. Indeed, La Menken began her stage career when the Tragic Mulatta and the Tragic Muse were at the height of their popularity in nineteenth-century transatlantic culture. In 1855, Rachel Félix, the Jewish tragedienne known as the Tragic Muse, left her native France to embark on her first American tour. "Tragic Muse" gained currency in the late eighteenth century to describe the chaste and matronly actress Mrs. Sarah Siddons. By the mid-nineteenth century, however, the title connoted the exotic beauty and sexual power of an actress typically figured as Jewish. Immortalized in the works of Benjamin Disraeli, Honoré de Balzac, Charlotte Brontë, George Eliot, and Henry James, Rachel offered a new image of Jewish womanhood. Instead of the beauty and self-sacrificing virtue that many associated with Walter Scott's Rebecca, Rachel came to embody artistic genius, sexual agency, and financial autonomy, a dangerous combination that garnered both praise and condemnation in the press. As Sentilles notes, the attention Rachel's career and private life generated might have inspired Menken to fashion herself into a Jewish actress in the hope that doing so would elicit comparisons to France's Tragic Muse. Sentilles speculates that Menken "knew a marketable identity when she saw one and probably realized that Rachel's Jewishness contributed to the moral latitude she was given by American spectators."[17]

By the time Menken first appeared onstage in New Orleans in 1857, the Tragic Mulatta had become a cultural phenomenon as images and stories circulated throughout the Atlantic world of "almost white" slaves who either died in childbirth or were driven to suicide to avoid sexual violation. Menken's rise to fame came at the end of a decade in which Hiram Powers's luminescent statue *The Greek Slave* generated controversy at England's Great Exhibition (fig. 2), and Harriet Beecher Stowe's *Uncle Tom's Cabin* (1852) inspired British sensation authors such as Captain Mayne Reid, Dion Boucicault, and Mary Elizabeth Braddon to write their own narratives in which mixed-race slaves were rescued from sexual violation and death. Mark Twain, who saw Menken's performance as Mazeppa in San Francisco in 1864, compared the actress to Powers's *Greek Slave* in his review: "She appeared to me to have but one garment on—a thin tight white linen one. . . . With the exception of this superfluous rag, the Menken dresses like the Greek Slave; but some of her postures are not so modest as the suggestive attitude of the latter." In fact, toward the end of Menken's visit to San Francisco, spectators titillated by the display of the actress's white body encased in a nude bodysuit and strapped to a "fiery untamed steed" could also see the white body of the mixed-race slave Zoe exposed on the auction block in performances of Boucicualt's *The Octoroon*.[18]

*Transatlantic Spectacles of Race* examines the cultural power of the Tragic Mulatta and the Tragic Muse, two crucial literary types from opposite sides of the Atlantic. Traditionally, the Tragic Mulatta is considered an American figure that grew out of the abolitionist short stories Lydia Maria Child published in the *Liberty Bell*, while the Tragic Muse

FIGURE 2. Hiram Powers, *The Greek Slave*, modeled 1841–43, carved 1846, marble, 66 × 19 × 17 inches. (Corcoran Gallery of Art, Washington, D.C. Gift of William Wilson Corcoran, accession no. 73.4.)

and her literary predecessor, the Beautiful Jewess, are primarily figures from British and French literary culture.[19] In studying the movement of textual bodies produced through cultural exchange, this book navigates a space that in the nineteenth-century imaginary and, until recently, in literary studies has been viewed as a barrier between American and British cultures. Opening up a neglected dialogue between the Tragic Mulatta and the Tragic Muse—female figures historically confined to separate literary histories—I examine how these literatures create and disseminate racial concepts across cultures. For example, although the Tragic Mulatta has been described as the "quintessential American," I read her as a transnantional figure created by British, French, and American authors whose travel narratives and novels circulated transatlantically in the late eighteenth and early nineteenth centuries.[20] Indeed, I argue that the cultural phenomenon of the Tragic Mulatta cannot be understood unless American narratives are studied alongside British and French representations of this figure. Similarly, the commodification and racial ambiguity of the Tragic Muse cannot be understood unless this figure is examined alongside representations of America's mixed-race slaves.

Amid the backdrop of American sensation culture in the 1840s and 1850s, representations of the Tragic Mulatta and the Tragic Muse overlapped in the transatlantic imaginary. In 1840, the nineteen-year-old Jewish actress Rachel Félix, who would eventually be crowned France's "Tragic Muse," began rehearsals for Alphonse Lamartine's play *Toussaint Louverture.* When Rachel, accompanied by her father, met with the other actors from the Théâtre-Français for a vigorous read-through of the drama, the first act was admired. However, when it became clear in the second act that Rachel's character, Adrienne, was a *mulâtresse*, Monsieur Félix left the room abruptly, taking his daughter with him. Although she overrode her father's objection to her playing the role of a sultan's mistress in Racine's *Bajazet*, Rachel declined the role of Adrienne, the mixed-race niece of Toussaint L'Ouverture described as "an abandoned child, the fruit of a treacherous love."[21] Perhaps Rachel, like her father, realized that playing the role of a West Indian *mulâtresse* did not require an elaborate costume of embroidered slippers and bejeweled turbans (fig. 3). If she took the role of Adrienne, it would not be her costume, but rather her unadorned Jewish features that would create the masquerade. And there was a more disconcerting affinity at work. As an actress, Rachel inspired a literary type that embodied the dangerous erotic fascination of the femme fatale, but also depended on the commodification of that allure onstage, making her disturbingly akin to the prostitute—even, perhaps, to the female slave. Of course she could insist that her artistic power was under her control, and that within the world of exchange she preserved her own agency. But how secure was that distinction between the Jewess and the *mulâtresse*? Although both Rachel and her father attempted to distance her image from that of the fair-skinned slaves who were becoming popular characters in the literature of the period, nineteenth-century culture played out powerful resemblances between the mixed-race slave and the Jewess.[22] For example, the Currier & Ives portrait *The Beautiful Quadroon* (ca. 1872–74) exoticizes the nameless subject by evoking associations with the Jewess and the Eastern woman (fig. 4). Instead of the simple white dress typically worn by quadroons and octoroons in illustrations from Stowe's *Uncle Tom's Cabin* and Reid's *The Quadroon; or, A Lover's Adventures in Louisiana*, the woman in *The Beautiful Quadroon* is adorned with rubies, emeralds, and gold. The bejeweld headpiece, necklace, and gold threading in her vest elicit comparisons to such images as Scott's Rebecca watching the tournament in *Ivanhoe* (fig. 13) and Rachel costumed as Racine's Roxane in *Bajazet* (fig. 3).

Defining the cultural and social situations in the United States and Britain that produced the Tragic Mulatta and the Tragic Muse, this project explores the transatlantic performance, commodification, and circulation of African American and Jewish women in the public and domestic spheres. My exploration of the Tragic Mulatta and Tragic Muse shows that women faced a crisis of visibility in the public sphere. While white women typically embodied an ideal of womanhood by remaining safely ensconced in the domestic sphere, the mixed-race slave and Jewish actress were public women on display. Their racial difference rendered them spectacles of sexuality and desire on the auction block and the stage. As Shawn Michelle Smith explains, the Tragic Mulatta, by virtue of her blackness, is denied the privacy and protection of the domestic sphere. At any time, regardless of whether she was a free woman of color or a slave, the Tragic Mulatta could be ripped from the home and exposed as an item for sale on the auction block, where she was the ultimate example of commodified female sexuality.[23] A sexually imperiled figure, the mixed-race slave conventionally committed suicide either because she had been raped or to avoid violence from the men who read her mixed-race blood as a sign of her sexual availability. Stripped of sexual agency, the Tragic Mulatta was trapped within a narrative that offered only two choices—sexual violation or death. The Tragic Muse, however, retains a disconcerting autonomy.

FIGURE 3. Henri Grévedon, portrait of Rachel as Roxane in *Bajazet*, 1840. (Bibliothèque nationale de France.)

Whereas the mixed-race slave on the auction block typically refuses to meet the gazes of her spectators, the Tragic Muse solicits the male gaze. The literary figure inspired by Rachel embodied both artistic power and the dangerous magnetism of the exotic femme fatale. Linking feminine autonomy, erotic spectacle, and material exchange, the Tragic Muse incarnated forces seemingly inimical to domestic womanhood. She either spurned the protection of the domestic sphere, like Eliot's Alcharisi in *Daniel Deronda*, or redefined it to accommodate her, like James's Miriam Rooth in *The Tragic Muse*. Although she was also a raced figure of exchange, the Tragic Muse operated from a position of autonomy and self-commodification.

FIGURE 4. *The Beautiful Quadroon*, Currier & Ives lithograph, ca. 1872–74. (The Historic New Orleans Collection, accession no. 1970.28.)

La Menken relished the power of the Tragic Muse. Describing her performance in *Mazeppa*, she writes: "Whether it be resting on the bare back of the leaping, dashing steed, and whirled up the mimic mountains of peril and danger, or wielding the combat sword with an energy that causes the strongest man to cover in dread . . . it is always said: 'She plays with her very soul.'" Menken is "as wild and as earnest" when she is off-stage. "Woe to the unlucky creature who displeases me, or opposes me in look or deed," she declares. "Everybody strives to please me as slaves do a master."[24] In August 1860, however, Menken discarded the femme fatale image often attributed to the Tragic Muse after her union with Heenan ended in scandal when the boxer refused to acknowledge their marriage upon returning from a championship match in England. She announced a performance at Hope Chapel, but instead of giving the poetry reading her spectators expected, she delivered the personal essay "Self Defence," in which she argues for the "public" woman's right to privacy and lays claim to the "purity of womanhood." She is again a "white maiden seek[ing] protection," but instead of running from Chief Eagle Eye, she is trying to escape from "editors who . . . busied themselves in scattering obscene and infamous items, blasting the heart and reputation of women of whom they knew *nothing*, and who, if compared to themselves, would appear as the whiteness of immaculate angels!"[25] Arraying herself "in simple and girlish white," Menken presented herself as a tragic victim left pregnant and at the mercy of the press by a husband who refused to claim her.[26] Like the Tragic Mulatta, she is denied the protection of the domestic sphere because the public "seek her in her humble home, amid her sorrows and her desolation, and there try to crush out her life and purity." In language that evokes the image of Eliza in *Uncle Tom's Cabin,* who is chased across the icy Ohio River with her baby clasped in her arms, Menken declares, "I am hunted to the river bank, and must speak or perish." She is careful to remind her audience that she is not "striving to lay the groundwork of some thrilling romance, to be read by schoolboys and sentimental chambermaids, who revel in the genius of Cobb and 'Ned Buntline.'" She is not the heroine of a sensation novel, but "a woman . . . wearing the God-given crown of daughter, sister, wife and mother, [who] humbly comes before you to vindicate truth and reality." Menken's awareness of genre in "Self Defence" frees her from the "time and circumstances" of the Heenan scandal, allowing her to be both Tragic Muse and Tragic Mulatta, sensation heroine and victim in a sentimental romance.[27]

By examining literary representations of the Tragic Mulatta and the Tragic Muse, as well as travel narratives, diaries, journalism, and illustrations, this book extends beyond literary, racial, and national boundaries to explore how nineteenth-century genres, such as abolitionist and sensation fiction, were shaped by the different ways in which fascinated British, French, and American spectators represented the bodies of the mixed-race slave and Jewish actress. As Michael McKeon explains, "Genres are formal structures that have a historical existence in the sense that they come into being, flourish, and decay, waxing and waning in complex relationship to other historical phenomena."[28] Studies of poetry, reform novels, slave narratives, and Victorian fiction in recent transatlantic scholarship show how exchanges within Anglo-American and transamerican cultures influenced the development of literary forms and genres.[29] In French, the words "gens" (people) and "genre" (type) share the same Latin root, "gen," which means to beget or create. My examination of the Tragic Mulatta and the Tragic Muse in the chapters that follow shows how the racial and textual "genres" of these figures were created and how they informed each other as they evolved within the nineteenth-century transatlantic imaginary.

My study of the Tragic Mulatta begins with British and French travelers' accounts of concubinage between white colonists and mixed-race Creole women in Jamaica and Saint-Domingue. While the mixed-race woman was often depicted as a grotesque figure in the travelogues of British travelers, such as Edward Long and Janet Schaw, in the French accounts of Médéric-Louis-Élie Moreau de Saint-Méry, Baron François Wimpffen, and S. J. Ducoeurjoly, she is lauded as an "American Venus." Both French and British texts emphasize her sexual agency and economic power, but Moreau's narrative is one of the first to speculate that perhaps the *mulâtresse* has been condemned to "the state of courtesan."[29] While the mixed-race West Indian woman is typically represented in eighteenth-century travel narratives as a wanton opportunist, she becomes a racially and sexually imperiled figure in British and American fiction published after the Saint-Domingue Revolution, such as *The Woman of Color*, which was published anonymously in 1808, and Leonara Sansay's *Zelica, the Creole* (1820). In British and French travel narratives, the nameless mixed-race West Indian women had both financial and sexual agency. As we move from travel narratives to epistolary and gothic fiction in chapter 1, the West Indian woman becomes a named heroine within a courtship narrative. Like the various Codes Noirs that sought to circumscribe the mixed-race woman's economic and social power, these novels, I argue, reflect an attempt to control both her fortune and her sexuality.

From the West Indies, I turn in chapter 2 to the New Orleans custom of *plaçage*, an institution that allowed free women of color to arrange unions with affluent white men. By examining a range of texts, from legislation, travel narratives, and editorials in local newspapers to abolitionist and sensation fiction, we see how racial ambiguity coupled with sexual and financial autonomy rendered New Orleans's free women of color a fascinating yet dangerous attraction in the city. The descriptions of the *placées,* or mixed-race concubines, in the travel narratives of British and European tourists, including Frances Trollope, Harriet Martineau, Alexis de Tocqueville, and Karl Bernhard, Duke of Saxe-Weimar-Eisenach, reflect the ways in which the tourists' romanticized descriptions of the free women of color in New Orleans prefigured what would become the conventional Tragic Mulatta narrative. As travel narratives merged with the abolitionist movement, authors constructed narratives that combined the freedom, class status, and refinement of the *placée* with the imminent public exposure and sexual violation of the "fancy girl," or fair-skinned slave. Travel accounts and abolitionist fiction sensationalized the mixed-race woman's plight by comparing *placées* and "fancy girls" to the Eastern houri, an association which, as the Currier & Ives portrait *The Beautiful Quadroon* shows, emphasizes the Tragic Mulatta's racial ambiguity (fig. 4). But whereas death is often the only means of escaping sexual violence in abolitionist narratives, such novels as Joseph Ingraham's *The Quadroone; or, St. Michael's Day* (1840) demonstrate how the sensation genre frees the mixed-race woman from this fate.

Although literary history has maintained a national divide between British and American sensation authors, I argue in chapter 3 that American abolitionist fiction gave rise to British sensation fiction. As travel accounts of the mixed-race women in the West Indies and New Orleans gave way to the abolitionist fiction of Lydia Maria Child, Harriet Beecher Stowe, and William Wells Brown in the 1840s and 1850s, the Tragic Mulatta became a transnational cultural phenomenon. While Child's "The Quadroons" (1842), Stowe's *Uncle Tom's Cabin* (1852), and Brown's *Clotel* (1853) portray the Tragic Mulatta as a sentimental figure of true womanhood whose compromised bloodline prohibits her from marrying her white suitor, she is transformed into a mysterious figure in the 1850s and 1860s. In lesser-known British texts, such as Captain Mayne Reid's *The Quadroon; or, a Lover's Adventures in Louisiana* (1856), Dion Boucicault's play *The Octoroon* (1859), and Mary Elizabeth Braddon's serial *The Octoroon; or, The Lily of Louisiana* (1861), the mixed-race slave becomes an embodiment of dangerous secrets as British authors, seeking to capitalize on the popularity of *Uncle Tom's Cabin*, coupled abolitionist sentiment with narratives of detection and discovery.

Chapter 4 explores the ways in which the power of self-commodification allowed the Tragic Muse to transcend the violent narrative of the Tragic Mulatta. The first part of the chapter examines the construction and presence of the *belle juive*, or Beautiful Jewess, as a literary figure that dominated perceptions of the "dark" woman in Britain, Europe, and the United States.[30] Like stories of the Tragic Mulatta, narratives of *belles juives*, such as Maria Edgeworth's *Harrington* (1817), Sir Walter Scott's *Ivanhoe* (1819), and Sir Edward Bulwer-Lytton's *Leila* (1838), subjected heroines to violence, commodification, and sexual exploitation. In the figure of the Tragic Muse, however, the *belle juive* gained both power and sexual autonomy—sometimes turning into the dangerous femme fatale. The second half of the chapter studies the Tragic Muse figures inspired by the Jewish tragedienne Rachel Félix in Honoré de Balzac's *Cousin Bette* (1846), Charlotte Brontë's *Villette* (1853), Mary Elizabeth Braddon's *Rupert Godwin* (1867), and George Eliot's *Daniel Deronda* (1876). While the Tragic Muse attained the public voice, class mobility, and sexual freedom that the Beautiful Jewess did not, the narratives evoked forms of energy and mobility that needed to be disciplined. Ultimately, the Tragic Muse was forced to make a choice: remain on the stage and perish or retire to the domestic sphere as wife and mother.

When the Tragic Mulatta's popularity intersects that of the Tragic Muse at midcentury, a new woman is born: the Tragic Mulatta who refashions herself into a Tragic Muse. Chapter 5 explores how Charles Kingsley's *Two Years Ago* (1857) and Lydia Maria Child's *A Romance of the Republic* (1867) revise the Tragic Mulatta narrative, granting the mixed-race slave freedom from slavery and sexual exploitation. Instead of succumbing to suicide or infanticide, the usual culmination of the Tragic Mulatta's career, Kingsley's Marie Lavington and Child's Rosa Royal embark upon successful stage careers as La Cordifiamma and La Senorita Rosita Campaneo. By rewriting the Tragic Mulatta as an actress, Kingsley and Child imbue their tragic heroines with an agency and mobility that most mixed-race women did not possess. In representing the Tragic Mulatta playing the Tragic Muse, Kingsley and Child explore the efforts of female subjects to escape subjection and degradation through their talent as performers, which offers them a sense of autonomy denied within slavery, but at the same time estranges them from the conventional womanhood affirmed through marriage. But whereas Kingsley's Marie invokes a male fantasy of the mixed-race woman as an undisciplined body whose desire needs to be restrained, Child's Rosa is a female fantasy of a "true" woman who can survive a sexual fall and financially support herself outside of marriage. Despite their differing investments, these novels share the same conclusion: the Tragic Mulatta eventually abandons her identity as the Tragic Muse to marry her white lover and enter the "cult of true womanhood." Anxieties about mixed-race slaves passing undetected into the domestic sphere inspired a set of little-known works in the 1870s that transformed the Tragic Mulatta from a spectacular victim into an exotic femme fatale who passes for white. Whereas Reid's, Boucicault's, and Braddon's Tragic Mulattas were exposed on the auction block, the mixed-race femmes fatales use the artistic genius and entrepreneurial powers of the Tragic

Muse to victimize white femininity by exposing the secrets of their white rivals in Alexandre Dumas *fils*'s *L'Étrangère* (1876) and Florence Marryat's *Daughter of the Tropics* (1888). However, unlike the villainous sensation heroines that preceded them, such as Lydia Gwilt and Lady Audley, the Tragic Mulattas of the fin de siècle evolve into adventuresses or exotic femmes fatales to escape narratives that seem to insist on their social exile or destruction.

I conclude by exploring the raced "New Woman" as represented in Emily Marion Harris's *Estelle* (1878), Henry James's *The Tragic Muse* (1890), Frances Harper's *Iola Leroy* (1892), and Pauline Hopkins's *Contending Forces* (1900). Like their white "New Woman" counterparts, Harris's Estelle Hofer, James's Miriam Rooth, Harper's Iola Leroy, and Hopkins's Dora Smith and Sappho Clark struggle to redefine "true womanhood" and to reconcile professional ambition and financial independence with personal desires for marriage and family. However, before they can resist the restrictive values of Victorian womanhood, these raced "New Women" must first demonstrate their claims to a "true womanhood" that is often denied them and negotiate an appropriate social space for their unstable racial and social identities. But whereas Kingsley and Child's mixed-race heroines and the fin de siècle femmes fatales examined in chapter 5 surrender or conceal their racial identities to pass into the domestic sphere, the Jewish and African American characters at the end of the century make no effort to conceal their racial origins. Indeed, the conclusion investigates a unique moment in nineteenth-century culture in which these raced "New Women" no longer felt the allure of passing, a sentiment reflected in Menken's poem "Myself," in which she laments, "Away down into the shadowy depths of the Real I once lived. / I thought that to seem was to be." This book follows the attempts of African American and Jewish heroines to resist the conventional narratives—the "scripts," as it were—of the Tragic Mulatta, the Beautiful Jewess, and the Tragic Muse in order to, as Menken declares in "Myself," "be known as I am."[31] Tracing the movement from "my heritage" to "myself" in representations of mixed-race African American and Jewish women in the nineteenth-century cultural imaginary, *Transatlantic Spectacles of Race* investigates the powerful connections between the development and circulation of literary genres, the construction of racial identity, and the trafficking of female sexuality in British, French, and American marketplaces.

# 1 / "Stamped and Molded by Pleasure": The Transnational Mulatta in Jamaica and Saint-Domingue

*All her kindred, and most commonly her very paramours, are fastened upon her keeper like so many leeches; while she, the chief leech, conspires to bleed him* usque ad deliquium.

—EDWARD LONG, *THE HISTORY OF JAMAICA* (1774)

*So therefore it's really to the state of courtesan that the mulattas are almost generally condemned. . . . This illegitimate commerce that offends religious manners and morals is, however, regarded as a necessary evil in the colonies, where white women are in small number.*

—MÉDÉRIC-LOUIS-ÉLIE MOREAU DE SAINT-MÉRY, *DESCRIPTION TOPOGRAPHIQUE, PHYSIQUE, CIVILE, POLITIQUE, ET HISTORIQUE DE LA PARTIE FRANÇAISE DE L'ISLE SAINT-DOMINGUE* (1797)

*To begin at the very source of my misfortunes, they proceeded from the beauty of my mother.*

—LEONARA SANSAY, *ZELICA, THE CREOLE* (1820)

In February 1789, three years before the Saint-Domingue Revolution began, Baron de Wimpffen made the following appeal in his travel narrative: "Let us introduce good morals into Saint Domingo. Let the planters, instead of attaching themselves to those black, yellow, livid complexioned mistresses, who brutify, and deceive them; marry women of their own colour; and we shall soon see the country assume, in the eyes of the observer, a very different aspect."[1] Wimpffen, who later settled on a coffee plantation near Jacmel, cites the prevalent custom of concubinage between white colonists and free women of color as the source of the colony's corruption. However, by May of that same year, his impression of "those black, yellow, livid" mistresses seems to have changed. Offering his readers an insider's view of a "coloured ball," Wimpffen writes: "These female mulattoes, who dance so exquisitely, and who have been painted to you in such seducing colours, are the most fervent priestesses of the American Venus. . . . They join to the inflammability of nitre, a petulance of desire, which, in despite of every consideration, incessantly urges them to pursue, seize, and devour pleasure, as the flame devours its aliment." Although "on every other occasion, these furious Bacchantes . . . scarcely seem to have strength enough to drag along their limbs, or articulate their words," they do possess "some skill in the management of a family, sufficient honesty to attach themselves invariably to one man, and great goodness of heart. More than one European, abandoned by his selfish brethren, has found in them all the solicitude of the most tender, the most constant, the most generous humanity, without being indebted for it to any other sentiment than benevolence."[2] So who was the mixed-race West Indian woman such travelers as Wimpffen, Médéric-Louis-Élie Moreau de Saint-Méry, Edward Long, Lady Maria Nugent, and Janet Schaw encountered in Saint-Domingue and Jamaica: an American Venus, a *fille de joye* (prostitute), a *ménagère* (housekeeper), or perhaps a complex combination of all three? This chapter examines how contradictory images of white and mixed-race Creoles in French, British, and American travel narratives created the Transnational Mulatta, an imperial figure who preceded the imperiled Tragic Mulatta in the eighteenth-century transatlantic imaginary.

The origins of the mixed-race West Indian woman as a literary type cannot be traced back to one particular nation. She was a transnational figure created by British, French, and American authors whose travel narratives and novels circulated transatlantically in the late eighteenth and early nineteenth centuries. Although the mixed-race West Indian woman has been examined in scholarship of the British and French West Indies, few scholars have read British, French, and American representations of this figure against each other.[3] By reading the mixed-race West Indian woman as a Transnational Mulatta, we will see that travel narratives that preceded the Saint-Domingue Revolution were populated with contradictory stereotypes that represented this figure as a deceptive adventuress, a monogamous devourer of pleasure, and a skillful housekeeper. But in British and American fiction published after the revolution, such as *The Woman of Color* (1808) and Leonara Sansay's *Zelica* (1820), the mixed-race West Indian woman is transformed from an imperial adventuress into an imperiled heiress. In this chapter, I argue that the transatlantic circulation of stories about the horrors of the Saint-Domingue Revolution transformed the way that British and American authors represented the mixed-race West Indian woman. In both travel accounts and legislation published before and during the revolution, the mixed-race West Indian woman is a nameless, voiceless figure defined by her body. Represented as an unruly public body, she embodied both fears and fantasies of life in the colonies. In fiction published after the revolution, however, the mixed-race West Indian woman whose well-publicized participation in concubinage had posed such a threat to the economic and moral well-being of the colonists in Jamaica and Saint-Domingue is enveloped in a more controlled domestic narrative that replaces her agency with dependence upon patriarchal authority.

## "*Filles de Joyes*"

The characteristics of intemperance, indolence, and sensuality that French, British, and American writers noted in both white and black Creoles were attributed to the effects of the "always burning sun."[4] Wimpffen, however, concedes that although the climate has "an astonishing power," "this insalubrity is to be attributed more to the excesses to which Europeans usually abandon themselves on their first arrival here, than to any inherent ill qualities in the climate. It is their own intemperance which renders a residence here so fatal to them."[5] Regardless of whether the atmosphere of moral laxity in the West Indies was created by the weather or the excesses of the colonists, most travelers used climate differences to distinguish "inhabitants of the Torrid Zone . . . from people of the Temperate Zones."[6] In other words, the climate provided an avenue for travelers to distinguish between the colonies and empire. As Jennifer Greeson explains, the "moral universe of late-eighteenth-century imperialism . . . dictated that colonial, tropical societies were inherently degenerate, holding a station in the order of nature and nations subordinate to that of metropolitan societies."[7] In fact, descriptions of the climate often led to the racialization of white Creole women. Speaking of the "caprices" of white Creole women in Jamaica, Edward Long advises his readers not to judge them too harshly because "if we consider how forcibly the warmth of this climate must co-operate with natural instinct to rouze the passions, we ought to regard chastity here as no mean effort of female fortitude; or, at least, judge not too rigidly of those lapses which happen through the venial frailty and weakness of human nature."[8] Evoking the image of the Eastern harem, Wimpffen echoes Long's description in his account of the female colonists who "have so much the more merit in living chaste, as the example of the males, and the education they receive leave them absolutely without resource against the influence of the climate, and the dangers of an eternal idleness. They pass their lives either stretched at length or, *cbinta*, that is, sitting in the oriental manner on mats, where their supreme delight is to have the soles of their feet tickled by a female slave." For both British and French travelers, the climate was also a way of explaining how male colonists, in Nugent's words, "are almost entirely under the dominion of their mulatto favourites."[9] As the French writer Michel-René Hilliard d'Auberteuil explains, "Mulâtresses . . . have claimed for themselves, over most of the Whites [men], an empire founded on libertinage."[10]

Describing the custom of concubinage in Jamaica as "a crime that seems to have gained sanction from custom, tho' attended with the greatest inconveniences not only to Individuals, but to the publick in general," Janet Schaw says that "the young black wenches lay themselves out for white lovers, in which they are but too successful. This prevents their marrying with their natural mates, and hence a spurious and degenerate breed, neither so fit for the field, nor indeed any work, as the true bred Negro."[11] Before travelers such as Long, Schaw, and Moreau recorded accounts of the mixed-race women in their travel narratives, the mixed-race population was documented in legislation that attempted to regulate relationships between colonists and the black and mixed-race population. Karen Weierman explains that "in 1644 the Antigua Assembly passed a law forbidding 'Carnall Coppullation between Christian and Heathen,' the latter being defined as Negro or Indian." Bermuda passed a law in 1663 "banning marriages between 'his Maiesties ffree borne subjects' and 'blacks' in 1663," and, as Weierman explains, "Antigua was probably the only colony in the British West Indies to pass miscegenation laws in the seventeenth century."[12] As reflected in the accounts of Jamaica recorded by Long, Schaw, and Nugent in the late eighteenth century, attempts to legislate interracial relations had not slowed the growth of the mixed-race population. As Schaw observes, the "licentious and even unnatural amours" of the colonists "appears too plainly from the crouds of Mulattoes, which you meet in the streets, houses and indeed every where."[13]

While the British government legislated against interracial marriage and sexuality in the late seventeenth century, the French government encouraged it. In the 1660s, the focus of the legislation was to prevent concubinage between masters and slaves on plantations. In her examination of interracial relationships in the "libertine colony" Saint-Domingue, Doris Garraway explains that in 1669 Lieutenant General de Bass "instituted new punishments for masters who had children by their own slaves. In this case, the master would not only lose his mulatto child who would be freed, but also his female slave, subject to 'confiscation' by colonial authorities." While loss of "property" was supposed to punish the father, the Superior Council of Gaudeloupe "rescinded the provision for automatic manumission" a decade later in 1860 "on the grounds that it "encouraged the crime by rewarding the mother, whose offspring might be spared a life of slavery."[14] As Garraway explains, the Code Noir that was instituted in 1685 fined men "who had one or more children with their slave concubines to a hefty fine of two thousand pounds of sugar."[15] But in a revolutionary move, the Code went on to state that no punishment would be exacted if "the man, who was not married to another person during his concubinage with his slave, marries, in the form observed by the Church, his said slave, who will be freed by this means, and the children rendered free and legitimate."[16] The laws encouraging interracial marriage in the seventeenth century were contested by colonists in the early eighteenth century. In fact, as Garraway observes, in 1724 "the Superior Councils of the French Caribbean begged the royal authorities for the harsh antimiscegenation provisions contained in the Louisiana Code noir, and in 1727 the intendant requested a royal decree to suppress the second half of article 9, which pressured whites to marry their concubines."[17] Although the Code was modified by royal edict in 1733, a social tax was levied against those white men "guilty of *mésalliance*." As Colin Dayan explains, white men who participated in concubinage descended in rank and "were evicted from public life. King Louis XV declared that anyone 'who married a *négresse* or *mulâtresse* could not be an officer, or have any profession in the colonies.'" They were demoted to the status of the *affranchis*, or free people of color, and according to Hilliard d'Auberteuil, were viewed by the free people of color as inferior. Despite these measures, "three hundred white planters had married women of color by 1763."[18] Of the 500,000 people living in Saint-Domingue, as Garraway observes, there were "30,000 whites, an equal number of free nonwhites, and over 400,000 slaves." When the Saint-Domingue Revolution began at the end of the century, the population of free people of color in the colony exceeded free populations in other British and French islands in the West Indies.[19] "After all," Moreau notes, "the law is silent, while nature calls implacably."[20]

Despite the Code Noir, concubinage remained a visible and tantalizing part of life in the West Indies. In fact, concubinage was a phenomenon of the public sphere. Of the mixed-race women in Saint-Domingue, Moreau writes: "The greatest publicity accompanies her actions. Most of these women live with white men. There, under the little-deserved title of 'housekeepers,' they have all the functions of wives, without being much disposed to look after the duties of this office."[21] Although colonists often had a "charming spouse . . . who could have been the joy and felicity of his days," the traveler S. J. Ducoeurjoly explains, the white man "humiliates his sensible companion" and "makes a trophy of his victory, in all the eyes of the colony."[22] The large mixed-race population was not the only visual sign of this custom. Moreau observes that "the pride of the mulatto women consists above all in displaying their conquests. . . . Publicity, I repeat, is one of their sweetest joys and it is in pleasure that they find it, and to it is owed the custom, every evening, at bedtime, of seeing the colored girls set out from where they live, always lighted by a lantern carried by a slave, on their way to pass the night with the man they love the most—or who pays the best."[23] While Moreau's narrative is the only one to describe this public evening ritual, both French and British travelers reported on the mixed-race women's ostentatious display of clothing and jewelry, which offered a visual symbol of their fallenness.

Although writers visiting Saint-Domingue, Jamaica, Antigua, and Barbados recorded lengthy descriptions of the physical and moral qualities of the *mulâtresses* who seemed to enchant and control the white colonists, with rare exception, we almost never see the travelers interacting or conversing with the free women of color, and if they do so, the words of the women are never recorded. Indeed, Wimpffen goes so far as to tell readers that his knowledge does not come from firsthand experience.[24] Although Nugent does converse with the free women of color in her sitting room after dinner each evening during her visit to Jamaica, she does not provide any details of their individual histories. She simply writes: "Get to my room at 9.—Dismiss my mulatto friends as soon as possible, and go to bed. Several of them gave me their histories. They are all daughters of Members of the Assembly, officers, &c. &c."[25] Nugent does not need to provide a detailed history for her "mulatto friends" because by the time she was recording details of her visit in 1801, the plethora of travel narratives that preceded hers had already defined the narrative of the mixed-race West Indian woman. An embodiment of sexual and material excesses in the colonies, the West Indian *mulâtresse* was a figure created by travelers whose narratives sought to define and perhaps even undermine her sexual and economic power. But like Wimpffen's account, these narratives contained contradictory elements and differed depending upon the nationality and gender of the author.

Long's 1774 *History of Jamaica* reflects many of the contradictions that were often a part of the descriptions of mixed-race women in the

West Indies. Likening the black and mixed-race women in Jamaica to "common prostitutes," Long says that although the West Indian mistress might have one gentleman or "keeper," as he was often called, she uses his money to support both her family and her other lovers: "All her kindred, and most commonly her very paramours, are fastened upon her keeper like so many leeches; while she, the chief leech, conspires to bleed him" to death. She may be a financial leech, but as Long concedes, she is "in general, well-shaped, and . . . well-featured."[26] Comparing her to a stage actress, Long goes on to say: "In well-dissembled affection, in her tricks, cajolements, and infidelities, she is far more perfectly versed, than any adept of the hundreds of Drury." Although these women are in his words "lascivious," he admits that "considering their want of instruction, their behaviour in public is remarkably decent; and they affect a modesty which they do not feel." Although, according to Long, their modesty may be a public performance, he admits that they do "possess, for the most part, a tenderness of disposition, which leads them to do many charitable actions, especially to poor white persons, and makes them excellent nurses to the sick."[27] Like Long, Janet Schaw describes the mixed-race women as "wenches," "licentious," and "insolent" in her *Journal of a Lady of Quality* (1774–76). Providing a detail that has not been corroborated by other travel accounts, this lady claims that when a "a mulattoe child interrupts their pleasures and is troublesome, they have certain herbs and medicines, that free them from such an incumbrance, but which seldom fails to cut short their own lives, as well as that of their offspring. By this many of them perish every year." Yet, Schaw adds at the end of this account of abortion, "I would have gladly drawn a veil over this part of a character, which in every thing else is most estimable."[28]

In contrast to the grotesque view of the mixed-race women in British accounts such as Long's and Schaw's, French travelers romanticized the *mulâtresse*. She is not a lascivious leech but an American Venus who has "reduced voluptuousness to a kind of mechanical art," which she has "carried to the highest point of perfection."[29] While Long portrays her as a leech with many lovers, Wimpffen, as Garraway observes, defines the "erotic powers of the mulatto woman" through her ability to create "pleasure from her own resources, independent of her partner."[30] In other words, she does not need a "keeper" or lovers to "pursue, seize, and devour" the sexual pleasure Wimpffen implies. In a departure from British travelers, male French travel writers such as Moreau and Ducoeurjoly warned colonists that mixed-race women on the island were more sexually experienced. Moreau writes: "She also has what is definitely more dangerous: the talent for trying her hand at greater delights than even her partner could equal. She knows pleasures of which not even the code of Paphos," the birthplace of Aphrodite, "contains all the secrets."[31] Ducoeurjoly confirms this representation: "There is nothing that the male imagination can conceive when it comes to pleasure that the *Mulâtresse* has not presented, divined, accomplished."[32] Although Moreau says that "the entire being of a mulatto woman is given up to love, and the fire of this goddess burns in her heart, to be extinguished only with her life. This cult is her whole code, all of her votive offerings, her entire happiness," his ethnography of Saint-Domingue offers a new valence to representations of the *mulâtresse*. While his description echoes the rhetoric of voluptuousness and seduction in Long's and Wimpffen's narratives, Moreau's representation is one of the first to describe the *mulâtresse* as being "generally condemned to the state of courtesan."[33] Moreau describes concubinage as a necessary evil in the colony created by the shortage of white women, the undesirability of free men of color, whom Moreau characterizes as having a "lack of education and a jealous temperament," and, of course, the way in which the hot climate "irritates the desires."[34] In addition, unlike Long and Schaw, Moreau does not assume that all mixed-race women are fallen: "It should not be concluded from what I have said of the morals of the colored women that there are none who know goodness. Yes, there are some who by their conduct deserve to be taken as models. These are the ones who have at the least the right to expect credit for having resisted the example of their peers." He then goes on to say, "But these exceptions, are, sadly, quite rare."[35]

As Moreau and others observe, concubinage may have been a necessary evil, but it was also lucrative for both the *mulatresse* and her "keeper." Because her wealth was not legitimized by marriage but passed on to her as gifts or an inheritance from her white lover, the financial autonomy of mixed-race women undermined the patriarchal social order in the colony and threatened the imperial project. Wimpffen comments that those "female mulattoes . . . who join a spirit of economy to their other talents seldom fail of acquiring a fortune."[36] Although, as Moreau observes, the mixed-race mistresses invested most of their wealth in clothing and jewelry, the free women of color were so adept at managing the expenses of the households provided by their "keepers" that, toward the end of the eighteenth century, many colonists began to seek out wealthy free women of color for marriage. After all, concubinage provided a free woman of color with financial independence, but the only way a white colonist could gain access to her fortune was to marry her. Unlike Long, who depicts the *mulâtresse* as a leech bleeding both colonist and colony dry, Hilliard d'Aurberteuil, as Yvonne Fabella explains, "suggested that white men be taught to become wealthy through their own work, 'not in degradation, in the confusion of ranks [or] in the inversion of the public order.'"[37] For those white men who married free women color, by the 1760s, as David Garrigus explains, "women of color brought an average of 35 percent more property than their spouses to . . . [their] marriages while white brides brought slightly less property than their grooms."[38]

Since the distinction between mixed-race and white Creoles could not be created by a difference in wealth, French and British travelers attempted to differentiate the two groups of women in other ways. For example, Long and Schaw tell their readers that despite the hot sun, white Creoles retain their fair skin coloring. Reassuring his readers, Long writes: "Many of the good folks in England have entertained the strange opinion that the children born in Jamaica of white parents turn swarthy, through the effect of the climate; nay, some have not scrupled to suppose, that they are converted into black-a-moors. The truth is, that the children born in England have not, in general, lovelier or more transparent skins, than the offspring of white parents in Jamaica. . . . [T]hough exposed, as lively children necessarily must be, very much to the influence of sun-shine, their skins do not acquire the English tan, but in general grow pale, and of a fainter white."[39] While Long's account of the whiteness of the British colonists' skin is a scientific impossibility, Schaw offers her readers a more realistic reason, explaining that the women, whose skin is "as pure as the lily, and as pale," maintain the whiteness of their complexions because "from childhood they never suffer the sun to have a peep at them, and to prevent him are covered with masks and bonnets, that absolutely made them look as if they were stewed."[40] By emphasizing the whiteness of the colonists' skin, Long and Schaw inform their readers that the racial purity of the colonists has not been compromised by their proximity to slaves and free people of color in Jamaica. Long explains that the "bronze" West Indians his readers may encounter in England do not have a darker complexion because of "the fervour of the sun in the torrid zone." Long goes on to say: "The many Mulatto, Quateron, and other illegitimate children sent over to England for education . . . are often sent to the most expensive public schools, where the history of their birth and parentage is entirely unknown, [and] they pass under the general name of West-Indians. . . . But the genuine English breed, untainted with these heterogeneous mixtures, is observed to be equally pure and delicate in Jamaica as the mother country."[41] By attempting to reassure readers that the "genuine English breed" could be distinguished from those of mixed race, Long's statement reflects an anxiety that mixed-race West Indians could pass for white in England and threaten the purity of English blood by marrying into families who sought to improve their wealth by marrying their sons to a West Indian heiress.

In the colonies, Long suggests that making marriage to white Creole women more appealing would put an end to the custom of concubinage. After all, if white and mixed-race Creole women were essentially the same in behavior and even in complexion, what incentive did the white colonists have to marry within their race? Long explains: "We ought to remove the principal obstacles which deter them from marriage. This will be chiefly effected by rendering women of their own complexion more agreeable companions, more frugal, trusty, and faithful friends, than can be met with among the African ladies. . . . A proper education is the first great point. A modest demeanour, a mind divested of false pride, a very moderate zeal for expensive pleasures, a skill in economy, and a conduct which indicates plain tokens of good humour, fidelity, and discretion, can never fail of making converts. Much, indeed, depends on the ladies themselves to rescue this truly honourable union from that fashionable detestation in which it seems to be held."[42] The main obstacle to marriage, according to Long's description, is that the mixed-race mistresses are more frugal, trusty, faithful, modest, good-humored, and discreet than the white Creole women. If as William Beckford says, the wealth of the free people of color allows them to wear expensive "dress and ornaments" and "to disfigure themselves with powder and with other unbecoming imitations of the European dress," it falls to the white Creole women to create the distinction between the two races by dressing more modestly and living more frugally.[43]

Whereas British travelers struggled to articulate distinctions between the white and mixed-race populations, French visitors admitted that white and mixed-race Creole women were in fact very much alike. Offering this revelation as secret information, Wimpffen writes: "A female Creole, who has never been out of Saint Domingo, would be a creature of a particular species, were it not for the conformity which an education, similar in almost every instance, establishes between her and the female mulatto. Let this, however, be a secret between us: for you will easily comprehend that with the prejudices which exist here, such a comparison must be an inexpiable crime in the eyes of those whose dignity it compromises."[44] For Wimpffen, whose description of sameness racializes the white Creole women, the distinction to be made is between white women in the colony and those at home in France. In fact, Moreau transitions to the section of his narrative entitled "The Seductive Mulatto Woman," by simply saying, "Everything which I have written, in painting the white Creole woman suits [the mixed-race Creole] perfectly, if you refer to elegance of form and ease of motion."[45] In fact, whereas Beckford accuses the free people of color of imitating the whites, both Moreau and Wimpffen describe white women deliberately copying the behavior and manners of the *mulâtresses*. "Who would believe, by the way, that the women of mixed blood are often taken as models by the white women, in their careless reactions," Moreau asks. "It is surprising enough to see that in their attitudes, their bearing, and their behavior, many young Creole women consciously imitate the mulatto girls whom they despise so much." In fact, he says that the "greatest defects" of the free women of color are "their lack of education and their imitation of the vices and the ridiculous doings of the whites."[46] To reestablish their superiority, French colonists attempted to regulate the dress of free women of color. Laurette Ravinet recorded in her *Mémoires d'une Créole du Port-au-Prince* (1844) how the white Creoles appealed to the Superior Council of Le Cap to demand that something be done to distinguish them from the class of mixed-race courtesans. The council responded by issuing "an order that forbade this degraded class from wearing shoes. They then appeared in sandals, with diamonds on the toes of their feet."[47] In her account of the Saint-Domingue Revolution in *Secret History*, Leonara Sansay elaborates on this ordinance: "No woman of colour was to wear silk, which was then universally worn, nor to appear in public without a handkerchief on her head. They determined to oppose this tyranny, and took for that purpose a singular but effectual resolution. They shut themselves up in their houses, and appeared no more in public. The merchants soon felt the bad effects of this determination, and represented so forcibly the injury the decree did to commerce, that it was reversed, and the olive beauties triumphed."[48] Though Ravinet and Sansay may have exaggerated, their accounts emphasize the extent of economic power free women of color had in Saint-Domingue.

Since such ordinances were not a reliable way to define difference, the French devised other methods of distinguishing between white colonists and free people of color. Moreau's intricate racial taxonomy attempted to control uncontrollable shades of color by offering a list of racial gradations broken down into fractions. Meanwhile, Hilliard concluded that intermarriage and concubinage could not be prevented so he encouraged whites to marry those free women of color with the lightest complexions.

Fabella explains that he then proposed a "three-caste society based on colour, which would determine rank. The darkest-skinned people would be slaves, the lightest-skinned people would be full citizens, and those in between would be the intermediary class of 'Yellows.'"[49] Such a class system based solely on skin color would mean that no amount of wealth, education, or political power could help someone rise in class if they did not have white skin. Of course, when Saint-Domingue became Haiti, Dessalines solved the problem of racial distinctions in the 1805 Constitution, which decreed that "Haitians, whatever their color, would be known as *blacks*, referred to "only by the generic word *black*."[50] Mixed-race heroines, however, defied such "genre" constraints in epistolary and gothic fiction published after the revolution.

## From Mistress to Heiress

While the travel narratives of Long, Schaw, Wimpffen, and Moreau depict the mixed-race West Indian woman as a libidinous, avaricious mistress, she becomes a virtuous but sexually imperiled figure in British and American fiction published shortly after the Saint-Domingue Revolution.[51] As most histories of the revolution reveal, white, black, and mixed-race women were often the unnamed victims of violence during Haiti's struggle for independence. During Toussaint L'Ouverture's rule in the 1790s, stories circulated that the former slave had assembled a seraglio of white Creole women. In fact, when Napoleon's forces attempted to reclaim the island and restore slavery between 1800 and 1803, General Rochambeau, upon moving from "Port-au-Prince to Le Cap to take Leclerc's place . . . brought with him 'the old seraglio of Toussaint.' This 'infamous circle of fallen women' included those white women who had 'prostituted themselves' to 'the old negro.'" According to accounts, Rochambeau later struck out at the most powerful black and mixed-race people on the island by inviting the beautiful *mulâtresses* to a ball that took place while he "had their fathers, brothers, and imprisoned or suspected husbands drowned in a neighboring bay; then he had these women driven home in carriages by guides on horseback carrying torches" after informing them, "You just assisted in the funerals of your husbands and your fathers!"[52] The Tragic Mulatta grew out of this history of interracial violence in Saint-Domingue.

The West Indian mistress's transformation into an imperiled heiress in the novels of the early 1800s reflects an attempt to legitimize sexual relationships in the West Indies by transforming an erotic spectacle into a figure of ideal womanhood whose virtue, and perhaps most importantly, her wealth now made her suitable for marriage. As the examination of travel narratives in the previous section reveals, the mixed-race West Indian mistress threatened both colony and empire because her sexual and financial autonomy placed her beyond the reach of patriarchal control. However, when she is transformed into an heiress, she is placed in a narrative in which both her wealth and body are controlled by a courtship plot. Because she does not possess the autonomy of the mixed-race mistress, the heiress must rely upon a figure of empire to protect her body and wealth. In this section, I argue that the Tragic Mulatta emerges from this reimagining of the mixed-race West Indian woman in such novels as the anonymously published *The Woman of Color,* and Sansay's *Zelica, the Creole*, which call for France and Britain, in light of the Saint-Domingue Revolution, to redefine their relationships with their West Indian colonies.

Nineteenth-century British literature is replete with figures of mixed-race West Indian heiresses, such as Jane Austen's sickly Miss Lambe in *Sanditon* (1817), William Makepeace Thackeray's caricature of Rhoda Swartz in *Vanity Fair* (1847), and of course Charlotte Brontë's Bertha Mason in *Jane Eyre* (1847). In *The Woman of Color,* we see the transition from mistress to heiress in the author's description of the slave Marcia and her daughter, Olivia Fairfield. The author writes that "Marcia loved her master! She had not learnt the art of concealing her sentiments, she knew not that she was doing wrong in indulging them, and she yielded herself to her passion, and fell the victim of gratitude!" In becoming the mistress of Mr. Fairfield, Marcia's "understanding became enlightened, and her manners improved." In addition, she learns about Christianity and "starts with horror" at the crime she had committed in her concubinage with Mr. Fairfield. Marcia dies giving birth to Olivia, the heroine of the novel.[53] For Olivia, virtue is not something she must learn; it is an inherent quality. However, her father fears that she will be preyed upon by ill-intentioned suitors if she remains in Jamaica. Upon his death, he arranges for her to move to England with a dowry of "sixty thousand pounds . . . which is to become the property of [her] cousin Augustus Merton" a month after their marriage. If they do not marry, this fortune will be transferred to Augustus's older brother and sister-in-law, George and Letitia Merton. As Olivia tells one of her companions on the voyage, "Once I set my foot on your land of liberty, I yield up my independence—my uncle's family are then to be the disposers of my fate" (60, 66). Describing herself as a "mere state machine!" Olivia ironically notes, she was free in slaveholding Jamaica, but in England she and her inheritance will now become the property of a man she's never met (59).

Throughout the epistolary novel, the author highlights the ways in which various aspects of life in England embody the criticism often leveled against the West Indies. Instead of serving tea at breakfast, Mrs. Merton reclines on an ottoman like an "indolent" Creole and reads a fashion magazine. Olivia attends a ball with Augustus only to be gazed upon like the Hottentot Venus as one gentleman "placed his glass most leisurely to his eye" to examine her. While the men and women at the ball eyed Olivia "as if they had been admitted purposely to see the untamed savage at a shilling a piece," Olivia silently returns their gaze, providing the following scathing description:

> While Augustus was engaged in conversation at a little distance, I heard one of these animals say to another—
>
> "Come, let's have a stare at Gusty's black princess!"
>
> And with the greatest sang froid they slouched (for it could not be called walking) up to me. . . . As he looked, he said—
>
> Pauvre diable! How I pity him!—a hundred thousand wouldn't be enough for the cursed sacrifice!—Allons Alex. Let's 'keep moving.' (85)

Olivia maps onto the British attendees at the ball the stereotypes such travelers as Long and Schaw used to characterize West Indian colonists. These representatives of the British Empire are animals who slouch up to her and whose speech is broken with French phrases. Whereas the colonists' proximity to slaves and free people of color was believed to corrupt their speech and posture, Olivia attributes the defects in the demeanor of the British to France's influence. Olivia concludes after the ball, "I am disappointed in England: I expected to meet with sensible, liberal, well informed and rational people, and I have not found them" (88).

Although his peers render Olivia a racial spectacle, Augustus holds her in high esteem. And though he is the second son in need of a fortune, he is more enamored with her "numerous and unrivalled virtues and perfections" than he is with her dowry. They marry, but Olivia says that after saying their vows, "at the moment when I felt the hand of Augustus, a flash of vivid lightning came from the window over the altar; it was followed by a loud and tremendous peal of thunder" (93, 95). Many months of undisturbed happiness pass, but as in Brontë's *Jane Eyre* forty years later, this ominous flash of lightning eventually leads to the discovery that Augustus is already married. Both Augustus and his impoverished bride, Angelina, were the victims of Mrs. Merton. Unaware that his son had married Angelina, Augustus's father sent him to "Ireland to transact some commercial business of an urgent nature which would necessarily detain him some time." While Augustus was away, Mrs. Merton informed Angelina that "she had been . . . ruined by a villain, under the stale pretext of a false marriage" (177, 178). When Augustus returned, he was told that Angelina had died in a shipwreck.

Anticipating Tragic Mulatta narratives of the 1840s and 1850s, the author shows how Olivia is stripped of her domestic identity. Through Mrs. Merton's treachery, the heiress is no longer a wife but has been returned to the role of mistress. And, as decreed by her father's will, now that her marriage to Augustus is void, her fortune is transferred to Mr. and Mrs. Merton, who offer to let Olivia live with them but do not offer to return her fortune despite Augustus's pleas. As Olivia's black servant Dido observes, "My poor Missee was happy in our own dear Jamaica; there every body knew she was Mr. Fairfield's daughter—good Massa's child" (141).

Unlike other tragic mixed-race heroines, Olivia does not die of grief or commit suicide. Instead, she recasts herself as Augustus's widow and returns to Jamaica. Published shortly after Saint-Domingue became Haiti and Britain abolished the slave trade, *The Woman of Color* shows several ways in which the interracial relationship between Augustus Merton and Olivia Fairfield mirrors the relationship between England and the West Indies. In this text, we see that Olivia, a mixed-race West Indian woman, is celebrated as an ideal figure of womanhood, and Augustus Merton is portrayed as a progressive figure of England. Although he's the second son (with past misdeeds) in need of a substantial dowry, he does not seek to exploit Olivia. But his attitude is overshadowed by that of his mercenary family members who see Olivia as nothing more than her £60,000 inheritance, which they wish to appropriate for themselves. Although the Mertons rob Olivia of her fortune and the legitimacy of her marriage, Olivia's return to Jamaica offered nineteenth-century readers a new way of viewing the relationship between colonizer and colonized. Instead of suffering enslavement, violation, or death, Olivia returns to Jamaica, which we might read as a sign of her finally gaining the independence she desired but also as a call or warning to England that freeing Jamaica and Antigua might prevent the bloodshed witnessed in Saint-Domingue.

The American author Leonora Sansay traveled to Saint-Domingue in 1802 with her husband, Louis, to reclaim the plantation he'd sold to

Toussaint L'Ouverture before fleeing to New York to escape the revolution. Before Sansay and her husband returned to the island, which had since been reinvaded by the French to remove Toussaint from power and reestablish slavery, she had been assured by her former lover, Vice President Aaron Burr, that order would be restored in weeks. However, in an 1803 letter to him, she reports: "Do you recollect having told me, that order would be established here in less than three weeks after my arrival—alas we have beheld months after months passing away & we are still far from that tranquility so much desired—when Toussaint was arrested, it was suppos'd the war was finish'd & it would have been had vigorous measures been immediately pursued."[54] Sansay's epistolary novel *Secret History; or, The Horrors of St. Domingo* records the violent struggle between black revolutionaries and French forces. Published in 1808, four years after Dessalines declared Haiti's independence, her novel is told through the letters of Mary, who travels to Saint-Domingue with her sister, Clara, and brother-in-law, St. Louis, who has returned to the island in the hope of regaining the estate he lost during the early years of the revolution. As Michael Drexler explains, "Clara" was an alter-ego Sansay first created in her letters to Burr to describe her adventures on the island.[55] In *Secret History*, the Saint-Domingue Revolution becomes a catalyst that triggers Clara's escape from her jealous and increasingly abusive husband.

Sansay's depiction of white and mixed-race Creole women in *Secret History* adheres closely to the stereotypes readers would have encountered in the late-eighteenth-century travel narratives of Long, Wimpffen, and Moreau. Indeed, at many moments, Sansay seems to be paraphrasing Moreau, with whom she may have crossed paths in Philadelphia after he relocated there to escape the revolution. Other than a passing reference to Zuline, a mulatto girl who helps colonists escape the revolution by arranging passage for them to America, Sansay does not give detailed descriptions of mixed-race women in *Secret History*. She says only that "the mulatto women are destined from their birth to a life of pleasure" and contends that "to the destiny of the women of colour no infamy is attached; they have inspired passions which have lasted through life, and are faithful to their lovers through every vicissitude of fortune and chance."[56] Sansay's account of life in Saint-Domingue does, however, offer vivid details of the indolent fierceness, to borrow Laetitia Barbauld's words, of the white Creole women. Whereas Moreau speaks in generalities about the white Creole wife who will "In her jealous fury . . . do anything to serve her vengeance" if she discovers that a slave "has (perhaps as a result of her husband's command) defiled the marital bed," Sansay provides the following anecdote. "One lady, who had a beautiful negro girl continually about her person," Sansay writes, "thought she saw some symptoms of *tendresse* in the eyes of her husband, and all the furies of jealousy seized her soul. She ordered one of her slaves to cut off the head of the unfortunate victim, which was instantly done. At dinner her husband said he felt no disposition to eat. . . . She rose and drew from a closet the head of Coomba. The husband, shocked beyond expression, left the house and sailed immediately for France, in order never again to behold such a monster." As Elizabeth Dillon argues, one of the secret "horrors" of Sansay's *Secret History* is that everyone—white and black, man and woman—is implicated in the events that lead to the Saint-Domingue Revolution.[57]

A little over a decade later, the events Sansay described in *Secret History* appeared in a new form. In the 1821 novel *Zelica, the Creole*, the events depicted in *Secret History* are intertwined with the narrative of the eponymous mixed-race heroine whose white father supports the revolution, threatening to disinherit her if she does not marry General Christophe. In fact, the year before *Zelica* was published, Henri Christophe, who had proclaimed himself president and then King Henri I of northern Haiti, after Dessalines's murder, had committed suicide after suffering a paralytic stroke. Sansay may have seen the death of Christophe as an opportunity to refashion *Secret History* into a new narrative she could resell. However, because the epistolary structure has been removed and the new narrative revises Clara and St. Louis's relationship, depicting him as an inattentive rather than violent husband, Drexler questions whether Sansay wrote *Zelica*. Whether the author is Sansay or someone else reappropriating her work, the change in genre and narrative structure from *Secret History* to *Zelica* is worthy of consideration.

An epistolary travelogue with moments of gothic terror, *Secret History* is like many of the travel narratives of the period in its attempts to define differences between the white and mixed-race Creole women. *Zelica*, however, is a novel in which all efforts at categorization and differentiation are futile: French colonists are mistaken for British sailors, women disguise themselves as men, and whites paint their faces black to escape the revolution. In this gothic romance propelled by the threat of interracial sexual violence, the author subverts the typical Tragic Mulatta's narrative in which the mixed-race slave is threatened by sexual violation from white men who read her mixed-race blood as a sign of her sexual wantonness.[58] In Zelica's narrative, she and the white heroine,

Clara, are pursued by General Christophe and his fictional second-in-command, Glaude.

Indeed, no one knows that Zelica is the quadroon daughter of a former slave until the second volume of the narrative. While her name connotes an exoticism that elicits associations with the East, inclusion of "Creole" in the title of the book maintains the ambiguity of her racial identity since this term could refer to white, black, and mixed-race West Indian women. In addition, not only is Zelica virtuous, but she is also the legitimate child of her father. Though her mother was a slave, her parents married and Zelica was educated in France. The author concedes that Zelica "had not been deprived, by a long abode in France, of the gracefully indolent movements that are the distinguishing characteristics of the creole ladies—formed by nature to fascinate, and furnished by education with all the powers of pleasing. [She] was a perfect enchantress, but she appeared wholly insensible to the flattery or gallantry of [Clara's husband,] St. Louis."[59] Zelica also wholly rejects General Christophe's attempts to court her even though her father will disinherit her if she doesn't marry him. Faced with disinheritance or marriage to a man for whom she feels "an unsuperable dread," Zelica asks her father, a French colonist and fervent supporter of the revolution, "Why . . . is your unfortunate daughter the only creature whom you would deprive of the freedom of choice which you say is the inherent right of every human being?"[60]

Thwarting patriarchal authority in *Zelica* leads to economic and sexual peril for both the mixed-race and white heroines. Zelica is pursued by Christophe, who "panted to obtain [her], [but] even in his dreams [she] eluded [his] grasp."[61] Clara, whose husband rapes her and threatens to disfigure her with nitric acid in *Secret History,* is imperiled in Zelica by the sustained threat of Glaude's desire for her. In her construction of the black soldier's desire for the white heroine, Sansay's language reflects both the titillation and anxiety of an interracial union. She writes: "General Glaude . . . with his eyes fixed on Clara, could with difficulty resist the desire he felt to seize her at once, and bear down all the obstacles that opposed themselves to his happiness. During the day, his ever-ready hand had assisted her in moments of weariness. The guards were by his order continually seeking the finest fruit—the clearest spring to refresh her; and whilst love softened into an approach to civilization his wild and haughty character—his passion, hourly increasing in violence, resembled a torrent breaking down all the barriers that impeded its course."[62] To help Clara escape Glaude's plan to kidnap her, Zelica devises a plan in which they will switch clothes and Clara will go into hiding. The ability of Clara and Zelica to switch places reflects the ambiguous nature of Zelica's racial identity, as well as underscores the many ways in which these women, though from different races and nations, mirror each other. *Zelica* shows that, despite the efforts of travel narratives and Sansay's earlier novel to create distinctions between white and mixed-race women, there's no difference between them; they are both imperiled by patriarchy and empire. In the ending of *Secret History*, Clara escapes her abusive husband, and she and her sister Mary are reunited in Jamaica. Preparing for their return to Philadelphia, Mary writes to Burr, telling him: "Clara and myself will leave [Kingston] for Philadelphia, in the course of the ensuing week. There I hope we shall meet you; and if I can only infuse into your bosom those sentiments for my sister which glow so warmly in my own, she will find in you a friend and a protector, and we may still be happy."[63] There is no one—neither an American vice president nor a French colonist—to protect Clara in *Zelica*.

The novel's conclusion is precipitated by Dessalines's proclamation of Haiti's independence and that all Haitians would be referred to as black. To escape the violence that ensues, Sansay's characters attempt to seek passage to America. However, despite Zelica's plan to protect Clara, Glaude kidnaps her. When Zelica's father tries to free her, Glaude "plunged his sword into the breast of De la Riviere; and the dagger of De la Riviere had been so surely aimed at the heart of Clara, that she expired without a groan." Clara's death at the end of the narrative is unexpected, especially since this is typically the fate of a Tragic Mulatta figure like Zelica. When Zelica comes upon the bloody tableau in Sansay's novel, she attempts to exit the narrative through death: "She gave one wild heart-broken shriek, flew to the edge of the rock, extended her arms to heaven, and plunged into the waves."[64] However, she is rescued by a British ship, on which St. Louis and others first mistake her for Clara. Ironically, the ship captain tells St. Louis not to worry about his wife, "'Your wife . . . as an American lady, can be in no danger; they will not dare to offer her any harm." But in this narrative, the American lady is left behind in a grave in Haiti, a casualty of the revolution. Zelica, however, is reunited onboard with her French fiancé, who had come to Saint-Domingue in search of her. Once Zelica and her fiancé transfer to an American vessel, we are not told what their future holds. The way that Lastour clasps Zelica "to his breast with the violence of one resolved never again to forego his hold" implies that the interracial couple will be together when they reach the United States.[65] However, we are not told what Zelica's identity will be when she reaches America. If she and Lastour landed in New Orleans, as did many colonists and free people color escaping the revolution, antimiscegenation laws would prevent them from marrying unless Zelica passed for white, carrying the secrets of Saint-Domingue to the shores of America.

# 2 / "Fascinating Allurements of Gold": New Orleans's "Copper-Colored Nymphs" and the Tragic Mulatta

*There walks one, the representative of a class whose look and every movement, whose whole existence is love. Related by blood to two of the races into which the human family is divided, she is excluded from each, and stands alone. . . . She has known from childhood her true position, and might teach the Roman poet his own art.*

H. DIDIMUS, *NEW ORLEANS AS I FOUND IT* (1845)

*Many commit suicide: more die broken-hearted.*

HARRIET MARTINEAU, *SOCIETY IN AMERICA* (1837)

If the ship carrying Zelica and her betrothed, Lastour, had docked in New Orleans in April 1804, the couple from Leonara Sansay's novel might not have been allowed to disembark immediately. Like many other refugees from Saint-Domingue who immigrated to New Orleans in the early 1800s to escape the aftermath of the revolution, Zelica and Lastour might have been forced to stay on board as officials inspected the ship "in order to prevent 'the illicit entrance of negroes and colored people, coming from the Antilles, and particularly from San Domingo.'"[1] Jennifer M. Spear explains that members of the New Orleans city council "expressed apprehension over the abuses and dangers to 'Public safety' that could occur if 'colored people of all kinds and from all countries' were admitted into Louisiana. They sought a ban on all 'black or colored persons' from entering 'into this province under pretext of being servants or any other reason,' allowing exceptions only for those 'negroes decidedly recognized as uncivilized' who arrived directly from Africa and were uncontaminated by revolutionary ideologies emanating from the Caribbean."[2] The circulation of revolutionary ideas was not the only threat to "Public safety." The city council's willingness to admit Africans because they were "decidedly recognized as uncivilized," their unmixed blood making it easier to determine their legal status, reflects a larger fear that mixed-race refugees could potentially carry the racial secrets of Saint-Domingue into New Orleans. The fear that mixed-race free people of color, or *gens de couleur libre,* from the West Indies could pass into the white population undetected reflects the city council's anxiety that New Orleans citizens would be unable to read the bodies of mixed-race refugees to determine who was free or enslaved and, perhaps more crucially, who was white or mixed-race.[3]

Despite Governor William Claiborne's "attempt to prevent 'free people of Colour of every description' from relocating to Louisiana" because, as he declared, "We have already a much greater proportion of that population, than comports with our interest," the population of *gens de couleur libre* in New Orleans continued to grow in the early 1800s, increasing from "almost five thousand in 1810" to "fifteen thousand in 1840, mostly through natural increase, although manumission and migration continued to play minor roles."[4] The ambiguous racial and social identities of the *gens de couleur libre* captivated visitors to New Orleans. British and European writers who visited New Orleans in the 1830s, such as Frances Trollope, Harriet Martineau, Alexis de Tocqueville, and his traveling companion, Gustave de Beaumont, were fascinated by accounts of *plaçage*, an institution that allowed free women of color to arrange unions with affluent white men. As in Jamaica and Saint-Domingue, the free women of color were the most powerful members of the free population.[5] Indeed, the financial power and social status free women of color gained from the system of *plaçage* was reflected in the names given to streets in the French Quarter. Shirley Thompson explains that "although they've since been changed to correspond with Burgundy and Rampart Streets . . . Rue d'Amour and Rue des Bon Enfants (Love and Good Children streets) designated thoroughfares associated in public knowledge with the practice of *plaçage* and the partial inheritance of a white father's estate by his natural children of color."[6] However, as travel narratives merged with the abolitionist movement, accounts of *plaçage* mingled with descriptions of "fancy girl" slave markets where eager bidders paid more for a fair-skinned slave or "fancy article" than a good field hand. Visitors to New Orleans depicted the *placées* as women without sexual agency, thereby setting the stage for the development of the Tragic Mulatta in popular fiction of the 1840s. This chapter examines how free women of color were transformed in the cultural imaginary from *placées* participating in self-marketing and self-commodification to the stereotypical Tragic Mulatta, who had no sexual agency and possessed no ownership of her body.

Popularized in Lydia Maria Child's "The Quadroons" (1842) and "Slavery's Pleasant Homes" (1843), Harriet Beecher Stowe's *Uncle Tom's Cabin* (1852), and William Wells Brown's *Clotel; or, The President's Daughter* (1853), the Tragic Mulatta occupied a liminal space in which she was both a model of domestic virtue and a "public" woman on the auction block. Represented as being both white and black, chaste and wanton, free and enslaved, the Tragic Mulatta's mixed-raced blood was believed to imbue her with the fair skin and refined manners of her white sisters, but beneath the surface lingered a trace of Africa that supposedly incited passion and sexual wantonness. A sexually imperiled figure, the mixed-race slave committed suicide either because she had been raped or to avoid violence from the men who read her mixed-race blood as a sign of her sexual lassitude. Although Child has been credited with inventing the Tragic Mulatta in her 1842 story "The Quadroons," this chapter argues that the Tragic Mulatta emerged from travel accounts of British and European writers who visited New Orleans in the 1830s. In *Society in America*, for example, Martineau relates the story of three sisters, the daughters of a *placée*, who are taken from the protection of the private sphere upon the death of their parents and sold on the auction block as "fancy articles." While Martineau leaves her readers to imagine the ending of each sister's narrative because, as she explains, "where each is gone, no one knows," Brown expands upon this sensational episode in *Clotel*, his depiction demonstrating that death was the only means of escape from imminent sexual violation.[7] In their attempts to persuade readers of the horrors of slavery, abolitionist authors sensationalized the mixed-race slave's predicament, often comparing her plight to that of the Eastern harem slave. Joseph Ingraham's 1840 sensation novel *The Quadroone; or, St. Michael's Day*, which is examined in the final section of the chapter, traces the ways in which the Tragic Mulatta's narrative is transformed into an oriental romance. Although the abolitionist fiction of Child and Brown depicts the Tragic Mulatta as a figure trapped within a narrative that offered only two choices—sexual violation or death—Ingraham's novel demonstrates how the sensation genre frees the mixed-race woman from this fate.

## Placing *Placées* in Fact and Fiction

As travel narratives, newspapers, and literature from the early nineteenth century show, free women of color were one of the main attractions that visitors to New Orleans wanted to see. Indeed, in selecting the following passage from Maria Edgeworth's *The Absentee* (1812) as the epigraph for her chapter on New Orleans in *Retrospect of Western Travel* (1838), Martineau aptly summarizes travelers' attitudes toward the city's custom of *plaçage*: "Though every body cried 'Shame!' and 'Shocking!' yet every body visited them." These women, who in William Faulkner's words were "created of by and for darkness," were reluctant spectacles whom visitors, having already heard accounts of their beauty and their illicit liaisons, sought out to either admire or judge.[8] However, any attempt to search beneath the public image of the *placées* for information about the actual free women of color who inspired the imaginations of travelers and such authors as Child, Faulkner, George Washington Cable, Grace King, and Kate Chopin only reveals that these women were as nameless and faceless as Charles Bon's spectral mistress in Faulkner's *Absalom, Absalom!* Like the mixed-race West Indian woman, New Orleans's *placées* were a cultural construction, a fantasy. With the exception of some legal documents, such as wills that show the women inheriting portions of their lovers' estates and the records of court cases in which white family members contested this inheritance, it is difficult, if not impossible, to locate the real women behind the romance.[9] Thus, it is necessary to provide a brief historical background of the population of free women of color in New Orleans to establish how the mixed-race women were perceived and how they lived before they became the subjects of local folklore and legends.

Attitudes toward the *gens de couleur libre* and interracial concubinage shifted throughout the eighteenth century. When the French settled New Orleans in 1718, there were more white men than white women, so many of the settlers formed liaisons with Native Americans and slave women. As Caryn Cossé Bell explains, "the Code Noir and church doctrine forbade interracial marriage and concubinage," but by midcentury, "interracial liaisons were commonplace, and parish registers indicated the church's acceptance of social patterns within the city."[10] To try to address the problem of interracial unions, the French government transported marriageable girls, called "casket girls" because of the shape of their government-issued trunks, to New Orleans to become suitable wives for the colonists. However, the population of *gens de couleur libre* continued to increase as colonists freed their mistresses and mixed-race children. When the city became a Spanish colony in 1763, the free population steadily rose from natural reproduction, as well as from an influx of free blacks immigrating to America to escape the political rebellion led by Toussaint L'Ouverture in Saint-Domingue. During this period, the free women of color were described as a public nuisance. In fact, the Spanish governor Esteban Miró issued his 1786 Bando de buen gobierno, which "warned the free women of color that their idleness, 'resulting from their dependence for a livelihood on incontinence and libertinism,' would not be tolerated. He ordered them to employ themselves in honest labor, threatened to have sent out of the colony all who failed to do so, and further warned them that he would consider 'excessive attention to dress as an evidence of misconduct.'"[11]

Like similar ordinances in Saint-Domingue, Miro's Bando reflects anxiety about the finery, or more specifically, the economic status, that the free women of color's liaisons with affluent white men afforded them. Travel narratives written during the Spanish period depict the quadroons' dress in negative terms. Writing in the late eighteenth century, the physician Paul Alliot says that the free women of color "inspire such lust through their bearing, their gestures, and their dress, that many well-to-do persons are ruined in pleasing them." Here, the quadroons are opportunistic adventuresses who do not commit suicide or die brokenhearted, as Martineau would have them do. Instead the mixed-race concubines ruin their lovers financially, and when they "perceive that the men with whom they live have nothing more, they desert and abandon them, and take up with another [white] man. Those among them who have children, are very careful to rear them in the same sentiments."[12] The increasing wealth of the free population meant that many of them could afford to dress, house, and entertain themselves in a manner that matched, and in some cases exceeded that of white Creoles. When money and miscegenation made it difficult to separate the citizens of New Orleans into neat racial categories, Miro's Bando interceded by banning the free women of color from wearing jewelry and plumes.[13] Instead, they were instructed to go back to covering their hair with a brightly colored handkerchief, known as a toque, the purpose of which was to mark them as nonwhite.

This anxiety that the free population might become indistinguishable from the white Creoles is also reflected in ordinances regulating entertainment in the early 1800s. In 1800, the Spanish attorney general, Pedro Barran, petitioned the city council, asking them "to reduce the number of public dance halls in order to lessen disorder." Barran was specifically concerned with the "tricolor balls," which were attended by free people of color, white Creoles, and slaves. Though Barran's primary complaint was that the balls admitted a large number of slaves, his true concern is that "these dances, by a ridiculous imitation have placed themselves to the same level of those given at . . . the Conde Street Ballroom," where "the luxury and ways of the white people were 'impudently imitated.'"[14] The free population was accused of "aping" the manners and customs of the white Creoles, but the main anxiety was that they had the money to do so. The traveler Christian Schultz remarks that the white gentlemen preferred the quadroon balls because they "at all times surpasse[d] both in the elegance of its decorations, and the splendour of the dress of the company" the white masquerades.[15]

The economic equality of the *gens de couleur libre* continued to be a threat throughout the early nineteenth century. However, by the time the city came under American governance with the Louisiana Purchase in 1803, attitudes toward the free women of color had subtly shifted. This change in perception may be accounted for by the introduction of quadroon balls in 1805. Advertised in the November 1805 *Moniteur* as dances where "*les hommes de couleur libre ne feront pas admis*," their exclusivity transformed the quadroon women, who were seen as being little better than prostitutes during the Spanish period, into a romantic, forbidden fantasy. Excluding free men of color from the balls had two consequences. First, the free women of color were romanticized and treated as a rare delicacy. Second, unlike mixed-race courtesans in the West Indies, they were perceived as having no agency in their participation in *plaçage*. Whereas in the eighteenth century they had been opportunists, in the age of abolitionism they were victims of anti–interracial marriage laws that prohibited them from legally marrying their lovers. In the minds of the travelers who visited the balls, the quadroons and *plaçage* represented everything that was wrong with the institution of slavery.

However, the exploitation of mixed-race women did not keep tourists from attending the quadroon balls, their imaginations transforming the public dance into an exotic spectacle. When M. August Tessier began holding quadroon balls in the St. Philip Street ballroom in 1805, he played up the exoticism of the event by renaming his ballroom the "Salle Chinoise." Observing the quadroons with the same anthropological gaze with which European travelers toured Eastern seraglios, visitors to New Orleans felt as though they had walked into an American harem where the women resembled "the higher order of women among the Hindoos" and embodied "the *beau-ideal* of female loveliness in the Oriental form." According to H. Didimus, who visited New Orleans in the winter of 1835, the quadroons represented a "class whose look and every movement, whose whole existence is love."[16]

Though Didimus described their countenances as "sensuality moulded into beauty," the quadroons differed from a sultan's houris in that reports of their sensuality were coupled with descriptions of their grace, dignity, and intelligence.[17] Offering a general description of the quadroons in New Orleans, Bernhard, the Duke of Saxe-Weimar-Eisenach, says that several of them "possess handsome fortunes" and "have enjoyed the benefits of as careful an education as most of the whites; they conduct themselves ordinarily with more propriety and decorum, and confer more happiness on their 'friends,' than many of the white ladies to their married lords." These sentiments are echoed in his account of the mixed-race women he encountered at the balls: "The coloured ladies were under the eyes of their mothers, they were well and gracefully dressed, and conducted themselves with much propriety and modesty." Though he emphasizes the propriety and modesty of the women, the duke is compelled to explain his interest in the balls. He reassures his readers that he felt compelled to go because "a stranger in my situation should see every thing, to acquire a knowledge of the habits, customs, opinions and prejudices of the people he is among."[18] In case readers begin to think that his multiple visits to the balls are because he is attracted to the quadroons who "addressed [him], and coquetted with [him] some time, in the most subtle and amusing manner," he explains that "it was pure curiosity that carried [him] a third time to the masquerade."[19]

While it is not surprising that male visitors were enchanted by and eager to defend the grace and beauty of the quadroons, female tourists such as Frances Trollope and Harriet Martineau also found themselves mesmerized by the free women of color. As Trollope describes them in *Domestic Manners of the Americans* (1827), the quadroons are "exquisitely beautiful, graceful, gentle, and amiable." Trollope explains that these beautiful and refined women "cannot marry . . . yet such is the powerful effect of their very peculiar grace, beauty, and sweetness of manner, that unfortunately they perpetually become the objects of choice and affection."[20] The repetition of grace, decorum, propriety, intelligence, and modesty in the travel narratives of Bernhard, Schultz, and Trollope reflect their surprised fascination. How was it possible for "black" women living as concubines to possess the accomplishments and deportment usually attributed to upper-class white women? This was indeed "peculiar," to borrow Trollope's term. Another "peculiar" element in the accounts of Bernhard, Schultz, and Trollope is that the *placée* is described as a woman without options. Because of antimiscegenation laws, Schultz explains, "necessity has compelled them to resort to the practice of forming temporary engagements with those whom they may fancy."[21] However, the free women of color did have options: they could have married free men of color. But in the minds of travelers writing about these "almost entirely white" women crippled by their compromised bloodlines, being the concubine of a white man was preferable to being the wife of a man of color.[22]

While travel writers could not remove the strain of blood that banished the quadroon ladies from polite white society, they could remove the stain of concubinage by emphasizing the fidelity of the *placées* and portraying them as victims of a racist legal system that rendered them concubines instead of wives. Both male and female travelers stressed that the *placées* were faithful women. Explaining that the liaisons typically lasted "for a month or a year, or as much longer as the parties may be pleased with each other," Schultz informs readers that "during any engagement of this kind, it is in vain to solicit improper favours: they are generally as strictly continent as the marriage ceremony could possibly make them."[23] Acknowledging that the quadroons "regard the negroes and mulattoes with contempt, and will not mix with them," Bernhard explains that in their liaisons with their white "friends," the *placées* view their "engagement as a matrimonial contract, though it goes no farther than a formal contract by which the 'friend' engages to pay the father or mother of the quadroon a specified sum. The quadroons both assume the name of their friends, and as I am assured preserve this engagement with as much fidelity as ladies espoused at the altar."[24] In these travel narratives, it is impossible for the *placée* to be mistaken for the prostitute who sells her body in the public marketplace because, as James Stuart explains in his 1833 travel account, the quadroon's "attachment . . . is so constant, and [her] conduct so free from stain."[25]

While the majority of travel accounts written between 1810 and 1837 emphasize the fidelity of the quadroons, the narratives vary in their descriptions of whether and how the interracial liaisons end. According to Schultz, the *placées* form new liaisons when their lovers leave. Unlike Alliot, Schultz does not disparage the quadroons for forming new connections. He simply explains, "When the term is expired, or the lover gone, they accept the next best offer that may be made to them." Trollope, on the other hand, says that the unions are "often lasting and happy, as far as any unions can be so to which a certain degree of disgrace is attached."[26] Though she associates *plaçage* with shame, Trollope does not allow for the possibility that the quadroons seek new lovers after their previous liaisons have ended. Martineau, however, envisions a different fate for the mixed-race woman who resorts to *plaçage* because she is forbidden to marry. In *Society in America* (1837), Martineau informs her readers that, although some of the liaisons last until death, more typically the concubinages are only sustained for several years. In a description that establishes the traits that would become recognizable tropes in fictionalized representations of the Tragic Mulatta, particularly in Child's "The Quadroons," Martineau says: "When the time comes for the gentleman to take a white wife, the dreadful news reaches his Quadroon partner, either by letter entitling her to call the house and furniture her own, or by the newspaper which announces his marriage. The Quadroon ladies are rarely or never known to form a second connexion. Many commit suicide: more die broken-hearted."[27] Martineau's description of *plaçage* is one of the only travel accounts that ends with the demise of the quadroons. Blaming the institution of slavery rather than the morals of the quadroon women, Martineau romanticizes their unions, shifting the terms of the *placées'* narrative. She gives these "almost white" ladies a tragic ending because to show them surviving and forming new connections would have garnered only scorn from white readers, whereas death at the hands of a system that prohibited *placées* from marrying elicited sympathy.

Whereas tourists saw the free women of color as victims of slavery and prejudice, New Orleans locals were less sympathetic because the free women of color threatened their social order in two ways. First, many of them were, as Bernhard describes them, "almost entirely white: from their skin no one would detect their origin; nay many of them have as fair a complexion as many of the haughty creole females."[28] If the skin color of the quadroons was no darker than that of the white Creoles, whose Spanish and Native American ancestry sometimes resulted in dark hair, eyes, and golden skin, what traits would be infallible enough to distinguish the free population from white society?

Second, like the mixed-race mistresses in Jamaica and Saint-Domingue, New Orleans's *placées* enticed white men away from white women. While travel narratives romanticized *plaçage*, newspaper articles and editorials criticized white men for participating in this "vice." In September 1810, for example, Lucinda Sparkle submitted an editorial to the *Louisiana Gazette* in which she laments that she "has witnessed the depravity which exists among the unmarried gentlemen of this city—greater part of the evil arises from their not associating with the best female society." Desiring to "promote the cause of matrimony," Sparkle asks the city councilmen to create "public walks . . . with fine avenues of trees, decorated with all the allurements of art, and let every inducement be held out to our most beautiful and accomplished females, to frequent it." She believes that the public walks will encourage young men to pursue the "feelings of the most pure and tender nature [that] are often excited" during Carnival season, but that dissipate when the "carnival ends, and the period of female seclusion again returns." Sparkle is a bold young woman to publicly express her disapproval of *plaçage*. However, she maintains her ladylike propriety by genteelly using a clever euphemism to refer to the quadroons and concubinage. "The charms of female modesty and virtue," she writes, "are unfortunately too little force, when brought into contact with the grosser passions, and the fascinating allurements of Gold."[29] Taken out of its cultural context, it would be easy to interpret "Gold" as a reference to the gambling dens where young men squandered the money they could have used to establish themselves. But placed within the context of *plaçage*, it is clear that Sparkle is alluding to the warm complexions of the free women of color.

The extent of the distraction created by the quadroons is evident in the travel narratives of male tourists, such as the duke and John H. B. Latrobe, who describe how they and their friends circulated between the quadroon and white balls. The duke leaves the white Creole ball he is attending to investigate the quadroon ball to which he's been invited. However, he explains, "I did not remain long there that I might not utterly destroy my standing in New Orleans, but returned to the masked ball and took great care not to disclose to the white ladies where I had been." He observes that because a large number of gentlemen had "hasted away to the quadroon ball," the white ladies "were obliged to form 'tapestry'" to entertain themselves.[30] An article published by a concerned citizen in a December 1826 issue of *L'Argus* complained that the popularity of quadroon balls reduced the attendance of gentlemen at a white masquerade ball held on the same night. Describing the women attending the "mixed" balls as "bold women / Enticing in their walk, their favors free," the article anxiously concludes that "the men of New Orleans . . . were neglecting 'the white privets to gather black grapes.'"[31]

The men who sought mistresses at the quadroon balls were doing more than merely satisfying their curiosity and sexual appetites. As a male respondent to Lucinda Sparkle's editorial remarks, they were reacting against the strict courtship customs in Creole society. The gentleman's main complaint is that young couples are too closely chaperoned: "Females whilst single, are treated as weak mortals destitute of every principle of virtue, and young men as villains destitute of every principle of honor, not to be trusted for a moment in the society of each other, unless in the presence of, or under the guardian eye of parents." Advising the "fair petitioner," Lucinda Sparkle, "to turn her attention to the reformation of the manners and customs of the society of New Orleans," the writer accuses the parents of marriageable daughters of "choosing husbands for them, which choice is generally influenced, not by the qualities of his person, but that of his estate."[32] As Frederick Olmsted observes in *The Cotton Kingdom* (1856), many young men felt that they were not financially prepared for marriage because they needed a fortune "to support the extravagant style of housekeeping, and gratify the expensive tastes of young women, as fashion is now educating them." Olmsted was informed by one young man that "it was cheaper for him to *placer* than to live in any other way which could be expected of him in New Orleans" because "his placée did not, except occasionally, require a servant; she did the marketing, and performed all the ordinary duties of housekeeping herself; she took care of his clothes, and in every way was economical and saving in her habits." The *placée* hoped her economy would make her lover "more strongly attached to her," giving him less reason to leave her for a legal wife.[33] In addition to looking for an economical alternative to marriage while they established themselves professionally and socially, young men were also searching for a woman with whom they could be at ease. The gentleman responding to Sparkle's editorial advises her to "persuade young ladies to be more sociable themselves, when in the company of young gentlemen" or else "the company of the *fair belles* [would be] deserted for that of the *copper-colored* nymphs."[34] Of course, such descriptions that favored the "friendly" quadroons over the "haughty creole females" perpetuated stereotypes of the warm-blooded, sensual woman of color and the cold, prim white woman.[35]

Though they were perceived as occupying opposite ends of the moral spectrum, the quadroons and white Creoles were both on the market. Just as the editorial responding to Sparkle's complaint accuses parents of treating their daughters "as an object of traffic to sell to the highest bidder," various accounts of *plaçage* implicated quadroon mothers in the exploitation of their daughters. In a comment that belies reality, Stuart reports, "The tales which have been told of the assemblage of beauties on the levee at sunset, where the mother or female relation makes the best bargain she can for her daughter or her ward, are, I am quite satisfied, merely travelers' stories."[36] Though Stuart's narrative refutes this rumor, his description reflects the extent to which the mothers' "selling" or placing of their daughters had become a part of the cultural imagination by the 1830s. Describing this economic transaction between the mother and her daughter's "friend" or "protector," Olmsted explains that a *plaçage* was sanctioned by the mother only after ensuring that the suitor could "support her daughter in a style suitable to the habits she had been bred to, and that, if he should ever leave her, he will give her a certain sum, for her future support, and a certain additional sum for each of the children she will then have."[37]

While some believed the mothers and their quadroon daughters were victims of a racist legal system, such writers as Gustave de Beaumont and many free men of color depicted the free women of color as greedy social climbers. In *Marie; or, Slavery in the United States* (1835), the novel inspired by Beaumont's travels through America with Tocqueville, the women who participate in *plaçage* desire a better social status. Explaining why the quadroons choose white men over the free men of color they could have married legally, Beaumont says: "She might, according to law, have married a mulatto, but such an alliance would not raise her out of her class. Also, the mulatto has no power to protect her; in marrying a man of color she perpetuates her degradation; she raises herself by prostituting herself to the white man." In Beaumont's description, the quadroon mothers are portrayed as merchants aware of the market value of refined, fair-skinned girls. Eager to capitalize on their daughters' bodies, particularly their virtue, the mothers bargain "shrewdly, demanding more or less as a price according to whether her daughter is more or less of a novice." When the union dissolves, as Beaumont says it inevitably does, "the girl of color sells herself to another man."[38]

Though the free men of color occupied the periphery of travelers' observations about *plaçage*, local literature written by mixed-race men shows that many of them were vehemently opposed to the tradition of interracial concubinage in New Orleans. However, whereas the majority of white travelers viewed the institution of slavery as the culprit for the degradation of mixed-race women, the free men of color blamed the quadroon women, particularly the mothers, who in Beaumont's words, encouraged and "rejoiced in" these interracial unions.[39] The works of Armand Lanusse, who edited *Les Cenelles*, a collection of poetry written by free men of color, contained severe critiques of *plaçage*. In his 1843 story "Un Mariage de Conscience," or "A Conscientious Marriage," Lanusse criticizes the quadroon mothers who force their daughters into concubinage and condemns the church officials who allow priests to officiate at such sacrilegious ceremonies. In the story, a young *placée* becomes insane after her lover abandons her for a white wife. The jilted girl was a reluctant *placée* who only agreed to a union with her white lover after her mother convinced her that it would be a "conscientious marriage" or, as the quadroon explains to her daughter, a "vow of marriage with no legal basis, but the priest officiates just like it were a legitimate wedding."[40] Lanusse's story ends violently with the forsaken girl running into the streets where she is trampled by the carriage carrying her former lover and his new wife. His portrayal of a quadroon mother confessing her sins in the 1845 poem "Épigramme" is even more ruthless in its attack on mothers trafficking their daughters. The quadroon tells the priest that she will repent her

> substantial list of weighty sins. . . .
> But before the first glimmer of grace
> Purges my soul of all sinful desires,
> Can I only, pastor . . . place my daughter?[41]

Despite condemnation from free men of color, the market for free women made New Orleans's mixed-race demimonde a significant part of the city's economic and social life.

"Eager cabmen," Henry Kmen explains, "vied with one another to solicit passengers by proposing to convey them to quadroon balls."[42] Indeed, most male visitors could expect their hosts to take them to a quadroon ball to observe and dance with the city's free women of color. Even newspaper advertisements for the balls in the 1830s reflected the way in which the balls had become a conventional form of entertainment. Quadroon balls, however, were never advertised as such; the advertisements did not refer to "Bals de Couleur" or "Bals des Quarteronnes." Interested parties learned by word of mouth whether a ballroom held mixed balls. In the 1830s, ads for the Washington Ballroom, a popular venue for the quadroon balls, offered a clever clue to solicit business. Placed among advertisements for runaway slaves, new books, sugar, and theater bills in the December 2, 1834 *New Orleans Bee*, an advertisement for the Washington Ballroom announced, "There is found in the interior of this establishment, which is the most splendid of the kind in the United States, all the commodities one can desire" (fig. 5). Without explicitly mentioning the quadroon women, the owners told readers of the *Bee* that more than just food and drink could be purchased at their establishment. Kmen notes that some of the ballrooms in the early 1800s "provided carriages at the door, and for utmost convenience . . . rented rooms right on the premises."[43] Whether this was still the case in the 1830s is uncertain, but this detail reveals a discrepancy between the reality of the ballrooms and

ORLEANS BALL-ROOM.
(For the opening.)
ON SATURDAY, 5th DEC. 1834,
GRAND
Dress & Masquerade Ball.
Admittance for gentlemen,........................$1 50
Ladies will not be admitted without an invitation ticket, delivered by the administration.
All persons will be compelled to unmask themselves, and none will be admitted with arms. dec 1

WASHINGTON BALL-ROOM.
St. Philip street, between Royal and Bourbon streets.
On Wednesday Evening, Dec. 3. 1834,
GRAND FULL DRESS & MASQUERADE
BALL.
Entrance for Gentlemen........................$1 00
There is found in the interior of this establishment, which is the most splendid of the kind in the United States, all the commodities one can desire. Eating Rooms, Bar, depot for hats, cloaks and canes, a store of Costumes and Masks, &c. &c. dec 2

FIGURE 5. Advertisements for the Orleans and Washington Ballrooms, *New Orleans Bee*, December 2, 1834. (© 2011 The Times-Picayune Publishing Co. All rights reserved. Used with permission of *The Times-Picayune*.)

the romanticized image presented in travel narratives that described the ballrooms as a setting in which long-term liaisons were established. The Washington Ballroom was also unique in that it was owned by Salomon Sacerdote, a Jewish businessman whose partner was Antoine Jonau, a free man of color.[44] Though the quadroon ballrooms prohibited free men of color from attending, they apparently were not prevented from profiting from those white men who desired mixed-race flesh.

Described by Tocqueville as "a sort of bazaar," the balls were transgressive spaces where appearances could be deceiving.[45] In his vivid 1834 description of a quadroon ball, John H. B. Latrobe reports that "the handsomest person male or female at the Ball was a Spanish gentleman who was dressed as a woman, and was not discovered, although he wore no mask, until many of his own sex had been introduced to him, some of his acquaintances among the number, and proceeded to make love to him as a female." While the other men were fooled, he "had observed that the Lady had the habit of spitting on the floor and putting her foot on it." As it was a masquerade ball, many of the men wore costumes, some of which evoked exotic images of Eastern sultans. Along with "several Turks," there was a "conspicuous . . . fellow in flesh coloured clothes fitting tight to the skin, and with ornaments of a Peruvian Indian as we sometimes see them in pictures."[46] While the male patrons were costumed as Turks and Indians, Latrobe reports that the mixed-race women wore "no other disguise to the person than a domino," or hooded cape, and a mask.

In Latrobe's narrative, the Washington Ballroom is a space that blurred gender and race distinctions, a space where men could be women, where white men could masquerade as "natives," where raced women "bore no mark of [their] descent." Though Latrobe attests that there were "no white women present," how could he be certain?[47] If a quadroon could appear "almost entirely white," couldn't curious white women simply say they were quadroons, don a mask, and gain entrance? And even if they were asked to unmask themselves before being admitted to the ball, which was the policy of the Orleans Ballroom, white women could still pass into "mixed" society undetected because of the quadroons' racial ambiguity. In fact, white women attending the quadroon balls had become such a public concern that articles addressing the problem were published in the *New Orleans Bee* and the *New Orleans Times-Picayune*. The authors of a November 1835 article in the *Bee* reported, "On Saturday night we paid a visit to the Washington ballroom in St. Philip St.; and tho we found great regularity prevail, we were certainly surprised to find that two-thirds of the females present were white women; and doubly so when we were informed . . . that there were many white ladies present who are usually considered respectable in their sphere of life."[48] While Latrobe reports that a ball he attended at the Orleans Ballroom was frequented by "white women of the lowest order," this was not the case in the Washington Ballroom, where, according to the article, "many married women were present."[49]

While it is possible that some of the women gained access to keep an eye on their husbands, it is also probable that they were drawn by the same fascination expressed by Stuart, Trollope, and Duke Bernhard. They wanted to see the golden women whose reputed beauty and graceful dancing lured husbands and suitors away from the white masquerades.

The *Bee* article gently chastises the curious ladies, reinscribing the tenets of ideal womanhood by which the true woman was never disguised, but was always supposed to be virtuously transparent in thought and action. The author also tells the interlopers that they should not risk tainting their delicate feminine sensibilities by experiencing those freedoms condoned by quadroon balls: "However disposed we may be to esteem ladies and gratify their curiosity, etc, we do not like to see them disguised in liquor or dress. What they may be permitted to do at a fancy ball, respectably 'got up' can scarcely afford a precedent to unrestrained freedom at masked balls for colored people two or three times a week." The white women attending the balls also posed an economic threat. If it became commonplace for white ladies to frequent the quadroons' venues, the balls would lose their exotic allure or "eligibility," as the article refers to it, and thereby risk losing patrons who came to socialize exclusively with the quadroon women.[50]

White women attending the balls had become such a problem that by 1837, the *Picayune* reported that the city council had "made it a penal offence to give a masked ball, and admit 'white and colored women together.'" But how could such an ordinance be enforced if skin color was not guaranteed to define someone's racial categorization? Addressing this question, the 1837 article asserts, "We are inclined to think it would require more ingenuity than any of the Aldermen of the First Municipality possess, to discover the *color* of some who attend; they go so habited that there is no discovering whether they are black or white."[51] Implicit in this remark is a question of whether the officials would be able to discern a woman's race if she wore neither costume nor mask. As Latrobe explains in his description of the "light quadroon whose person bore no mark of her descent," the "degradation" that resulted from her being categorized as a woman of color "was a matter of tradition only."[52] Here Latrobe echoes Beaumont, who upon seeing a "young woman of dazzling beauty, whose complexion, of perfect whiteness, proclaimed the purest European blood," asks the person sitting next to him why this woman is sitting in the theater's mulatto section. His neighbor responds, "she is colored . . . local tradition has established her ancestry, and everyone knows that she had a mulatto among her forebears." Beaumont asks the same question of a woman who is "the same color as the mulattoes" to which his neighbor answers, "She is white . . . local tradition affirms that the blood which flows in her veins is Spanish."[53]

Although Latrobe is critical of the role "local tradition" played in determining the race of the women he encountered, he is more troubled by the racial fluidity of the quadroons, particularly their performance of whiteness. Observing the masks worn by the quadroons, he says: "Nearly all had masks—white masks. Those who had not were young girls as yet destitute of a keeper, and who it seemed to me shewed their faces as a merchant shews samples of his wares to entice purchasers."[54] Whereas the young "almost white" women without masks search for suitors to provide them with social legitimacy and stability, the white masks worn by the quadroons who have acquired "protectors" or "keepers" reflect the new social and perhaps racial status they achieved from *plaçage*. The white masks suggest that quadroons who became *placées* had in some small way renegotiated their racial categorization: they were now "white" instead of "almost white." Purchased with the price of their bodies, the white masks denote the performative nature of the quadroons' racial identities. While emphasizing their white ancestry, the masks also exaggerate their nonwhiteness. According to Frantz Fanon, "all these frantic women of color in quest of white men" achieve "the great dream" of interracial unions through performance, or as he describes it, their "overcompensating behavior": "Their need to gesticulate, their love of ridiculous ostentation, their calculated, theatrical, revolting attitudes, are just so many effects of the same mania for grandeur," or, more specifically, whiteness. Indeed, as Fanon explains, the mixed-race woman who marries a white man "was no longer the woman who wanted to be white; she was white. She was joining the white world."[55] While the southern legal system ensured that the *placées* would be unable to "join the white world" through marriage, the *placées* in New Orleans's mixed-race demimonde were one step closer to the whiteness they coveted.

The quadroons' refashioning of their racial identity makes Latrobe anxious. Although he acknowledges his compassion for the mixed-race women whom the "white man's sins makes infamous, and devotes to prostitution from their cradle," after leaving the ball he reminds himself that, even if the *placées*' degradation stemmed from tradition rather than a visible, tangible cause, the women he observed were racially tainted. He says, "I could not get it out of my mind that those women that I saw were negroes nothing more or less."[56] Perplexed by the quadroons' "peculiar" beauty and its power to defy racial and social categories, Latrobe employs racist stereotype to distinguish the *placées* from white ladies. Though he admits that "curiosity kept [him] looking on for sometime" at the "graceful and elegant dancers," the smell of the ballroom serves as a reminder that the mixed-race ladies were, as he says, "negroes nothing more or less": "Towards the end of the ball the room became very warm and the smell of the heated quadroons and mulattoes most disagreeable to one not accustomed to it. I could not bear it and went away."[57] Because skin color is an unreliable indicator of racial difference, Latrobe uses smell to reinscribe their race.

The fascinated sympathy that Latrobe, Trollope, Martineau, and other visitors expressed toward New Orleans's *placées* hinges upon the quadroons' nonwhiteness, which, in the minds of these travelers, renders mixed-race women victims. Though Martineau and Trollope romanticize the free women of color as tragic victims of white men's affection, it is possible that some of the mixed-race demimonde preferred concubinage to marriage. Whereas married women could not own property, the *placées* were able to keep in their names whatever property or income their lovers bequeathed to them. Martineau even notes that when the *placée*'s lover decides to marry, she is "entitl[ed] to call the house and furniture her own."[58]

Court cases in which the white relatives of a quadroon's lover contested his will offer some insight into the degree to which *placées* profited financially from their liaisons. In the 1848 case of *Macarty et al. v. Mandeville*, the relatives of Eugene Macarty contested the property (a house on Barracks Street and $12,000) he left Eulalie Mandeville, with whom he lived in concubinage from 1796 until his death in 1845. The defense for Mandeville asserts that "all the property in the possession of the defendant belongs exclusively to her . . . the result of her industry and economy during half a century. . . . [S]he had, in all respects, rendered her condition as reputable . . . as it could be made." A daughter from "one of the most distinguished" families in Louisiana, Mandeville had also received "a tract . . . three acres front and forty in depth on each side of the bayou . . . and we think it clear her family gave her money." Of course, if Mandeville had been a white woman who had married Macarty legally, her money and land would have become his. However, since she was a free woman of color prohibited by law from marrying her white lover, Mandeville was able to take the property from her family, as well as her inheritance from Macarty, and use it to buy slaves and engage in the dry goods business. Because of her business savvy and reputation as an upstanding citizen of New Orleans, the courts ruled that "the property claimed by the plaintiffs appears to us to be in the bona fide possession of the defendant and exclusively so. . . . [W]e find no warrant . . . for disturbing her in the enjoyment of the fruits of the labor and thrift of a long life."[59] Unencumbered by marriage laws that placed all property in the husband's name, Eulalie Mandeville and other free women of color were able to use the property they received from concubinage to better their social positions, and more importantly, to establish themselves in the New Orleans business world.[60]

Though *plaçage* gave free women of color a purchase on whiteness and a certain degree of protection and economic freedom, their proximity to slavery was a constant threat to their way of life. If slave owners could prove that a *placée* and her children were the descendents of slaves and had not been legally freed, mixed-race women who had been living as free citizens could be repossessed and sold as slaves. This racial peril is demonstrated in Martineau's account of the three sisters who were auctioned off to pay their father's debts. Though they had been raised as free women of color without official manumission papers, they were removed from the protection of the private sphere to the public humiliation of the auction block. In this story, Martineau describes how a New Hampshire gentleman bought a plantation in Louisiana and took a quadroon mistress, who was known as a "well-principled, amiable, well-educated woman." However, unlike the *placées* described elsewhere in Martineau's chapter, this woman lived as the gentleman's wife for twenty years. She warned her "husband" that she was descended from slaves and had not been manumitted; however, he neglected to secure free papers for her and their daughters. When he and his wife died, the daughters, who Martineau says had "no perceptible mulatto tinge" and were "to all appearance perfectly white," were reclaimed as property to pay his debts. Martineau describes how the creditors saw the sisters as "'first-rate articles' too valuable to be relinquished" to the uncle who wanted to take them back to New Hampshire, where they would pass into white society. Alluding to how the sisters were sold as "fancy girl" slaves or concubines, Martineau writes, "They were sold . . . at high prices, for the vilest of purposes: and where each is gone, no one knows."[61]

Like the proprietors of venues that specialized in quadroon balls, New Orleans slave traders sought to capitalize upon white men's desire for mixed-race women by trafficking fair-skinned slaves, or "fancy girls." At "fancy girl" slave auctions, eager buyers paid more for a fair-skinned slave, or "fancy article," than they did for a good field hand. Monique Guillory notes that the virtue of the "fancy girl" added to her value since "some adolescent females of mixed race were sold as 'virgins.'"[62] Like the "almost white" *placées* whom tourists crowded into quadroon balls to observe, the "fancy girls" offered a sexual fantasy to slaveholders. While her fair skin, refinement, intelligence, and virtue earned her a place as a "lady's maid," "housekeeper," or "cook," her main purpose was to gratify her master's sexual desires. As Walter Johnson explains, the word "fancy" suggests that slave traders were trafficking a fantasy made flesh. Noting that slaveholders paid excessive prices "ranging from $2000 to $5233" for a "fancy" girl, Johnson asserts: "The high prices were a measure not only of desire but dominance. No other man could afford to pay so much . . . no other man's desires would be so spectacularly fulfilled." While the *placées* were hidden away on the outskirts of the French Quarter, the "fancies" reflected their masters' "power to purchase what was forbidden and the audacity to show it off."[63]

However, though their positions in the plantation home were conspicuous, the fancies, like their free quadroon sisters on Rampart Street, were an "unspeakable" presence in slaveholding society.[64] If a slaveholder's treatment of a fancy became too preferential, he was shunned by polite society. Describing the political fall of a Kentucky war hero, Richard Johnson, Catherine Clinton explains that his liaison with his "housekeeper" Julia Chinn became a political scandal because he publicly acknowledged his daughters rather than keeping them secret. Unlike the New Orleans newspaper editor who "entertained his dinner guests at a house inhabited by his 'Quadroon mistress' and the couple's child," the Kentucky politician made the mistake of "accord[ing] his mulatto family the privilege of white status."[65] As in the world of the French demimonde, it was permissible for a gentleman to entertain guests at the home he purchased or rented for his mixed-race mistress as long as he kept a separate home for his legitimate family. Johnson, however, did not have a legitimate white family to shield his indiscretions, which made many fear that if Johnson made it to the White House, "the colored will have an Esther at the foot of the throne . . . who may not only dictate modes and fashions to the female community, but may deliver her people from civil disabilities, break down the barrier of prejudice which separates the two races, and produce an amalgamation."[66] The fear of amalgamation aside, the criticism lodged against Johnson also reveals a deeper anxiety that interracial intimacy would lead to social reform. Because of their race and gender, mixed-race women did not have a public voice, but Johnson's critics feared that they would influence men in power who could speak for them.

The figure of the Tragic Mulatta that grew out of travel narratives and abolitionist literature had neither voice nor agency. She was a spectacle whose sexual fall was ventriloquized by fascinated travelers and outraged abolitionists. As Martineau, Child, and Brown began constructing the Tragic Mulatta's narrative in the 1830s and 1840s, the real women who lived as *placées* or who were sold as "fancy girls" faded into the shadows. Like Charles Bon's "octoroon mistress," who never utters a word but floats through *Absalom, Absalom!* in an ethereal cloud of silk and perfume, the mixed-race women who inspired the Tragic Mulatta's narrative were rendered romantic specters. Eliding the sexual and economic complexities of the mixed-race woman's experience, authors of the Tragic Mulatta constructed a simple narrative that merged the freedom, class status, and refinement of the *placée* with the imminent public exposure and sexual violation of the "fancy girl." Inviting "white readers to identify with the victim by gender while distancing themselves by race," the Tragic Mulatta's narrative hinged on the mixed-race woman's seeming lack of agency.[67] Stripped of sexual agency, death becomes the only means of escaping sexual violence: the violation Child's Xarifa suffers renders her a "raving maniac" who dies after fracturing her head "in a frenzy of despair" while Brown's Clotel dives into the Potomac rather than return to her master.[68] Ingraham's sensation novel *The Quadroone; or, St. Michael's Day,* however, offers the Tragic Mulatta a different resolution.

## "Advancing Towards Orientalism"

Travelers and authors such as Schultz, Buckingham, Martineau, Ingraham, and Child sensationalized the mixed-race woman's lack of sexual agency by comparing the South's slaves and concubines to the harem wives they encountered in such works as the *Arabian Nights,* Racine's *Bajazet,* the letters of Lady Mary Wortley Montagu, and Byron's poetry. To those in the West, harem women were, in the words of Thomas Moore's 1817 narrative poem *Lalla Rookh,* sexual delicacies secreted away in palaces

> Where thro' the silken net-work, glancing eyes,
> From time to time, like sudden gleams that glow
> Thro' autumn clouds, shine o'er the pomp below. . . .
> . . . commissioned from above
> To people Eden's bowers with shapes of love,
> (Creatures so bright, that the same lips and eyes
> They wear on earth will serve in Paradise).[69]

Explaining the "lure of the unknown and the forbidden" that harems held for Europeans, Ruth Bernard Yeazell observes that the women, as they were imagined by various male authors and artists, were "at once theatrically exposed and withheld from view."[70] Just as the harems and its inhabitants were, as Yeazell argues, "primarily structures of fantasy," the *placées* waltzing at a quadroon ball or the "fancy girl" slaves exposed on the auction block were also more fantasy than flesh.[71]

While oriental imagery in the travel narratives of Schultz and Buckingham, as well as in Currier & Ives's *The Beautiful Quadroon* (fig. 4), enhance the exoticism and romance of the mixed-race women represented, Martineau used images of harem women to emphasize the *placée* and fancy girl's degradation at the hands of slavery. Though it would be almost a decade before she traveled to the Eastern harems, Martineau describes the exploitation of slave women on plantations where "every man . . . may have his harem, and has every inducement of custom, and of pecuniary gain" to "rear as many as possible, like stock, for the southern market."[72] She goes on to describe the wife of a slaveholder who referred to herself as "the chief slave of the harem." Describing the plantation harems and the extreme dependence of indolent plantation mistresses on their husbands, Martineau expresses fear that southern society is "advancing towards orientalism."[73]

While she pities the white southern women and mixed-race concubines and slaves who were victims of the patriarchal slavery system, she does not extend the same sympathy to the harem women she encountered during her visit to Egypt in 1846. Explaining this discrepancy in attitudes, Deborah Anna Logan asserts that while Martineau "could certainly comprehend women's sexual victimization by a system beyond their control," she was not sympathetic to "the material luxury and sensory overindulgence that marked harem women's lives and that clearly served as compensation for their sexual enslavement."[74] Whereas New Orleans's quadroon concubines are "highly educated . . . beautiful and accomplished," the harem wives Martineau encounters have "no trace of mind" and are "dull, soulless, brutish."[75] While she reproaches harem wives for fearing disgrace if their daughters remained unmarried after the age of eleven, Martineau's sentimentalized description of the *placées* neither condemns the role quadroon mothers played in the exploitation of their daughters nor acknowledges the likelihood that they formed new liaisons instead of resorting to suicide when a lover left them. Though southern white women, New Orleans's *placées*, and Eastern harem wives all lived an "ornamental existence aimed exclusively at 'conspicuous display,'" Martineau is sympathetic only toward the mixed-race concubines who were, in her mind, attempting to lead respectful, moral lives in a society that accorded them neither virginity nor legal marriage.[76]

Early fiction about *placées* and mixed-race slaves, such as Ingraham's *The Quadroone; or, St. Michael's Day* and Child's "The Quadroons," use Eastern images to emphasize the Tragic Mulatta's racial ambiguity and her equivocal sexuality (at once virtuous and wanton). Depicting the Tragic Mulatta as an American houri, Ingraham's obscure sensation novel takes as its starting point France's surrender of New Orleans to the Spanish in 1766. Set against a backdrop of political upheaval, Ingraham's novel follows the intricate machinations of the quadroon Ninine, a femme fatale figure who rivals Balzac's deadliest courtesans. Ninine is the *placée* of the Marquise de la Caronde, the French governor of Louisiana, and before the marquise's wife gave her husband a son, Ninine was the "favoured mistress. . . . The Marchioness of Caronde wore only his name. Ninine held the cords of his will, and governed him as her caprice pointed." Poisoned by envy and a monomaniacal obsession with revenge, Ninine attempts several times to poison the legitimate heir of the marquise. She eventually succeeds in murdering the marchioness, but the child survives. So great are the quadroon's powers of fascination that though the marquise suspects that Ninine murdered his wife, "his love for the siren who had thrown about him her fatal net was stronger than his horror at the crime." Ninine soon gives birth to a son who drives her ambition to new extremes: "She now aspired to the title and estates of the father for her illegitimate son."[77] She begins a relentless search for the legitimate heir who has been hidden away by his father. Instead of murdering the child, Ninine decides to switch the half brothers. This plot, later repeated in Child's *A Romance of the Republic* (1867) and Mark Twain's *Puddn'head Wilson* (1894), results in the mixed-race son, Jules, being raised as an affluent gentleman, while the white son, Renault, is enslaved.

Ninine also has a daughter, Azelie, whom she hopes to "place" advantageously in the New Orleans demimonde. Jules Caronde is the quadroon's first choice for her daughter. The incestuous implications of half brother and sister becoming lovers emphasize the extent of Ninine's corruption by social ambitions. But when Jules falls out of favor with Ninine once the change in government renders him an outlaw, Ninine decides that the new Spanish governor, the Count of Osma, would be a more advantageous match. However, Jules refuses to surrender his desire for Azelie, claiming Ninine and Azelie as his slaves because the marquise died before filing manumission papers for Ninine and her children. Jules, therefore, claims Azelie as his slave so he can force her to become his concubine. When Jules is wounded in a revolt, Ninine sells Azelie to the Count of Osma. Azelie's lover, a Spanish cavalier, helps her escape from the count's home. The count holds a tribunal to regain his property; however, during the trial a further twist in the plot is revealed. Azelie is not a quadroon! She is the daughter of Zillah, a Moorish princess, whom the count secretly wed and then jilted for a Spanish wife. Zillah's servant rescued the child and pursued the count from Spain to Cuba, where she was captured by a pirate and sold at a New Orleans slave auction. Upon seeing the young Azelie at the slave auction, Ninine purchased the child, "contemplating the wealth and consideration her charms would bring her when she should grow into the bloom of girlhood."[78]

Ingraham thus transforms the Tragic Mulatta's narrative into an oriental romance propelled by the conventions of the sensation genre. By juxtaposing the *placée* and the houri, he emphasizes the mixed-race concubine's status as a woman who exists only for man's pleasure. Spectacles of raced femininity, exotic objects of the white male gaze, the harem wife and the *placée* have neither agency nor voice. The Count of Osma explains that the quadroon's "destiny is the same with the maidens of the east" who are not "degraded by the fulfillment of a destiny which they have ever been taught to be the summit of happiness."[79] Ingraham complicates his juxtaposition of the *placée* and houri, however, by aligning the mixed-race concubine with another figure of exoticized femininity—the Moorish princess or maiden. Unlike the houri, who is made for love, the Moorish maiden is virtuous. However, like the Tragic Mulatta, the Moorish maiden is often a sexually imperiled figure.

In revealing that Azelie is the daughter of a Moorish princess, Ingraham emphasizes the racial ambiguity of the Tragic Mulatta. Though it would seem that he has erased Azelie's race by removing her African ancestry, she remains nonwhite—indeed, the religious difference of the Moors and Spaniards was often depicted as a racial difference, which implies that Azelie is "mixed." Contemporary narratives often used oriental details to accentuate the racial ambiguity of the mixed-race *placée* or slave. In "The Quadroons," published two years after Ingraham's romance, Child invokes the Orient and the harem when she explains that Xarifa's name came from a Moorish ballad: "It was Edward's fancy to name their eldest child Xarifa; in commemoration of a Spanish song, which had first conveyed to his ears the sweet tones of her mother's voice."[80] Alluding to "The Bridal of Andella," in which Xarifa refuses the balladeer's request to come to the window and watch her lover wed another, Child maps the romantic exoticism of the East onto her quadroons, Xarifa and her mother, Rosalie. Ignoring the implications of naming his daughter after a ballad in which a woman is abandoned by her lover, Edward perceives his *placée*, Rosalie, as an exotic fantasy made flesh. His fancy does not anticipate the tragic consequences that will ensue when he abandons her for a white wife.

While highlighting parallels between the tragic narratives of the jilted Moorish maiden and the mixed-race concubine, Child's allusion also emphasizes the racial ambiguity of the octoroon Xarifa. The Moorish origin of Xarifa's name, Child explains, "was most appropriate to one so emphatically 'a child of the sun.'"[81] Though Ingraham and Child incorporate oriental details into their Tragic Mulatta narratives, with the exception of the works of Captain Mayne Reid and Charles Kingsley, this dimension of the Tragic Mulatta figure disappears in subsequent texts that instead emphasize the mixed-race heroine's proximity to white womanhood. Writing in the late 1850s, both Reid and Kingsley observe in their physical descriptions of the Tragic Mulatta that the mixed-race slave's features were, as Reid explains, "of a strange type—its strangely-beautiful expression, not Caucasian, not Indian, not Asiatic," but perhaps a changing kaleidoscope of all these elements.[82]

As orientalism underscores the exoticism of the Tragic Mulatta, it also helps Ingraham to explain the custom of *plaçage*. In the preface of *The Quadroone*, Ingraham compares New Orleans concubinage to Eastern harems: "While their laws were singularly severe against legal amalgamation, they openly practiced a system of concubinage that has been without a parallel even in Oriental countries." Invoking the Eastern seraglio, Ingraham emphasizes the "oriental elegance" of Ninine's apartments in the French Quarter, full of "rich and luxurious decorations of ivory, marble, and ebony" and "hangings of damask, and divans of blue and crimson silk."[83] Like the Circassian parent, however, Ninine views this interior, and the disposal of her daughter, "as a natural and suitable one." The count similarly invokes the harem when he imagines himself to be a sultan and Azelie his houri. Justifying his purchase of Azelie to his horrified daughter, Estelle, the count asks: "Is the Sultan of Orient guilty of crime for filling his harem with the houris of Circassia? This is the destiny of the females of that land, and such concubinage is their only wedlock."[84] Of course, part of the allure of both the houris and quadroons is that neither of these women have the agency or opportunity to voice their dissent.

Like Beaumont and Lanusse, Ingraham condemns *plaçage*, particularly the role quadroon mothers played in the exploitation and sexual violation of their daughters. As Renault explains, the quadroon mother's greed and ambition for social status results in the prostitution of her daughter. He admonishes his mother: "Cease to educate your daughters as baits to criminal passion, and their conditions will be less unequal. It is your pride, your love of display and finery, your female ambition and envious desire to surpass wives and honourable mothers" that renders "female virtue . . . an article of merchandise." Indeed, without her virtue, the *placée* is not a marketable commodity. As Ninine tells her daughter: "Thou art too lovely a treasure, child, to be lightly guarded. One stain upon thy maiden honour, and the poorest bourgeois of the town would not accept thee. As thou art, a prince might kneel for thee."[85] Even the count, who is eager to possess Azelie, is surprised by the cold calculation with which Ninine bargains. When Ninine demands ten thousand crowns before allowing the count to carry away his property, he responds, "Wouldst thou sell thy daughter like a slave, woman?"[86]

As commodities in a sexual market in which they are trafficked by their mothers, the houri and the *placée* are trapped in narratives in which they "have no alternative but death or splendid misery." Though Azelie's Moorish identity allows her to escape sexual violation and suicide, Ingraham's sensation novel highlights similarities between the narratives of America's doomed mixed-race slave and the tragic houris and Moorish maidens of the East. Indeed, the fate of Azelie's mother, Zillah, resembles that of the Tragic Mulatta. After Zillah secretly weds the Count of Osma, he forsakes their marriage vows and returns to Spain. She follows him and confronts him as he is about to wed another. After ordering "his servants to bear off the mad woman, and cast her forth into the storm," the count resumes his wedding to a Spanish lady and Zillah dies in childbirth.[87]

Further connections between the Tragic Mulatta and women of the East can be seen in Ingraham's allusion to Scott's *Ivanhoe*. Ingraham's description of Azelie nursing the wounded cavalier Don Henrique echoes Scott's portrayal of Rebecca's attraction to Ivanhoe. Both Rebecca and Azelie present an image of the tragic exotic woman who has loved where it's forbidden. Like Rebecca, who watches over the sleeping Ivanhoe and attempts "to fortify, her mind . . . against those treacherous feelings which assailed her from within," Azelie looks upon the Spanish cavalier and laments: "Such should the youth be whom my soul would obey, and my poor heart love. But alas! I am outcast and degraded, and can look on this noble brow only with dishonour."[88] The racial obstacle to marrying the men they love also renders them objects of illicit sexual desire. In the eyes of the men who desire them, Rebecca and Azelie possess what might be described as a wanton or sensual innocence. In an extended erotic description of Azelie, Don Henrique muses: "What can compare with the glossy softness of those tresses, or the blackness of their hue! It concealed all her face and bosom like a veil, having escaped in its wantonness from a wreath of wrought silk that had been gracefully bound above her forehead." The cavalier continues his description of the beautiful "houri" by observing that "sleep in her innocence had permitted one foot and ancle to escape from her robe, and unconsciously display so much of the beautiful limb as betrayed the matchless perfection of her divine figure."[89]

Ingraham couples the erotic images of Azelie's wanton hair and exposed ankle with a reminder of her innocence, noting the "chaste expressive beauty of the whole reposing countenance!" Indeed, he explains that without her innocence, Azelie would lose the beauty that fascinates him: "Innocence is written on each lineament; is part and parcel in the compound of her beauty; wanting which, it would lose its better principle." This blend of sensual beauty and innocence tempt even the best men to violate the raced woman's virtue. Although he declares that he will not "profane" the "virgin purity" of Azelie's lips, "though the temptation had wellnigh but now overcome [his] better feelings," Don Henrique resolves to steal a kiss, but is prevented from doing so by Azelie's brother, Renault.[90]

The sensual innocence of the Tragic Mulatta and other raced women ultimately leads to their deaths. However, though the narratives of these raced figures often end in their suicide, death may be either victory or defeat. In early Tragic Mulatta narratives, such as Child's "The Quadroons," suicide is an act of despair, while in the Moorish maiden's story, death is an act of honor. Unlike the Tragic Mulatta whose innocence is violated, the Moorish maiden dies to prove that she has remained virtuous despite the sexual peril she has suffered. Indeed, the eponymous heroine of Lady Barbarina Dacre's tragic 1821 drama *Xarifa* thrusts a dagger into her breast and tells her father, "I die—a virtuous queen—and spotless—wife—."[91] For the harem wives who have no virtue to preserve, suicide is an act of defiance and a sign that they have reappropriated their bodies from the sultans who have imprisoned them. In Montisquieu's *Lettres persanes* (1721), suicide is a declaration of independence. After her affair has been discovered, the houri Roxane leaves a suicide note for the sultan in which she declares, "I may have lived in servitude, but I have always been free . . . and my sprit has always kept itself independent."[92] Unlike the houris and Moorish maidens, however, the Tragic Mulatta is destroyed by grief and despair. If she doesn't die by her own hand, then she dies giving birth to the child that is a result of her sexual violation.

Though Ninine is an evil presence in the novel, her machinations reflect her attempt to break free from the Tragic Mulatta's narrative—and thus point toward a different development of the figure. A forerunner of the exotic femmes fatales we see in sensation fiction of the 1860s and 1870s, such as Mary Elizabeth Braddon's *Aurora Floyd*, Wilkie Collins's *Armadale*, and H. Rider Haggard's *She*, Ingraham's treacherous quadroon anticipates the mixed-race villainesses in such fin de siècle texts as Alexandre Dumas *fils*'s *L'Étrangère* (1876) and Florence Marryat's *Daughter of the Tropics* (1888).[93] While Ninine thwarts her daughter's desire for Don Henrique, even going so far as to drug Azelie before selling her to the Count of Osma, she herself reflects a strong sense of autonomy and sexual agency. Accepting her position as a mixed-race woman who will never be able to marry a white man, Ninine refuses the tragic role of the abandoned lover. Instead, she is empowered by her sexuality and the financial security that self-commodification grants her. She tells the count: "Our beauty purchase for us the hearts and fortunes of men! The proudest wife can boast no more." In fact, she declares that she prefers concubinage to marriage because, as she explains, a *placée* "has all the luxuries and privileges of a wife without its obedience and slavish duties. I would rather be thy father's concubine than his wedded wife."[94] Ninine's attitude is a dramatic departure from the romanticized depictions of *plaçage* in which the mixed-race concubine commits suicide or dies of grief when she is abandoned by her lover. Rather than destroy herself, Ninine sets out to murder the marquise's wife and son. Through murder and manipulation, Ninine defies the tragic narrative in which she, as a mixed-race concubine, has been placed.

# 3 / "Oh Heavens! What Am I?": The Tragic Mulatta as Sensation Heroine

*"I—I—oh Heavens! what am I? A slave—a slave—whom men love only to ruin."*

—CAPTAIN MAYNE REID, *THE QUADROON; OR, A LOVER'S ADVENTURES IN LOUISIANA* (1856)

*"Julia—Julia is a slave! I am Julia; I am a slave; poor slave!"*

—VAN BUREN DENSLOW, *OWNED AND DISOWNED; OR, THE CHATTEL CHILD* (1857)

Published the year before *Lady Audley's Secret*, Mary Elizabeth Braddon's *The Octoroon; or, The Lily of Louisiana* (1861) opens in a crowded ballroom during the London season of 1860. Cora Leslie, an American girl born on a plantation near New Orleans but educated in England, has attracted the interest of Gilbert Margrave, a British engineer celebrated for inventing machinery to replace slave labor. Pointing out Cora's beauty to Mortimer Percy, an American planter, Gilbert asks his acquaintance if he knows who the lovely beauty is. Mortimer responds: "No. But I can do more. I can tell you *what* she is." The southerner then explains to the naïve British gentleman that Cora is the daughter of a slave: "Had you been a planter, Gilbert, you would have been able to discover, as I did, when just now I stood close to that lovely girl, the fatal signs of her birth. At the extreme corner of the eye, and at the root of the finger nails, the South[ern] American can always discover the trace of slavery, though but *one drop* of the blood of the despised race tainted the object upon whom he looked."[1] Gilbert is not the only character unable to read the signs of Cora's racial ancestry. While American Tragic Mulatta narratives traditionally pivot on the mixed-race woman's discovery that she is not free, Braddon's story revolves around a more shocking secret: Cora does not know she is an octoroon! Upon learning that her father has been injured in a slave revolt on his plantation, she returns to New Orleans ignorant of her racial ancestry. "The courted, the caressed, the admired beauty of a London season" soon learns, however, that she is not white.[2] Braddon's novel follows Cora's struggle to escape a narrative that offered only two choices to mixed-race women: sexual violation or death.

In American abolitionist texts, such as Lydia Maria Child's "The Quadroons" (1842), Harriet Beecher Stowe's *Uncle Tom's Cabin* (1852), and William Wells Brown's *Clotel* (1853), the Tragic Mulatta is a sentimental figure of true womanhood whose compromised bloodline prohibits her from marrying her white suitor. However, as British sensation authors such as Braddon capitalized on the popularity of *Uncle Tom's Cabin*, the Tragic Mulatta was transformed into a figure of mystery in the 1850s and 1860s. In lesser-known texts, such as Captain Mayne Reid's *The Quadroon; or, a Lover's Adventures in Louisiana* (1856), Dion Boucicault's play *The Octoroon* (1859), and Braddon's serial, the mixed-race slave becomes an embodiment of dangerous secrets as British authors coupled abolitionist sentiment with narratives of detection and discovery. Although literary history has maintained a national divide between British and American sensation authors, I argue that American abolitionist fiction gave rise to British sensation fiction. Indeed, although Wilkie Collins's *The Woman in White* (1860) is traditionally given as the starting point for British sensation fiction, this genre begins to emerge in the sensational American Tragic Mulatta narratives of the 1840s and 1850s.[3]

Although the abolitionist works of Child, Brown, and Stowe are traditionally categorized as sentimental texts meant to elicit tears and sympathy from readers, the realities of slavery interrupt these narratives by introducing mysterious identities, sexual transgressions, madness, and violence—elements that would later define British sensation fiction—into the genteel drawing rooms of characters and readers alike. In fact, a review in the *English Woman's Journal* expressed concern about the ways in which British consumer culture sensationalized the realities of American slavery. Citing recent abolitionist articles, the reviewer declares: "We are not at liberty to fancy or hope that the practice of the South in the matter of slavery is better than its theory. 'The Character of the Southern States of America,' by F. W. Newman, and 'The Essence of Slavery,' by Isa Craig, are but renewed attempts to make the English public realize that though 'Uncle Tom's Cabin' may be a sensation novel, the Key to it is a sad and trustworthy statement of the facts."[4] However, in Britain, Stowe's novel continued to be read as a work of sensation rather than realism. As British periodicals such as *Blackwood's Edinburgh Magazine*, *Quarterly Review*, and *Sixpenny Journal* sought to define sensation fiction in their reviews of such novels as *The Woman in White* and *Lady Audley's Secret*, reviewers compared the works of Collins and Braddon to Stowe's *Uncle*

*Tom's Cabin*.[5] "Wilkie Collins's extremely clever romance," writes one reviewer of *The Woman in White*, "we regard as the greatest success in sensation writing, with the single exception of Mrs Stowe's deservedly popular work."[6] Indeed, Stowe's Cassy, the brutalized quadroon slave on Simon Legree's plantation, could be read as an early sensation heroine. The violation Cassy endures at her master's hands "hardened womanhood within her," transforming her into a manipulative femme fatale who uses Legree's superstitions and guilt about his sadistic acts against him. In an unsettling scene of domestic intimacy between the quadroon and her master, the sensation genre serves as a means of Cassy's escape when Legree begins reading one of her books, "one of those collections of stories of bloody murders, ghostly legends, and supernatural visitations, which, coarsely got up and illustrated, have a strange fascination for one who once begins to read them."[7] Legree's reading of Cassy's penny dreadful makes him susceptible to her haunting of the garret, a gothic space in which Stowe asks readers to imagine the sexual violence and torture one of his previous victims suffered when she was confined there: "What passed there, we do not say; the negroes used to whisper darkly to each other; but it was known that the body of the unfortunate creature was one day taken down from there, and buried."[8] After masquerading as the ghost of Legree's dead mother and escaping in the disguise of a Spanish lady, Cassy is reunited with her son and daughter in a Canadian Quaker community. Stowe's ending reveals the previously unknown familial connections between the mother and children obfuscated by slavery.

Stowe's novel created such a sensation in Britain that, as Audrey Fisch explains, "Uncle Tom-mania" inspired illustrated songbooks, wallpaper, curio ornaments, dolls, paintings, a card game, a set of quadrilles, abolitionist stationery, not to mention the many theatrical and literary adaptations of the story. As a result of its commercial success, *Uncle Tom's Cabin* became a site of cultural conflict in Britain as reviews revealed "anxieties underlying Victorian questions about the definition and role of culture, of the expanding reading public, and about working-class revolt."[9] The *Spectator*, for example, described how "'the mob,' Victorian shorthand for the working classes, those without education and cultural taste, having 'read a popular book,' are 'rushing to see the leading personages placed in a visible shape before its eyes.'" In the *Times*, the author of an editorial worries: "I fear that the book will . . . be immortalized at the Victoria and Bower Saloon, and no doubt 'the Secret Chamber in Legree's house,' and the 'Death of Tom at the Whipping-post,' will be faithfully recorded; or, 'Legree, the Man of Crime and the Murderer of Uncle Tom,' will attract the unwashed inhabitants of the Transpontine districts. The book, which might have done worlds of good in other hands, will sink into the sewer of literature in penny numbers, and be turned to the worst instead of the best purposes."[10] Fisch observes that this battle between high and low culture in British reviews of *Uncle Tom's Cabin* reflects a deeper anxiety that Stowe's novel would "'excite the passions'" of the masses, "leading them to a dangerous state of excitement approaching anarchy."[11] The criticism leveled against *Uncle Tom's Cabin* in British reviews would be echoed in attacks on the sensation novel in the 1860s (although worries arose over the sensation novel's power to rouse women rather than working-class readers).

More than a decade before *Uncle Tom's Cabin* became an international "media event," to borrow William Warner's term, that inspired several British sensation narratives about imperiled mixed-race slaves, Britain was inundated with a range of American sensations. Shelley Streeby observes that this "culture of sensation" in 1840s America extended far beyond the popular fiction of George Lippard and Ned Buntline to the circulation of daily newspapers and "cheap, sensational story papers such as the *Flag of Our Union* and the *Star Spangled Banner*" via the railway (itself a symbol of sensation), along with various forms of popular entertainment such as blackface minstrelsy.[12] Although writers and critics in the United States almost never used the term to refer to their literature and culture, the British perceived "sensation" as a thoroughly American phenomenon. As a poem in an 1861 issue of *Punch* surmises:

Some would have it an age of Sensation,
If the age one of Sense may not be—
The word's not *Old* England's creation,
But New England's over the sea.

Described in the poem as a "land of fast life and fast laws," America was regarded as a place where everything from a steamer explosion or a senator "goug[ing] a friend / In the course of a lively debate" to the "last new sermon, or wash for the mouth, / New acrobat, planet or drama" was proclaimed a "sensation."[13] The "pois'nous exotic 'Sensation'" generated in America was quickly transported to Britain, where audiences eagerly crowded theaters to see P. T. Barnum's shows, which featured such spectacles as Tom Thumb, Jenny Lind the "Swedish Nightingale," and Mrs. Bloomer, "an American, whose revolutionary championing of a short skirt and long loose trousers fascinated British women, to the bemusement, and often derision, of British men."[14] British lecture halls in "small towns such as Ledbury and Ventnor in Hampshire and the Isle of Wight," as well as in "the major industrial centers such as Manchester, Birmingham, and Leeds" were also filled with spectators who came to see African American abolitionists, including Frederick Douglass, Henry "Box" Brown, William Wells Brown, and William and Ellen Craft, describe in vivid detail how they escaped the horrors of American slavery. Indeed, between his arrival in Liverpool in 1845 and his return to America in 1847, Douglass delivered at least three hundred lectures.[15] A blend of empirical inquiry and entertainment, the lectures allowed audiences to see the fugitive slaves display their scars along with instruments of torture while narrating their heroic flights to freedom.[16]

However, the popularity of Douglass, "Box" Brown, and the Crafts eventually raised questions about whether the abolitionists' message was overshadowed by the celebrity of the fugitive slaves. In 1851, the *Wolverhampton and Staffordshire Herald* accused "Box" Brown's show of offering a "gross and palpable exaggeration" of the institution of slavery, declaring that Brown's exhibition would not fail to "generate disgust at the foppery, conceit, vanity, and egotistical stupidity of the 'Box' Brown school."[17] The review concluded that Brown's show was detrimental to the cause of abolitionism and described those who attended as "wide-mouthed and wondergaping": "The editor 'deeply regret[s] that the public should be gulled' and 'caution[s] those who may attend, to expect only amusement, as the horrors related in the richest nigger style are as good as pantomine.'" The newspaper succeeded in turning away middle-class Victorians seeking a "balance between instruction and diversion."[18] According to an article published a week later in the *Wolverhampton and Staffordshire Herald,* "the nightly attendance has been meagre in the extreme . . . his nocturnal antics [played] to the delight and merriment of the juvenile rag-a-muffins who for the most part make up the 'darkey's' audiences."[19] In fact, attendance had decreased so dramatically that Brown later sued the newspaper for libel and received £100 in damages.

The sensation generated by "Box" Brown and his fellow abolitionists not only threatened to draw attention away from the abolitionist cause, but also threatened to turn other African American abolitionists into spectacles since, after Brown, their events were advertised by enthusiastic British abolitionists in a manner akin to the "oddities" who received top billing in Barnum's shows. During William and Ellen Craft's visit to Bristol, for example, the British abolitionist J. B. Estlin wrote to his American colleague Samuel May: "The Crafts . . . had kind but not judicious, (& some vulgar) advisers in the North of England, neither their interest nor respectability (Ellen's espy) being properly consulted. Some of their hand-bills have been headed 'Arrival of 3 Fugitive Slaves from America'!! as if 3 monkeys had been imported, and their public appearance has been too often of the exhibitive kind."[20] Ellen Craft in particular stoked British fascination as the "almost white" slave who, as an article in the *Liberator* described, "'may become a mother, but not a wife. . . . What passes under the name of marriage, is but a sort of concubinage, which exists not at the will of the parties, but at the will, the whim, caprice, or interest of another.'" Craft escaped this fate by running away to Philadelphia disguised as a white southern gentleman, her husband serving as her valet. However, the obsession with her whiteness recorded in the British press seems to reflect public curiosity in the concubinage (or sexual violence) between her master and mother that produced her fair complexion. Referring to her as a "gentle, refined-looking young creature of twenty-four years," the antislavery tract *Singular Escapes from Slavery* declared that Craft was "as fair as most of her British sisters, and in mental qualifications their equal too."[21] Both embodying and resisting the stereotype of the sexually imperiled mixed-race slave, Craft was a silent figure on the lecture hall's stage. Margaret McCaskill cites the following account of William Wells Brown and William Craft's joint lecture published in the *Scotland Advertiser:* "When the meeting was about to disperse, a general wish was expressed that Mrs. Craft, who was seated on the platform, should present herself to the audience. She seemed rather reluctant to do so, but on the persuasion of the Provost and several other gentlemen, she consented to offer a standing position on the left side of the former. . . . At first she seemed abashed, but the cheering continued, she courtesied [*sic*] gracefully, and retired." As McCaskill asserts, Craft had escaped the auction block only to be "displayed as a specimen of Victorian femininity" in the lecture hall.[22]

Indeed, shortly after the Crafts arrived in England in 1851, the American abolitionist Henry Wright suggested that they be showcased in the Great Exhibition: "Above all, an American slave-auction block must be there, with William and Ellen Craft on the block, Henry Clay as auctioneer, and the American flag floating over it. . . . Or, if they cannot be admitted into the Fair, with other specimens of American ingenuity and skill, they must be exhibited in some place outside, but near it, so that they can be seen and examined with convenience."[23] The Crafts resisted being reduced to mere spectacles by instead promenading through the Crystal Palace on the arms of their British abolitionist friends. William Farmer, who accompanied William Craft through the exhibit, remarked:

"This arrangement was purposefully made in order that there might be no appearance of patronizing the fugitives, but that it might be shown that we regarded them as our equals, and honored them for their heroic escape from slavery." Upon reaching the American section of the exhibit, the abolitionists encountered Hiram Powers's statue *The Greek Slave* (fig. 2). Farmer writes that William Wells Brown took a copy of the *Punch* cartoon *The Virginian Slave. Intended as a Companion to Powers's "Greek Slave,"* produced by one of their companions, and "deposited it within the enclosure by the 'Greek Slave,' saying audibly, 'As an American fugitive slave, I place this "Virginia Slave" by the side of the "Greek Slave," as its most fitting companion.'"[24] Brown's remarks underscore the disparity between the demure Greek slave with eyes cast downward and the weary Virginia slave with sorrowful eyes cast upward. Standing upon a podium decorated with crossed whips, the ebony slave is stripped to her waist, and her wrists are bound with thick shackles (fig. 6). "Unlike in Powers's work," Kate Flint explains, "the nakedness here cannot be seen as classical homage."[25] Whereas Powers's celebrated statue transmutes slavery into a classical form, *Punch*'s image of slavery is one of grotesque realism.

Why would the United States invite universal scrutiny by including Powers's statue in its section of the exhibition? The prominent display of *The Greek Slave* reflects America's failure to realize that slavery, specifically as it was embodied by the figures of "almost white" slaves, had become an inextricable feature of its national identity. To the United States, Powers's statue was the pinnacle of American artistic achievement, but to British critics, she was not a Greek slave, but one of the persecuted mixed-race slaves they'd heard about in the lectures of Douglass, William Wells Brown, and the Crafts. While America sought to defend its claim to the title of "model republic" under the critical eye of Mother England, in the years following the Great Exhibition and the publication of *Uncle Tom's Cabin,* novels, illustrations, songs, and dramas emblazoned with the word "quadroon" or "octoroon" saturated both American and British culture as readers and spectators consumed stories about "almost white" women forced onto the auction block.[26] Ironically, in Britain, this "octoroon fever" was fueled by the Irish authors Reid and Boucicault, whose appropriations of the Tragic Mulatta's narrative dramatized the efforts of an innocent British hero to rescue the mixed-race heroine from the sexual perils of American slavery. Perhaps their interest in America's octoroons and quadroons was inspired by similarities between Ireland's struggle for independence and the ambiguous status of the mixed-race slave's unstable colonized body.

FIGURE 6. John Tenniel, *The Virginian Slave. Intended as a Companion to Power's "Greek Slave," Punch*, 1851. (This item is reproduced by permission of The Huntington Library, San Marino, California.)

## Women in White

Born in Ireland, Reid sailed for New Orleans in 1839 at the age of twenty-one. In the ten years that followed, he migrated from New Orleans to New York, working a variety of jobs along the way, including those as a private tutor, storekeeper, actor, and soldier.[27] Although he left America in 1849, settling in London after being wounded in the Mexican-American War, he earned his living by publishing novels based on his adventures in North and South America, such as *The Rifle Rangers; or, Adventures of an Officer in Southern Mexico* (1850), *The Scalp Hunters; or, Romantic Adventures in Northern Mexico* (1851), *The Desert Home; or, The Adventures of a Lost Family in the Wilderness* (1852), and *The Boy Hunters; or, Adventures in Search of a White Buffalo* (1853). Reid's adventure novels were so popular in both Britain and America that Barnum announced in newspapers: "I have succeeded in engaging Captain Mayne Reid to write a series of plays, founded on his own novels, to be produced simultaneously in England and the United States. Captain Reid's picturesque romances are equally popular on both sides of the Atlantic; millions have read them, and few without feeling intense interest in the scenes and characters he has created."[28] In 1856, Reid published what is arguably his most influential work, *The Quadroon; or, A Lover's Adventures in Louisiana,* a tale that was a departure from his romances of the American frontier. In the preface, Reid declares that "the book is 'founded' upon an actual experience," but he is also careful to explain that he is not the quadroon's lover, informing his readers: "This book is a romance—nothing more. The author is not the hero." Although this novel capitalizes on the recent public obsession with mixed-race slaves generated by *Uncle Tom's Cabin* and the lectures of African American abolitionists touring Britain, Reid insists in a note to his preface: "The book . . . was written many years ago, and would have been then published, but for the interference of a well-known work, which treated of similar scenes and subjects. That work appeared just as the 'Quadroon' was about to be put to press; and the author of the latter, not willing to risk the chances of being considered an imitator had determined on keeping the QUADROON from the public."[29] But unlike Stowe's novel, which focused on reuniting Cassy with the children born from her concubinage with a New Orleans lawyer, Reid's text transformed the Tragic Mulatta's narrative from one of seduction to one of courtship. Indeed, his interracial courtship plot introduces several new elements to the Tragic Mulatta's narrative, which Boucicault and Braddon later borrowed in their adaptations.[30]

Written in the tradition of the travel narrative genre, these retellings begin with the hero, who is either a British gentleman or an American from the North, traveling to New Orleans, a transnational space that, as we saw in chapter 2, was imbued with an atmosphere of exoticism and mystery that often made signifiers of national and racial identity difficult to define. Here, the foreign hero falls in love with the mixed-race heroine and resolves to rescue her from slavery and marry her despite America's antimiscegenation laws. The English or northern gentleman's unfamiliarity with the American South renders him unable to read the mixed-race heroine's racial identity. As authors whitened the mixed-race heroine's body in texts published between 1855 and 1865, transforming her from a quadroon to an octoroon, detection of her racial identity became even more difficult. Indeed, in texts such as the American abolitionist Van Buren Denslow's *Owned and Disowned; or The Chattel Child: A Tale of Southern Life* (1857) and Braddon's *The Octoroon,* the heroine doesn't know her race. The allure of the "almost white" slave, as Reid's narrative reveals, was coupled with a fear that her mixed-race body could pass into white society undetected, a fear that becomes reality in Hannah Crafts's *The Bondwoman's Narrative* (ca. 1855) and Charles Kingsley's *Two Years Ago* (1857).[31] In Kingsley's novel, which is examined in chapter 5, a mixed-race slave, Marie Lavington, escapes slavery by refashioning herself into the Italian diva "La Cordifiamma," yet she lives in constant fear that her body will eventually betray the secret of her ancestry. Although Reid's, Boucicault's, Denslow's, and Braddon's heroines do not conceal the secrets of their bodies once their racial identities are discovered, later sensation narratives, such as *Lady Audley's Secret,* pivoted on the heroine's fear that her body would betray her true identity. Borrowing from the racial discourse of *The Octoroon,* Braddon writes that Lady Audley is anxious that the "dreadful taint" of madness she inherited from her mother will be discovered.[32]

In Reid's novel and the adaptations that followed, the British hero is unable to detect the secrets of the heroine's body on his own. When Reid's narrator, Edward Rutherford, travels to America in search of adventure on a steamer bound for St. Louis, he meets the Louisiana Creole Eugénie Besançon, whom he helps swim ashore when the ship capsizes. When he later awakens at her plantation, recovering from his wounds, it is with "an impression on [his] mind of having beheld amid this confusion a face of extraordinary beauty—the face of a lovely girl!"—but it was not the face of Eugénie. He is informed by one of her slaves that the mysterious face, "of a strange type—its strangely-beautiful expression, not Caucasian, not Indian, not Asiatic," instead belongs to Aurore, a quadroon slave. At first repelled by his discovery, Edward's interest returns when he learns that she is an accomplished lady who can read, write, and play the piano.[33] In Boucicault's adaptation, Zoe, the octoroon, is forced to reveal her racial identity to George Peyton, who was born in Louisiana but educated in Europe, when he proposes that she become his "wife—the sharer of my hopes, my ambitions, and my sorrows." Referring to herself as though she is a specimen of mixed-race, Zoe asks: "George, do you see that hand you hold? look at these fingers; do you see the nails are of a bluish tinge?" She points out a similar "faint blue mark" in her eyes.[34] Zoe's account of her body echoes the writings of eighteenth-century scientists, such as Jean-Baptiste Labat, who believed that fingernails could reveal signs of racial difference. However, the color of the mark varied from author to author. While Boucicault represents the mark as blue, Labat asserts that if a mark at the root of the nails is "white or nearly white, one may say with certainty that the child is a Mulatto."[35] After revealing signs of her racial difference, Zoe asks, "Do you know what I am?" When George declares that he does not know, Zoe, who exhibits more self-loathing than Reid's and Braddon's heroines, exclaims, "I'm an unclean thing—forbidden by the laws—I'm an Octoroon!"[36]

The Tragic Mulatta's crime was in her mixed blood, which placed her outside the conventions of ideal womanhood. She did not commit murder, adultery, or bigamy, but like later sensation heroines, such as Lydia Gwilt, Aurora Floyd, Lady Audley, and Lady Isabel Vane, the Tragic Mulatta was an affront to domestic stereotypes. As Lyn Pykett explains: "The sensation 'heroine' . . . offers a complex and contradictory range of significations, and is not simply the iconic embodiment of transgressive femininity, or a fantasy version of a feared or desired female power, as some critics have argued. If the sensation heroine embodies anything, it is an uncertainty about the definition of the feminine, or of 'woman.'"[37] The British adaptations of the Tragic Mulatta's narrative highlight this questioning of Victorian femininity by offering a reversal of Walter Scott's *Ivanhoe* in which Ivanhoe chose the fair Rowena over the Jewess, or "dark lady," Rebecca. In Reid's, Boucicault's, and Braddon's texts, the British hero chooses the slave over the beautiful white heroine who puts aside her own desires to help the hero rescue the octoroon.

Race is not the only secret that must be detected in these British retellings of the Tragic Mulatta's narrative. The mixed-race heroine, with the help of the hero, must uncover whether she is a slave or free. As in the later works of Braddon, Collins, and Mrs. Henry Wood in which the sensation heroine's true social class must be revealed, the Tragic Mulatta's identity is defined solely by paper. Indeed, the novel itself participates in the assignation of identity, the pages of the text solidifying the Tragic Mulatta as a recognizable figure of ideal femininity. During the height of the British sensation movement, the construction of Victorian identity in such works as *The Woman in White* frequently hinged on ephemeral documents such as parish registries. In *Lady Audley's Secret*, for example, Lucy Graham's extensive paper trail, which culminates in Robert Audley's discovery of a "dilapidated paper-covered bonnet-box" with labels bearing her previous names, proves that she is a bigamist.[38] However, without documents to prove otherwise, sensation characters could exchange an old identity for a new one. In Reid's novel, the question of Aurore's status begins as one of ownership—who owns Aurore? Eugénie Besançon or the villain, Gayarre? By the end of the novel, Reid reveals that neither of these people has a claim to Aurore because Eugénie's father had signed free papers for her, which Gayarre, a New Orleans lawyer, later stole and hid away.

Whereas Aurore believes that she is a slave and then discovers that she is free, Boucicault's stage drama reverses this plot. In *The Octoroon*, Boucicault depicts the mixed-race heroine, Zoe, as a free woman, who is later sold to pay off her deceased father's debts. Again stolen documents are central to the plot. In Boucicault's play, a letter releasing the Peyton plantation from debt has been stolen by the villain, M'Closky. The villain's theft of Zoe's free papers and a letter releasing the estate from its debt (a letter which he commits murder to obtain) is motivated by more than his desire to possess the octoroon. It is also a skirmish in class conflict: M'Closky declares: "Curse their old families—they cut me—a bilious conceited, thin lot of dried-up aristocracy. I hate 'em. Just because my grandfather wasn't some broken-down Virginia transplant, or a stingy old Creole, I ain't fit to sit down to the same meat with them. . . . I'll sweep these Peytons from this section of the country." The lower-class Irishman presumes that the not-quite-white heroine shares his hatred for the Peytons. In proposing to Zoe, he asks her to become both his lover and partner in ruining the family: "You shall be mistress of Terrebonne. . . . [T]hese Peytons are bust; cut 'em; I am rich, jine me; I'll set you up grand, and we'll give these first families our dust, until you'll see their white skins shrivel up with hate and rage."[39] Realizing that she won't come to him of her own free will, M'Closky steals her free papers so he can then purchase her as a slave. In the American version of the play, Zoe commits suicide before the discovery of M'Closky's crime is revealed, while in British performances, George discovers the villain's treachery in time to rescue her. In both Reid's and Boucicault's texts, the mixed-race heroine's fate hinges on whether the villain's theft of her free papers will be discovered.

While British authors like Reid and Boucicault were creating narratives in which the hero does not know the heroine's race, American authors such as Denslow were publishing sensational tales in which the heroine does not know her race.[40] In his description of Julia, the mixed-race heroine of *Owned and Disowned*, Denslow harkens back to the descriptions of Creole women in travel narratives from the West Indies and New Orleans: "The voluptuous loveliness of the creole, mingling perhaps, with the pride of the Spanish and the grace of the French, combine in Julia with the mentality of the American."[41] In the labyrinthine plot of Denslow's novel, Julia discovers that she is not white when her half sister Ada overhears their father arranging to sell Julia to the infamous pirate Defoe in order to save himself from bankruptcy. In a letter to Defoe, her father reveals that if the pirate had not demanded Julia as payment for the debt, "her intelligence and beauty, united as they are with the most amiable disposition, could not fail to secure for me through her an alliance, by marriage, with some of the 'first families' of the South—a connexion which would ensure me treble what I can get for her as a slave, even from you. Such was my design in rearing and educating her." Acknowledging that his debt "makes such benevolence too expensive a luxury," Julia's father confesses that "it would be nothing more or less than a cheat to deceive the world as to her rightful condition; and the best course is to let her occupy the position for which nature and her birth designed her."[42] Julia is informed by her half sister, Ada, that she is not white: "He whom you call your father is the father only of your shame. Nay, he has sold you, as he would a common negro, to yonder wretch, outlaw, pirate, fiend, Defoe, who is even now bantering with him about the price." In response to this news, in a scene that Denslow may have borrowed from Kingsley's *Two Years Ago*, which was published earlier the same year, Julia approaches the mirror, where "she turned and gazed earnestly upon her reflected likeness . . . as if to read there the hard story which her sister could not tell. Unloosing her hair from her comb, she brought her long jetty curls before her shoulders, until they covered her whole bosom, and fell down below her waist. . . . As she drew away her hand, she held that off, and scanned its pallid whiteness. Then her gaze wandered from feature to feature of her countenance, till at last it vibrated between her own rich ruby lips and black, lustrous, and passionate eye." Julia scans her body, looking for signs of blackness that aren't there. Looking at herself, she "murmured in a low, distant voice, as if her soul had been spirited away. . . . 'Julia—Julia is a slave! I am Julia; I am a slave; poor slave!'"[43] Unlike Reid's, Boucicault's, and Braddon's texts, Denslow's representation of the mixed-race heroine shows that there is not a single sign of difference, such as a blue tint in the fingernail or in the eye, which Julia can read to determine her racial ancestry. Denslow shows Julia dissociating from her body as it proves incapable of producing evidence of her racial difference.

Since her body is indecipherable, Julia turns to Ada for answers, but when Julia asks who her mother was, her half sister, who is described as "a doll-like, though lovely creature, whom no years could change from child to woman," cannot articulate how Julia came to be.[44] As a representation of ideal womanhood, Ada is unable to voice the relationship between their father and the slave woman that concluded in Julia's birth. Underscoring the role of social institutions such as the church and the legal system in determining racial identity, Denslow shows that Julia is only able to obtain the truth about her racial ancestry from a priest who shows her the title papers for herself and her mother. She then learns from the priest that her mother was a quadroon slave whose "father and owner had intended to free her, but died suddenly, and she was thrown into the market for sale." She was purchased by Julia's father, who did not inform her that he "was her owner, but visiting her as a friend, with honeyed words upon his lips, proposed to secure her liberty and make her his wife. So he gained her affections, and she yielded to her lover and affianced husband, what as her owner even he would blush to have enforced."[45] Rather than her narrative ending in death, Julia's mother contracts smallpox shortly after Julia's birth, the loss of her beauty freeing her from slavery. She retreats to a convent where she repents for her sins.

Like Denslow's Julia, Braddon's heroine, Cora, must not only detect her free status but also her race and the sexual transgressions that led to her birth. As Franny Nudelman explains in her examination of Harriet Jacobs's *Incidents in the Life of a Slave Girl* (1861), "The tragic mulatta is both the sign and site of sexual abuse: the color of her skin makes visible the fact that her forefathers raped her foremothers, and she is imagined as the object of the white man's continued violence."[46] In British versions of the Tragic Mulatta's narrative, the threat of sexual violence looms over the domestic space, but Reid's, Boucicault's, and Braddon's heroines do not suffer the physical or sexual violence that Child's Xarifa, Stowe's Cassy, or Brown's Clotel endure. Moreover, neither Reid nor

Boucicault provides any background about Aurore's and Zoe's mothers and the possible violation they suffered at the hands of their masters. Braddon's text, however, narrates the violence suffered by the heroine's mother, Francilia, who is the quintessence of the Tragic Mulatta stereotype. Upon returning to her father's plantation, Cora is informed by the planter Augustus Horton: "There is, perhaps, a secret; there is, it may be, a fatality which overshadows your young life. Be mine, and none shall ever taunt you with that fatal secret; be mine, and you shall be the proudest beauty in Louisiana, the queen of New Orleans. . . . [B]e mine, and the debt owed me by your father shall be canceled."[47] Cora dismisses Augustus, but asks Toby, Francilia's slave-husband, to reveal the secret of her birth: "One day, Francilia left for Saint Louis, with her master and mistress. They were absent some weeks. . . . When Francilia—returned—she . . . had become your father's mistress. She confessed all to me, with tears, and heart-rending grief!" After her daughter is sent to England, Francilia is sold because the "glance of those mournful black eyes became an eternal reproach, which irritated and tormented" her master.[48] She later commits suicide to avoid being raped by her new master. Cora, upon learning that she is the daughter of a slave, confronts her father and fiercely taunts him when he threatens to whip Toby for revealing the secret. "Strike me rather than him," she exclaims. "Prove to me, sir, that I am before my master; for if I am indeed your daughter, I demand of you an account of your conduct to my mother." When her father asks what more he could have done beyond trying to educate her abroad to protect her from the knowledge of her birth, Cora vehemently responds, "You could have refrained from giving me life!"[49]

Once discovered, the mixed-race heroine's bloodline jeopardizes her position within the domestic sphere. Exposure of the heroine's racial secret also highlights the representation of "black" and white femininity as these sensation narratives subvert traditional constructions of gender and race, as well as the role both mixed-race and white women play in the public and private spheres. Indeed, as the Tragic Mulatta struggles to return to the protection of the domestic sphere to maintain her virtue, we see the moral character of her white counterpart improved by participation in the public sphere. By juxtaposing the ideal white woman with the mysterious dark woman, the British authors establish early on that though their exotic beauties may have obscure origins, they also have the virtue, gentility, education, and refinement of their white counterparts. Though the English hero is aware of the white heroine's beauty, wealth, and social connections, he falls in love with the demure slave instead because she is the true representative of ideal Victorian womanhood. While Reid depicts Eugénie and the quadroon Aurore as equals, both Boucicault and Braddon show that the mixed-race woman is superior to her fashionable and worldly counterpart. Braddon contrasts her mixed-race heroine, Cora, to her white counterpart, Adelaide Horton, explaining: "There was a marked contrast between the two friends. Young as Adelaide Horton was, she had already all the finished elegance and easy confidence of a woman of fashion. Frivolous, capricious, and something of a coquette, she was born to charm in a ball-room, and to shine in a crowd." Whereas Adelaide is enamored with the social world, Cora, upon discovering her ancestry, rejects her fashionable life in London, accusing her father: "The purchase-money which you received for her perhaps served to pay for the costly dresses which you bestowed upon me! The diamonds which have glittered upon my neck and arms were perhaps bought with the price of my mother's blood."[50]

The white heroine's proximity to the evils of slavery brings her into contact with political debate and struggle. Yet, unexpectedly, it is through their public engagement that the white women in these narratives approach ideal womanhood. For example, Eugénie's cross-dressing in Reid's *The Quadroon* allows her to gain access to the gambling dens of men and to the exploitation and exchange of the slave auction. However, instead of these elements corrupting her, the agency she exhibits gives her the power to recover her father's estate. In imagining the fate of the ideal woman, Reid shows Eugénie living a life of chaste solitude because she lost her first "virgin love!" to her slave, Aurore. While Reid's narrator has established a concubinage with Aurore because anti-interracial laws forbid them to marry, Eugénie remains chaste: "Hers was a mighty will; and all its energies were employed to pluck the fatal arrow from her heart. . . . Her heart's young hope was crushed—her gay spirit shrouded—but there are other joys in life besides the play of the passions; and, it may be, the path of love is not the true road to happiness."[51] In Reid's narrative, the mixed-race slave's virtue is compromised by concubinage, while Eugénie resides in chaste solitude.

Boucicault also exposes his white heroine, Dora Sunnyside, to the evils of slavery, but this exposure changes her for the better. Dora's proximity to slavery emphasizes her own commodification on the marriage market, but instead of being "sold" by her parents, Dora recognizes her own worth. Knowing that the Peyton's plantation is facing financial ruin, Dora says: "George knows that I am an heiress; my fortune would release this estate from debt. . . . If he would only propose to marry me I would accept him." But as Dora soon discovers, George is in love with Zoe. She puts her desire for George aside in an attempt to purchase Terrebonne and all its slaves at the auction. Declaring to her father that she wants to buy Terrebonne, she asks him to sell her property at Comptableau and buy Terrebonne instead. When her father questions her, she threatens, "Do you want *me* to stop here and *bid* for it?"[52] To keep his daughter away from the auction scene, Mr. Sunnyside agrees to purchase Terrebonne for her. The slave auction takes place inside the Peyton home, but though it isn't in a public market, it's still construed as a space where ladies should not be present. Dora, however, returns to the auction and attempts to outbid the villainous M'Closky. When M'Closky outbids her and a fight erupts between him and George, the other men gathered remark: "Ain't we forgetting there's a lady present? . . . If we can't behave like Christians, let's try to act like gentlemen. . . . He didn't ought to bid against a lady." In the American version of the play, Dora's virtuous attempt to rescue Zoe from slavery is rewarded when the dying octoroon remarks: "I stood between your heart and hers. When I am dead she will not be jealous of your love for me."[53] Boucicault leaves audiences to believe that in time George and Dora will marry.

Adelaide Horton is also rewarded with marriage in Braddon's adaptation of Reid's novel. Like Boucicault's Dora, Adelaide does not initially exhibit abolitionist sentiment. However, while Dora doesn't display animosity toward Zoe, Adelaide spurns Cora's friendship upon discovering her ancestry. She even goes so far as to denounce Cora publicly on a steamship the octoroon has taken to visit her mother's grave. Jealous that the British hero has rejected her in favor of "the despised daughter of a slave," she accuses the captain of the ship of allowing "a mulattress to take her place on board your boat amongst the free citizens of New Orleans." However, her cousin, Mortimer Percy, admonishes her: "Oh! Adelaide, Adelaide . . . this is indeed despicable!"[54] The white heroine is eventually tempered by her exposure to the evils of slavery, which leads her to put aside her own desire for the English hero to help him rescue his beloved octoroon. She is later rewarded when her cousin proposes marriage—the first moment in which Mortimer feels love rather than obligation for his cousin, whom he previously felt bound to marry for "commercial interests."[55] As with Reid's Eugénie and Boucicault's Dora, commitment to abolitionism brings Adelaide closer to the rewards of Victorian domesticity. In most sensation fiction, the exposure of secrets and past transgressions is contained by the domestic sphere. In *Lady Audley's Secret*, for example, forced by Robert Audley to confess, Lady

Audley falls on her knees before her husband and admits all, including the "hereditary taint" of insanity from which she was desperate to escape. Everything in the novel has led up to this moment, when Robert Audley has gathered enough information to expose his aunt. However, instead of being tried for the attempted murder of her first husband, Lady Audley is placed in a private asylum. The transgressions that occur in the domestic sphere are resolved in the privacy of the home rather than in the public court of law. However, in British and American abolitionist tales of the Tragic Mulatta, the mixed-race heroine is ripped from the comfort and privacy of the domestic sphere and subjected to public exposure and sale on the auction block. Exposed on the auctioneer's platform, she is stripped of her whiteness.[56] She becomes a spectacle in which her white body is read as black. In *Scenes of Subjection*, Saidiya Hartman explains that the Tragic Mulatta's "white or near-white body . . . makes the captive's suffering visible and discernable."[57] On the auction block, the Tragic Mulatta's body becomes a blank screen upon which are inscribed all the wrongs of slavery.

The auction-block scenes in abolitionist fiction are sensational in two senses—not only is the body of the mixed-race slave exposed, but both spectators and readers are invited to witness her physical sensations. Stowe's Cassy is not subjected to a public sale, but is auctioned off in private, which was often the case with "fancy girls" (fig. 7). Her private sale indicates that she is dissociated from her body, which she prostituted to her lover's cousin in order to keep her children, who were inevitably sold. Since Cassy is a spectacle of fallen womanhood, Emmeline assumes the role of the virtuous and sexually imperiled Tragic Mulatta. Emmeline's exposure on the auction block is a figurative rape, yet the sensations she feels there make her more beautiful: "The blood flushes painfully in her otherwise colorless cheek, her eye has a feverish fire, and her mother groans to see that she looks more beautiful than she ever saw her before" (fig. 8).[58] She is "more beautiful" in her public shame because her flushed cheeks emphasize her whiteness. P. Gabrielle Foreman points out in her reading of Louisa Picquet's autobiography, *The Octoroon Slave and Concubine*, that Picquet "recognizes that enslaved women are placed in front of viewers not only to be bought, as she explains to Mattison derisively, but as spectacle, 'to be seen.'"[59] Indeed, the illustration of Stowe's Emmeline on the auction block depicts her posed in a manner similar to Powers's *The Greek Slave*.

While the slave auction scene is a sensational moment in both American and British abolitionist texts, it becomes a climactic moment of exposure in British versions of the Tragic Mulatta's narrative. In Reid's,

FIGURE 7. Hammatt Billings, untitled illustration of Cassy at private auction, *Uncle Tom's Cabin*, 1853. (The Historic New Orleans Collection, accession no. 85-363-RL.)

Boucicault's, and Braddon's texts, public exposure on the auction block immediately follows the heroine's discovery of her true identity. As in the novels of Stowe and Brown, Reid's Tragic Mulatta, Aurore, "beautiful as ever," creates a sensation among the crowd witnessing her auction: "Every voice became hushed, and every eye was bent upon her as she moved across the floor. Men hurried forward from distant parts of the hall to get a nearer glance; others made way for her, stepping politely back as if she had been a queen." Reid also invokes the image of *The Greek Slave* in his description of Aurore standing "upon the dais like a statue upon its pedestal—the type of sadness and beauty."[60] However, Aurore upsets this fantasy of exploited white womanhood because she wears the "head-dress . . . worn by all quadroons—the 'toque' of the Madras kerchief, which sat upon her brow like a coronet, its green, crimson, and yellow

FIGURE 8. Hammatt Billings, untitled illustration of Emmeline on the auction block, *Uncle Tom's Cabin*, 1853. (The Historic New Orleans Collection, accession no. 85–363–RL.)

checks contrasting finely with the raven blackness of her hair."[61] While the American edition of the novel depicts Aurore wearing the toque, the illustration that accompanies this scene in a British edition depicts the traditional image of the "white" woman for sale (figs. 9, 10). Aurore does not wear the toque in the sketch, and like Stowe's Emmeline, her hair is undone. While Reid's text uses the toque as a sign of Aurore's racial difference, the accompanying illustration in the British edition removes it, perhaps because the illustrator did not want to surrender the fantasy.

In Denslow's *Owned and Disowned,* however, the mixed-race heroine embodies the transgressive power of the sensation heroine by speaking out on the auction block. The slave market becomes a lecture hall as she cries out against the injustice of slavery. Speaking out in this manner disrupts the fantasy of the sale because she is no longer the image of refined and silent womanhood. Before Julia is brought to the block, the

FIGURE 9. Untitled illustration of Aurore wearing a headdress in an American edition of *The Quadroon* by Mayne Reid, 1856. (Courtesy of the Louis Round Wilson Special Collections Library, University of North Carolina at Chapel Hill.)

auctioneer says: "Now, gentlemen, we'll have [in] a little the nicest girl that ever went to market. I have sold things afore in my time, but I tell you—Boys, bring out No. Three. No, not often, gentlemen, you can buy such property as No. Three."[62] Departing from the traditional posture of the Tragic Mulatta on the auction block, Julia does not look down but meets the gaze of the spectators: "Disdaining the touch of the attendants who would have led her forth, with eyes not suffused with tears, but flashing with suppressed rage, Julia advanced with a firm, elastic

FIGURE 10. Untitled illustration of Aurore without a headdress in a British edition of *The Quadroon* by Mayne Reid, 1856. (Department of Special Collections, Charles E. Young Research Library, UCLA.)

step, and after upraising her dark orbs for a few moments, as if in prayer, to heaven . . . she turned and faced the curious and disgusting gaze of the wondering audience, with a dignity not unlike that with which a brave European princess, wrecked among savages, would have looked at her captors." In fact, when the auctioneer takes her "by the hand, he would have held it up after his manner with female slaves, as a tradesman would exhibit his stuffs," Julia shrieks, "'Hands off, low man!' . . . starting suddenly from him, and bending her eagle eye for a moment upon him, with a fierceness before which he quailed. 'Hands off, vile monster, I repeat.'" In Denslow's portrayal of the auction-block scene, Julia reappropriates her body and defines how it will be used in slavery. Rejecting the auctioneer's description of her as a "putty governess," a euphemism for "fancy girl" or concubine, Julia declares: "Silence, dog! be silent, I tell you. . . . Sell me, work me, lash me to your heart's content, if you choose, but dare not to insult me!"[63] Julia is punished for attempting to repossess her body when the auctioneer encourages the spectators to touch her. "Walk up an' look at her," he says. "Don't be afeared genmen, if she is shy. Feel of her, gentlemen." Whereas his contemporaries typically placed the octoroon on a pedestal, rendering her as silent and immobile as Powers's *Greek Slave,* Denslow emphasizes the physical peril women would have endured on the auction block. Heightening the sensationalism of an "almost white" woman being subjected to the physical and verbal insults of a slave auction, Denslow shows the auctioneer threatening to whip Julia: "Give me my whip . . . hold the white skinned wench, while I lash her." In Kingsley's novel, examined in chapter 5, Marie also defends herself on the auction block and is whipped for "speaking as a woman should speak"; however, before Julia is struck by the lash in Denslow's narrative, her betrothed rescues her.[64]

Similarly, Braddon also calls attention to the female slave's status as an object to be seen as well as possessed: "Eyeglasses were raised, spectacles put on, and looks of insolent admiration were fixed upon the unhappy girl." Not only is her body a spectacle, but it also becomes a focal point of social conflict as her British fiancé and his American rival feverishly bid against each other for ownership of her, one desiring her as his wife, the other as his mistress. However, whereas the slave auction is the pinnacle of Reid's and Boucicault's works, Braddon offers a different climax: Cora's confrontation with her new master, Augustus Horton. Though Cora briefly thinks of suicide, Braddon guides her away from the traditional fate of the Tragic Mulatta, explaining that, "to this girl, religiously educated, there was something horrible in the idea of suicide. It seemed a doubt of Providence even to think of this worst and last resource."[65] Instead, Cora decides to flee Horton's villa. Using the rope that bound her wrists at the slave auction, Cora climbs over the balcony and runs, but when Horton captures her, he says: "It is not the right of a master that I would exercise, but that of a lover. . . . The rigours of slavery are not for you. Reward my devotion with one smile, one word of encouragement, and a life of luxury shall be yours." Rebuffing him, Cora raises the rope that had previously bound her and says, "One step further, and it is I who will inflict upon you the chastisement of a slave, by striking you across the face" (fig. 11).[66] Instead of rebelling against Victorian womanhood sexually as Lady Audley and Aurora Floyd do, Cora rebels against a narrative that would inflict on her the fate of her mother. Although Cora defies her master verbally and threatens physical violence, her agency is short-lived. Before Horton can respond to her raised arm, her father and fiancé rescue her.

## Afterlives of the Tragic Mulatta

The later sensation fiction of Braddon, Collins, and Wood culminates in the removal of all threats to the domestic sphere and the assertion of middle-class virtues. (Lady Audley awaits death in a Belgian asylum, Lydia Gwilt commits suicide, and a repentant Lady Isabel Vane dies of grief.) Indeed, with few exceptions, these authors return both characters and readers to "a 'pure,' closed, middle-class" space.[67] But what of the mixed-race heroines who were rescued from the tragic fates of their American predecessors, such as Child's Xarifa, who fractures her head against a wall, or Brown's Clotel, who dives into the Potomac? Reid's, Boucicault's, and Braddon's heroines survive their narratives, but the authors diverge in the endings they give to these mixed-race slaves and their English lovers. While Braddon's ending explicitly alludes to marriage, Reid's conclusion is more ambiguous: "Would you have me paint the ceremony—the pomp and splendour—the ribbons and rosettes—the after-scenes of perfect bliss? Hymen, forbid! All these must be left to your fancy, if your fancy deign to act. But the interest of a 'lover's adventures' usually ends with the consummation of his hopes—not even always extending to the altar—and you, reader, will scarce be curious to lift the curtain, that veils the tranquil after-life of myself and my beautiful QUADROON."[68] Although he seems to give readers license to imagine Aurore and Edward united in marriage or in concubinage, the couple remains in Louisiana where antimiscegenation laws prohibit marriage. Reid's

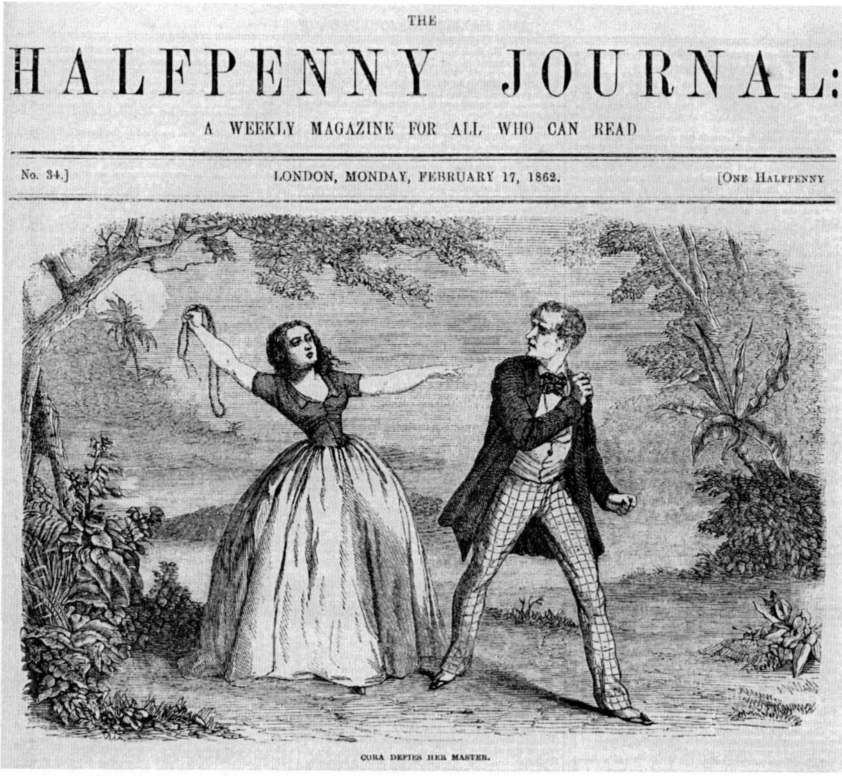
THE
HALFPENNY JOURNAL:
A WEEKLY MAGAZINE FOR ALL WHO CAN READ
No. 34.] LONDON, MONDAY, FEBRUARY 17, 1862. [ONE HALFPENNY
CORA DEFIES HER MASTER.

FIGURE 11. *Cora Defies Her Master, Halfpenny Journal*, 1862. (Department of Special Collections, Charles E. Young Research Library, UCLA.)

reluctance to imagine a definitive ending for the quadroon reflects the conflict between sensation fiction, which transformed America's mixed-race slaves into romantic figures, and the abolitionist project seeking to expose the horrific truths of slavery. In Reid's novel and the adaptations that followed, British literature subsumed America's sensational abolitionist fiction and thereby changed the terms of the Tragic Mulatta's consumption. Both Reid and Braddon obscure the realities of slavery to offer their mixed-race heroines romantic endings.

Boucicault, however, resolved to give his octoroon a realistic conclusion. In the original version of the play performed for American audiences in 1859, Zoe commits suicide to escape the sexual violence that awaits her at the home of her new master, M'Closky. Zoe's death not only restores order on the Peyton plantation by leaving George free to marry the white heroine he rejected in favor of the octoroon, but it also erases the "fatal mark" of difference from Zoe's eyes. "Dat's what her soul's gwine to do," remarks a fellow slave. "It's going up dar, whar dere's no line atween folks."[69] In this ending, Boucicault condemns an institution and its adherents who would rather see the mixed-race slave kill herself than marry her white lover. British audiences, however, rejected this ending when the play premiered in London in 1861. Responding to pressure from the public and the press, Boucicault revised the play's final act. In what has become known as the English ending, George walks onstage after the infamous steamboat explosion, carrying an unconscious Zoe in his arms. Many spectators welcomed this change, including Reid, who praised Bouciault for having "had the good taste to alter [the ending], restoring the beautiful quadroon to the happier destiny to which the romance had consigned her."[70] But as Boucicault explains in a letter to the London *Times*, this new ending rang false: "In the death of the Octoroon lies the moral and teaching of the whole work. Had this girl been saved, and the drama brought to a happy end, the horrors of her position, irremediable from the very nature of the institution of slavery, would subside into the condition of temporary annoyance. . . . Has public sentiment in this country veered so diametrically on this subject . . . that the feeling of the English people is taking another course?"[71] Indeed, a decade earlier, interracial unions between Englishmen and mixed-race West Indian women had been the source of gothic horror in *Jane Eyre* (1847) and racist caricature in *Vanity Fair* (1847).[72] Although Zoe survives, her unconscious state in the English ending seems to indicate a refusal on Boucicault's part to allow the sensation genre to diminish the realism of American slavery and antimiscegenation laws.

Braddon's narrative, however, offers readers the ending that both Reid and Boucicault resist: "Cora is a happy wife in our dear native land—happy in the society of the father she loves, secure in the devotion of her proud English husband."[73] Denslow's novel also ends with Julia's marriage to her childhood friend, Walter; however, the wedding celebration is interrupted by her father, who, "stung by remorse, overwhelmed by rage, shame and chagrin, having no motive to survive his irrecoverable disgrace . . . had returned to the scene of the wealth he had abused and the opportunities for good which he had prostituted to evil—to blow out his brains."[74] Through the sensational death of Julia's father, Denslow's narrative symbolically eradicates patriarchal slave society. Julia and Walter eventually relocate to the North, where, in the last scene of the novel, they tell their history to their mixed-race daughter. Although

Braddon makes the interracial marriage of Cora and Gilbert explicit, she does not allude to any children in the novel's conclusion. As Kimberly Harrison argues: "Braddon's narrative is less forceful in its antislavery design. . . . While [Gilbert] Margrave goes to America with the goal of mitigating slavery, the novel ends without reference to a large-scale vision of abolition."[75] Instead, after a brief visit to Francilia's grave, Cora and Gilbert travel to England, where American slavery is the subject of sensation dramas and penny dreadfuls rather than a way of life. Cora is reabsorbed into Britain's domestic sphere, but Braddon does not explain how Cora's race fits within her new identity as an English wife. Do her British neighbors know she is a former slave? Or is this a secret of omission protected by her husband and father?[76] Instead, Cora passes into the domestic realm, carrying the secrets of American slavery and miscegenation into her middle-class English home, where she becomes what Henry James describes as one of "those most mysterious of mysteries, the mysteries which are at our own doors."[77]

# 4 / "I Wonder What Market He Means That Daughter For": The Beautiful Jewess and the Tragic Muse

*My daughter! O my ducats! O my daughter!*
*Fled with a Christian! O my Christian ducats!*
*Justice, the law, my ducats and my daughter!*

SHAKESPEARE, *THE MERCHANT OF VENICE* (1596)

*I am making myself commercial, I take and I pile up the dollars.*

RACHEL TO LOUISE DE SAIGNEVILLE, BOSTON, OCTOBER 8, 1855

Before the Jewish actress Rachel Félix debuted at the Théâtre-Français in 1838, the title "Tragic Muse" stood for a figure English, white, chaste, and matronly. These traits were embodied by the famous tragic actress Mrs. Sarah Siddons, who became "'the most public woman of the day' without sacrificing her claim to private respectability." Unlike most actresses or "public women" who were tainted by their profession, Mrs. Siddons deflected this stigma through the title of wife and mother: "In 1786, following a particularly brilliant performance as Belvidera in *Venice Preserv'd*, she was discovered at home, 'at her sick child's cot, rocking it with her foot and holding another at her breast, her new rôle in hand, which she was learning.'"[1] Immortalized in Joshua Reynolds's 1784 portrait *Sarah Siddons as the Tragic Muse*, Siddons sits in a pose that recalls "the posture of the prophet Isaiah as rendered by Michelangelo in the Sistine Chapel."[2] Her white skin is illuminated against shadows in which the Aristotelian figures of pity and fear loom behind her (fig. 12). Though the lack of color in her cheeks is in character with her portrayal of Melpomene, the Tragic Muse in Greek mythology, the whiteness of her complexion also represents her Englishness and her virtue.

Unlike Mrs. Siddons, Rachel Félix was known only by her first name. Her lack of affiliation implied immorality and instability, and hence a dangerous mobility. In Rachel, ideas of nationalism, ethnicity, and sexuality were united and spectacularized in one young body. As James Agate

FIGURE 12. Sir Joshua Reynolds, *Sarah Siddons as the Tragic Muse*, 1783–84. (Courtesy of the Huntington Art Collections, San Marino, California.)

wrote in his 1928 biography of Rachel, France's Tragic Muse was "first a great Jewess, second a great actress, and third a great lover."[3] She achieved iconic status as both a French actress and as a spectacle of Judaism. While texts such as Benjamin Disraeli's *Tancred* (1847) and George Eliot's *Daniel Deronda* (1876) pivot on the secret of Jewish ancestry, Rachel never hid her heritage. Rachel's Jewish identity invited both adulation and anti-Semitic stereotypes. As Rachel toured Europe, England, and the United States, her image also circulated in the nineteenth-century cultural imagination as a raced figure of power and sexual autonomy. She came to embody a certain "type" of "legendary, literary, tragic Jewish Woman. . . . After Rachel, women like her would be seen as a type in France; someone thin, dark, Jewish, nervous, passionate, serious, and maybe a little desperate might be called *une vraie Rachel.*"[4]

This chapter investigates how "Tragic Muse" was transformed from a title associated with the chaste and matronly Mrs. Siddons into one that connoted the exoticism, beauty, and sexual power of the Jewish actress. Her image grew out of a long tradition of the *belle juive,* or Beautiful Jewess, as a literary figure that dominated perceptions of the "dark" woman in Britain, Europe, and the United States. The Tragic Muse narratives explored in the second section of the chapter reflect how the Jewish actress used this racial ambiguity to her advantage. While the Beautiful Jewess was typically a victim of violence either from her father or from the European men who wanted to possess her, the Tragic Muse used her powers of performance to escape this fate by moving between racial and social identities. Examining the Rachel-inspired Tragic Muse figures in Honoré de Balzac's *Cousin Bette* (1846), Charlotte Brontë's *Villette* (1853), Mary Elizabeth Braddon's *Rupert Godwin* (1867), and Eliot's *Daniel Deronda* shows how the *belle juive* took on both power and sexual autonomy—sometimes turning into a dangerous femme fatale who was empowered by her intelligence and artistic genius. But though the Tragic Muse attained the public voice, class mobility, and sexual freedom that the Beautiful Jewess did not, the narratives featuring her often disciplined her disruptive body. In the end, the Tragic Muse was forced to make a choice: retire to the domestic sphere and assume the roles of wife and mother or remain on the stage and perish.

## A "Wanton Beauty"

Before Rachel brought images of sexual power and self-commodification to representations of the Jewess, this literary figure was a paragon of virtue, devotion, and fortitude. Inspired by the beautiful and noble Jewesses in the Bible, such as Rachel, Esther, and Ruth, the dramatists of the sixteenth and seventeenth centuries transformed the biblical Jewess into a tragic heroine. In the works of Marlowe, Shakespeare, and Racine, the *belle juive* was constructed in much the same way as the Tragic Mulatta would be represented centuries later. The beautiful Jewess embodied both virtue and sensuality. As Livia E. Bitton describes her, the Jewess was "at once the symbol of virginal purity, of carnal desire and of fetal yearning for the supreme maternal intimacy."[5] But despite her associations with virtue and selfless maternity, as embodied by the biblical heroines, the Jewess was an object of desire. As Jean-Paul Sartre explains, "There is in the words 'belle Juive' a very special sexual signification."[6] Like the Tragic Mulatta, the Jewess was an identity grounded in sexuality. Her exotic allure was believed to have the power to bewitch the British and European men who were attracted to her. In turn, the Jewess's sexuality is often exploited by her father. In such texts as Christopher Marlowe's *The Jew of Malta* (1590), Shakespeare's *The Merchant of Venice* (1596), Walter Scott's *Ivanhoe* (1819), and Sir Edward Bulwer-Lytton's *Leila* (1838), the Jewess's father acts out of calculated commercial self-interest, and treats his daughter as a commodity that, like the Tragic Mulatta, could be traded and sold to further his own financial and political interests. Because of their social marginality and rootlessness, the Beautiful Jewess and her father were regarded with suspicion and associated with a world of superstition and violent irrationality. The Jews were also depicted as a social threat because their intelligence was often linked to dissembling. As Michael Ragussis explains, Disraeli was often described as an actor "'that never took off his wig or rouge or robes,' an 'Eastern showman.'"[7] When paired with an ambiguous racial identity, the anxiety surrounding the Jew's powers of deception created the stereotype of the "cunning Jew" who could disguise her Jewish ancestry.

The narratives of the Beautiful Jewess that grew out of the Renaissance dramas of Marlowe and Shakespeare are propelled by the Jewess's father, who believes he has been wronged financially or politically. His daughter, specifically her virginity, becomes a political tool by which he attempts to destroy the Gentiles who have wronged him. The Beautiful Jewess, like the Tragic Mulatta, was property—her life and body belonged to her father. Though nominally every daughter was her father's property, the patriarchal emphases of Judaism encouraged a typology of the Jewish daughter who was more than usually at the mercy of a father who was condemned for his utterly unscrupulous commercial self-interest. For example, in Marlowe's *The Jew of Malta*, when the Christian rulers of Malta take Barabas's money and transform his house into a nunnery, his daughter, Abigail, becomes Barabas's tool in retrieving a fortune he has hidden away in his home. When her father urges her to disguise herself as a convert who seeks to enter the nunnery, Abigail hesitates: "Thus father shall I much dissemble."[8] But since he is her father, she dare not resist, and after agreeing to disguise herself as a novice, she carries out his wishes. In lines that resonate in Shakespeare's Shylock, Barabas exclaims: "Oh my girl, / My gold, my fortune, my felicity . . . Oh girl, oh gold, oh beauty, oh my bliss!" The repeated conjunction of "gold" and "girl" conflates Abigail and her father's gold, a sentiment that is repeated in *The Merchant of Venice* when Shylock bemoans the loss he has sustained when Jessica disappears with his jewels and money: "My daughter! O my ducats! O my daughter! / Fled with a Christian! O my Christian ducats! . . . my ducats and my daughter!"[9]

As her father's property, Abigail is soon called on to take part in his plan of revenge against the Christian governor of Malta. Barabas asks his daughter to prostitute her affections in order to lead two Gentile suitors (one of whom she loves) to kill each other. Although she is virtuous, her beauty is constantly sexualized. Her lover, Mathias, declares upon seeing her enter the nunnery:

> . . . Fair Abigail the rich Jew's daughter
> Become a nun? . . .
> Tut, she were fitter for a tale of love
> Than to be tirèd out with orisons:
> And better would she far become a bed
> Embracèd in a friendly lover's arms,
> Than rise at midnight to a solemn mass.[10]

Barabas wants his daughter to remain virtuous, but he also sees a power in her beauty, which can attract the Christian men who seized his fortune and his home. Although Barabas has promised his daughter to Mathias, he also promises Lodowick, the governor's son and Mathias's friend, that he may wed Abigail. When Lodowick coyly inquires whether Barabas can "help [him] to a diamond," hoping that he might convince the Jew to let him "have a sight of Abigail," Abigal's father responds, "The diamond that I talk of, ne'er was foiled . . . Lord Lodowick, it sparkles bright and fair."[11] After Barabas invites Lodowick to a viewing of the "diamond" at his home, the two men walk to the marketplace so that Barabas can purchase a slave. The sequence points up Abigail's own status as property.

Though she is not a slave, Abigail is not free to disobey her father's request that she entertain Lodowick even though she loves Mathias:

> Entertain Lodowick the Governor's son
> With all the courtesy you can afford;
> Provided, that you keep your maidenhead . . .
> . . . Kiss him, speak him fair,
> And like a cunning Jew so cast about,
> That ye be both made sure ere you come out.[12]

Barabas must make sure that Abigail keeps her virginity because without this diamond she is worthless and loses her value in the marriage market.

The beauty of the Jewess, especially when paired with her virtue, was of such a quality that it inspired Christian suitors to toss aside cultural difference to pursue her. However, the relationship between the Jewess and her Gentile lover was a doomed affair that often led to the Jewess's death, sometimes by her own hand, but more often by the hand of her father. Like the Tragic Mulatta, the Beautiful Jewess's "matchless beauty and selfless innocence render [her] tragic death especially painful."[13] With the exception of Shakespeare's comedy *The Merchant of Venice*, in which Shylock's daughter survives her conversion to Christianity, texts featuring *belles juives* end with the woman's death or rejection by her lover due to political or familial pressures. In Barabas's request that Abigail play the "cunning Jew" and prostitute her affection, Marlowe invokes the image of the Jewess as a seductress or femme fatale who makes men feel desire while she feels only the power of making them love her. When Abigail protests that she loves Don Mathias, her father replies: "Yet I say make love to [Lodowick]; / Do, it is requisite it should be so." When she learns that her duplicity has led to the deaths of Lodowick and Mathias, who have fought over her, Abigail returns to the nunnery. This time she converts in earnest. Ironically, just as her Jewish beauty renders her an object of desire, becoming a novice also carries a sexual connotation. Like the Beautiful Jewess and the Tragic Mulatta, the novice is also defined in terms of her sexuality—or rather, its repression—which in turn fuels salacious rumor. Her father's slave responds to Abigail's decision to return to the nunnery, "Have not the nuns fine sport with the friars now and then?" Enraged that his daughter has defied him, Barabas declares: "Ne'er shall she grieve me more with her disgrace; / Ne'er shall she live to inherit aught of mine."[14] He sends a batch of poisoned porridge to the nunnery, murdering Abigail and the other nuns. Though she dies a Christian, Abigail does not hate her father or regret her Jewish heritage. In *The Merchant of Venice*, however,

Shylock's daughter, Jessica, is a "most beautiful pagan, most sweet Jew!" who looks upon her Jewish blood as a curse: "Alack, what heinous sin is it in me / To be ashamed to be my father's child. / But though I am a daughter to his blood, I am not to his manners."[15] Playing the "cunning Jew" to outwit her father, Jessica escapes from Shylock's house and is rewarded with both autonomy and, in the end, her father's entire fortune, which will revert to her upon his death.[16]

*The Jew of Malta* places the Beautiful Jewess in a conversion narrative that eventually leads to her death at the hand of her father. However, if the Jewess chooses not to convert, her narrative typically ends in self-exile as in Racine's *Berenice* (1670), which portrays the Beautiful Jewess as a woman who "loves too well" her Christian lover, but inevitably suffers his rejection. Racine's tragedy tells the story of a Jewish queen who is poised to become the wife of Titus, the Roman emperor. Although Berenice may be a worldly woman, her positive moral influence redeems the future ruler of the Roman Empire. Titus owes his success and welcoming by the Roman people to Berenice's influence:

> Brought up in Nero's court, I went astray
> Through bad example, following the way,
> In youth, of pleasure down its easy slope.
> Then I met Berenice.

Berenice's influence has benefited the Roman Empire, making Titus "hear the voice of duty," but she has two marks against her.[17] She is a Jewess and she is a monarch. Not only do the Romans fear the powerful and autonomous Berenice, but if Titus marries Berenice, then Rome becomes susceptible to the rule of a Jewess who, even though she does not make laws or doctrine herself, will have influence over the man who does. Throughout the play, Racine refers to the five years that Berenice and Titus lived together before his return to Rome to take over the empire after his father's death. The repetition of five years insists on Berenice's virtue. She is not physically chaste as Abigail and Jessica are, but she is faithful, which is evinced by her sustained, loving relationship with Titus. Racine does not depict her as wanton or as a femme fatale trying to gain control of the Roman Empire, but he does describe her relationship with Titus in sexual terms: "My sole crime was loving thee too well."[18] Although Titus eventually resolves to marry her despite the political consequences, Berenice rejects his offer and returns to Palestine.

Nineteenth-century narratives of the Beautiful Jewess retain the theatricality of the Renaissance dramas. The Beautiful Jewess, like the

Tragic Mulatta, is a private figure continually made spectacle as fascinated spectators attempt to discern the secrets of her identity. Indeed both mixed-race and Jewish ancestry is represented, Ragussis explains, "as a suspicion or rumor that haunts certain characters . . . Jewish origins are hidden, suppressed; Jewish identity is a secret identity, in need of ferreting out. . . . [T]he most meaningless detail of one's life can lead to the erroneous charge of Jewish identity. . . . Jewish identity is grasped from the outside; it is guessed at, pieced together, measured by certain (not altogether reliable) rules of physiognomy or behavior."[19] In such nineteenth-century fiction as *Harrington* (1817), Maria Edgeworth's novel of manners, and the historical romances of Scott and Bulwer-Lytton, detection of the Jewess's identity becomes a plot convention that renders the *belle juive* a site of conflict through which the relationship between Judaism, national identity, and ideal womanhood is examined.

Although the Jewess was not a prominent figure in American literature, readers in the States were fascinated with British portrayals of the figure. As Martineau writes in *Society in America:* "Scott is idolized, and so is Miss Edgeworth, but I think no one is so much read as Mr. Bulwer. I question whether it is possible to pass half a day in general society without hearing him mentioned."[20] In fact, Bulwer-Lytton's *Leila*, as well as other works such as *Zanoni* (1842), probably appealed to American readers who devoured the work of such American sensation writers as George Lippard and E.D.E.N. Southworth.[21] Edgeworth's *Harrington* is prefaced by a note to the reader from the author's father, Richard Lovell Edgeworth, in which he explains that *Harrington* was written in response to "an extremely well-written letter, which Miss Edgeworth received from America, from a Jewish lady, complaining of the illiberality with which the Jewish nation had been treated in some of Miss Edgeworth's works."[22] In her letter, Rachel Mordecai responds to the representation of the villain, Mr. Mordicai, in "The Absentee." After Edgeworth responded to Mordecai's criticism with the positive portrayal of the Jewish gentleman Montenero in *Harrington*, the two women became lifelong correspondents.[23] Berenice Montenero is not the first Jewish heiress to be featured in Edgeworth's work. Old Thady, the narrator and butler in *Castle Rackrent* (1800), offers the following description of the Jewess who takes up residence in his home: "The bride might well be a great fortune—she was a *Jewish* by all accounts, who are famous for their great riches. . . . [W]hat will become of him and his, and all of us, with this heretic Blackamore at the head of the Castle Rackrent estate. . . . I took care to put the best foot foremost, and passed her for a Nabob, in the kitchen, which accounted for her dark complexion, and everything." Though her husband says that he once called her "my pretty Jessica," Thady cannot see how the Jewess, who is eventually imprisoned in her room by her husband, could elicit these words from him.[24] Edgeworth's representation of the Jewess in *Castle Rackrent*, as well as in *The Absentee* (1812), led Mordecai to write the following: "Relying on the good sense and candour of Miss Edgeworth I would ask, how it can be that she, who on all other subjects shows such justice and liberality, should on one alone appear biased by prejudice: should even instill that prejudice in the minds of youth! Can my allusion be mistaken? It is to the species of character which whenever a *Jew* is introduced is invariably attached to him. . . . In those parts of the world where these people are oppressed and made continually the subject of scorn and derision, they may in many instances deserve censure; but in this happy country, where religious distinctions are scarcely known, where character and talents are all sufficient to attain advancement, we find the Jews to form a respectable part of the community. They are in most instances liberally educated, many following the honourable professions of Law, and Physick, with credit and ability, and associating with the best society our country affords."[25] Edgeworth not only paraphrases this letter in *Harrington*, giving the words to the heroine, Berenice, but she also represents America as a haven of religious tolerance.

Describing *Harrington* in a response to Mordecai as her "atonement and reparation" for the past, Edgeworth creates a narrative in which the hero, William Harrington, overcomes his anti-Semitism.[26] Harrington has grown up with an aversion to Jews because a maid threatened to let a Jewish lamplighter carry him away "in his great bag" if the boy did not stop protesting and go to bed quietly. The innocent lamplighter becomes a figure of monstrosity that the maid uses to discipline young Harrington: "The threat of 'Simon the Jew' was for some time afterwards used upon every occasion to reduce me to passive obedience. . . . [My maid] proceeded to tell me, in a mysterious tone, stories of Jews who had been known to steal poor children for the purpose of killing, crucifying, and sacrificing them at their secret feasts and midnight abominations." Mapping his maid's stories of how a Jewish couple in Paris baked "the flesh of little children" into pork pies onto the image of the Jewish lamplighter he sees outside his window, Harrington says that upon going to bed, "I saw faces around me grinning, glaring, receding, advancing, all turning at last into one and the same face of the Jew with the long beard, and the terrible eyes, and that bag in which I fancied were mangled limbs of children." Soon his phobia of Jews, which was treated as "a medical . . . a metaphysical wonder," transforms him into a spectacle in his parents' social circle, giving him a feeling of power over spectators who try to puzzle out the reason for his phobia.[27]

Harrington's phobia is supported by his parents' prejudice against the Jews. He grows up hearing discussions among his parents and their visitors about the Jewish Question. By deconstructing stereotypes, such as those embodied by the maid's tale of the Jewish lamplighter and Shakespeare's Shylock, Edgeworth shows Harrington beginning to question his phobia. Through an acquaintanceship with Jacob, the lamplighter's son whom Harrington and his classmates bullied in grade school, Harrington meets Mr. Montenero, a Jewish gentleman bearing no resemblance to Shylock. He learns that Mr. Montenero left Spain to escape the Inquisition and "had been fortunate enough to carry his wealth, which was very considerable, safely out of Spain, and had settled in America, where he had enjoyed perfect toleration and freedom of religious opinion. He had travelled in almost every country in Europe, and joined extensive knowledge of books and a cultivated taste for the arts with a thorough knowledge of mankind and of the world." Edgeworth writes against the Shylock stereotype in her representation of Mr. Montenero as a cosmopolitan gentleman who is "dignified, courteous and free from affectation," but she retains many of the tropes from the Renaissance dramas in her depiction of his daughter, Berenice.[28]

Although Berenice, named for the Jewish queen in Racine's play, is no actress, she is reduced to a racial spectacle in her theater box as Harrington and the members of his party watch her and discuss her racial origins during a performance of *The Merchant of Venice.* One lady conjectures that Berenice is "an East Indian . . . by her dark complexion." The truth of her Jewish ancestry is revealed when the play that Berenice's party came to see is replaced at the last moment with *The Merchant of Venice.* Although the rest of the party are dismayed—"How unlucky! . . . What can we do?—Better go away—carriage gone!—must sit it out—Maybe she won't mind—Oh! she will—Shylock!—Jessica!—How unfortunate!—poor Miss Berry!"—Harrington notices that Berenice is embarrassed by the attention: "I looked, and saw the Jewess! She had turned away from the young ladies her companions, and had endeavored to screen herself behind the pillar against which I had been leaning."[29] Noting the "great sensibility, painfully, proudly repressed" in her countenance, Harrington's fixed gaze causes "a sudden and deep colour [to] spread over her face." He watches Berenice during the Jessica scenes, eventually turning away from the stage to become a voyeur of her emotions: "I was so placed that I could see her, without being seen; and during the succeeding acts, my attention was chiefly directed to the study of all the changes in her expressive countenance. I now saw and heard the play solely with reference to her feelings; I anticipated every stroke which could touch her, and became every moment more and more interested and delighted with her, from the perception that . . . I perfectly knew how to read her soul, and interpret her countenance."[30] The Jewess grows pale and almost faints under Harrington's gaze, offering him the opportunity to escort her out of the theater.

Not only is Berenice depicted as a racial spectacle, but she is also commodified when her chaperone responds to Harrington's wish to inquire after her health the next day: "The young lady no doubt's well worth inquiring after—a great heiress, as the saying is, as rich as a Jew she'll be, Miss Montenero." While the hero has no designs upon Berenice's fortune, his friend Lord Mowbray does, even though he has formed a liaison with the actress who played Jessica in the production of Shakespeare's play. Mowbray does not respect or admire Berenice, but he would not mind possessing her fortune now that expenses to support his actress have eaten into his income. He tells Harrington: "I have no great taste for matrimony or for Jewesses, but a Jewish heiress in the present state of my affairs—Harrington, you know the pretty little gipsy—the actress who played Jessica that night . . . my little Jessica has, since that time, played away at a rare rate with my ready money." Ironically, though Lord Mowbray's actress is not Jewish, he refers to her only by the name of Shylock's daughter; the identity of the actress is never revealed, which reflects the way in which Mowbray views both the Jewess and the actress as sexually available figures of womanhood. He concludes: "'Twould be poetic justice to make one Jewess pay for another, if I could. Two hundred thousand pounds, Miss Montenero is, I think they say."[31] In Mowbray's mind, Berenice is her fortune; her identity and her inheritance are inextricable.

In acting the part of a desperate lover, Mowbray meets with Berenice and tells her that her influence has made him a better man. As in Racine's representation of Berenice's relationship with Titus, the Jewess exudes a positive moral influence over her Christian suitor. Mowbray discloses to Montenero that his daughter has "given him a taste for refined female society, disgusted him with his former associates." When Berenice is not moved by Mowbray's moral transformation, he attempts to seduce her with his title and class status: "Miss Montenero was a stranger, a Jewess, just entering into the fashionable world—just doubting . . . whether she would make London her future residence, or return to the wilds of

America. Lord Mowbray wished to make her sensible that his public attentions would bring her at once into fashion," granting her a social legitimacy in the fashionable circles.[32]

Even though Mowbray talks of converting to Judaism, Berenice rejects him and eventually accepts Harrington as her husband. However, unlike Jessica in *The Merchant of Venice*, Berenice is not required to convert because the question proves superfluous: Berenice turns out to have been a Christian all along. Her father, who raised his daughter in the Protestant faith of her English mother, led Harrington to believe that Berenice is a Jewess in order to test his morals: "I have tried you to the utmost, and am satisfied both of the steadiness of your principles and of the strength of your attachment to my daughter—Berenice is not a Jewess." Although Edgeworth presents a positive image of the Jew and condemns English anti-Semitism, by revealing that her Jewish heroine is actually a Christian, she does not allow Harrington and Berenice to embody intermarriage.[33] Ironically, America is represented as a space where intermarriage among Christians and Jews is more acceptable than it is in England: "In some cases, more frequently on the continent and in America than in England, Jews have married Christian women, and the wives have continued undisturbed in their faith."[34] Upon reading Edgeworth's novel, Mordecai wrote to her expressing "much satisfaction" and hope that "in England, where from circumstances related in that work, we must believe prejudices carried to an excess, hardly conceivable to us in America, it will doubtless be productive of much good." Despite praising the "many excellencies of the work," Mordecai does "confess with frankness": "In one event I was disappointed. Berenice was not a Jewess. I have endeavored to discover Miss Edgeworth's motive for not suffering her to remain such. . . . I have at length adopted an opinion suggested by my dear father, that this circumstance was intended as an additional proof of the united liberality and firmness of Mr. Montenero's principles. He had married a lady of different religious persuasion, without being inclined to swerve in the least from his own; and he had brought up his daughter in the belief of her mother, but with an equal regard for both religions; inculcating thereby the principle that, provided the heart is sincere in its adoration, the conduct governed by justice, benevolence, and morality, the modes of faith and forms of worship are immaterial; all equally acceptable to that Almighty Being, who looks down on all his creatures with an eye of mercy and forgiveness. . . . It would be gratifying to us to know how far our impressions regarding Berenice are correct."[35] In her reply, Edgeworth does not offer an explanation for her decision to make

Berenice a Christian. She tells Mordecai: "I wish you would thank your kindhearted father for the reason he gave for my making Berenice turn out to be a Christian. It was a better reason than I own I had ever thought up." Perhaps the controversy surrounding Edgeworth's attempt to publish the courtship between a West Indian gentleman and the eponymous heroine in *Belinda* (1801) made her reluctant to portray intermarriage again.[36]

In a letter to Joanna Baillie, Scott described Edgeworth's novel as "delightful," but revealed, "I own I breathed more freely when I found Miss Montenero was not an actual Jewess." He viewed Edgeworth's representation of Berenice's father as a cosmopolitan gentleman as an impossibility, telling Baillie: "Jews will always to me be Jews. One does not naturally or easily combine with their habits and pursuits any great liberality of principle although certainly it may and I believe does exist in many individual instances. They are money-makers and money-brokers by profession and it is a trade which narrows the mind."[37] Scott, who was greatly influenced by Edgeworth's works, took up the Jewish Question two years after the publication of *Harrington*, creating the unforgettable heroine Rebecca, who became a prototype for exotic, "dark" nineteenth-century heroines such as Eliot's Maggie Tulliver in *The Mill on the Floss* (1860). Scott's character of a Jewess separated from her Christian suitor by religion and race was modeled on Rebecca Gratz, an American who rejected Samuel Ewing, her Christian suitor, because she refused to marry outside of her faith. Scott never met Gratz, but was reportedly told about her matchless beauty by her friend Washington Irving. Scott transports the image of Gratz to twelfth-century England, when the Anglo-Saxons are living under the French Normans' rule.

*Ivanhoe* is framed by scenes that represent Rebecca's body as a sexual and racial spectacle. Rebecca is introduced to readers during a tournament where her father audaciously claims a front-row seat in the gallery "without respect either to his descent, equality, or religion." This scene of disruption recalls the scene in *Harrington* in which Berenice's gauche chaperone, Mrs. Coates, settles her wards into seats in such a way that Berenice becomes a spectacle to the aristocrats already seated. Prince John's attention is drawn toward Rebecca, who "might have compared with the proudest beauties of England. . . . Her form . . . was shown to advantage by a sort of Eastern dress, which she wore according to the fashion of the females of her nation. Her turban of yellow silk suited well with the darkness of her complexion."[38] The alluring exoticism of Rebecca's appearance catches the attention of both the prince and the

FIGURE 13. Albert Henry Payne, untitled engraving of Rebecca watching the tournament, *Ivanhoe*, 1851. (Edinburgh University Library.)

proud English dames seated above her, who "scoffed and sneered . . . but secretly envied" her. The attention that Scott draws to the jewel clasps on her vest also sexualizes her: "Of the golden and pearl-studded clasps which closed her vest from the throat to the waist, the three uppermost were left unfastened on account of the heat, which something enlarged the prospect to which we allude." Her unbuttoned vest, revealing a diamond necklace that conspicuously decorates her neck, heightens Rebecca's sexuality (fig. 13). Prince John describes Rebecca as "the very model of perfection whose charms drove frantic the wisest king that ever lived."[39] Scott's use of "frantic" in this description imbues Rebecca with the "wanton beauty" which Bulwer-Lytton ascribes to his Leila. Prince John is so taken with Rebecca's beauty that he wants to name her the "Sovereign of Love and of Beauty," but the members of his party are scandalized at this suggestion, deeming it an insult to the "lovely Saxon,"

Rowena. As a racial spectacle, Rebecca's body becomes the site of political conflict between the "liberal" prince and his conservative followers who inform him, "Those who follow your Grace in the paths which you tread . . . acquire the right of counsellors; for your interest and safety are not more deeply gaged than their own."[40]

Rebecca's body becomes a public spectacle a second time in the novel when a letter sent to the current Grand Master identifies Rebecca as a "Jewish sorceress" whose "black eyes have seduced" De Bois-Guilbert, the knight who kidnapped her. The Grand Master orders that Rebecca be tried as a witch, exclaiming, "I will teach her to throw spell and incantation over the soldiers of the Blessed Temple!"[41] When she is brought to trial, Rebecca's body once again becomes the site of conflict as De Bois-Guilbert struggles between the expression of his autonomy, which is represented by his forbidden love for Rebecca, and his ambition to become Grand Master of his Order. He tries to exchange his ambitious plans to become Grand Master with a new plan to embark for Palestine, where he and Rebecca will rule: "Thou shalt be a queen, Rebecca: on Mount Carmel shall we pitch the throne which my valour will gain for you, and I will exchange my long-desired baton for a sceptre!" However, just as Edgeworth's Berenice rejects Lord Mowbray, Rebecca tells the desperate knight, "I will never . . . esteem him who is willing to barter these ties, and cast away the bonds of the order of which he is a sworn member, in order to gratify an unruly passion for the daughter of another people."[42] When the knight realizes that Rebecca has rejected him, he chooses ambition and says that he cannot save her by appealing to King Richard.

As Rebecca awaits her fate in front of the public, her impending death is more than the "bloody spectacle" of a witch being burned at the stake. She is also a racial spectacle, which is emphasized by the presence of four black slaves standing next to the platform: their "colour and African features, then so little known in England, appalled the multitude, who gazed on them as on demons." In language reminiscent of John Gabriel Stedman's *Narrative of a Five Years Expedition against the Revolted Negroes of Surinam* (1796), in which the teeth of African slaves are cited as evidence of their cannibalism, Scott describes the slaves as showing "their white fangs, as if they grinned at the thoughts of the expected tragedy."[43] Stripped of her "Oriental garments," Rebecca's placement next to the burning pile of wood is nonetheless conspicuous. She wears a "coarse white dress, of the simplest form" and "no other ornament than her long black tresses" (fig. 14). Waiting in front of the crowd for a knight to ride forward as her champion, Rebecca is a tragic and abandoned

FIGURE 14. R. Westall, "Rebecca at the Stake," *Ivanhoe*, 1820. (Edinburgh University Library.)

figure, rescued only when Ivanhoe appears at the last moment to fight for her honor. The death of Bois De-Guilbert, who dies not from any blow struck by Ivanhoe but from "the violence of his own contending passions," and the reappearance of King Richard distract the crowd from Rebecca, who is able to steal away with her father.[44]

However, before she departs, Scott reveals Rebecca's desire for Ivanhoe to see her as more than a Jewess. As the crowd gathers around the knight, Rebecca's inability to articulate her gratitude emphasizes her desire: "O no—no—no; I must not at this moment dare to speak to him. Alas! I should say more than—." Throughout the novel, Scott teases his readers with the possibility that Ivanhoe might feel something more for his Jewish nurse than gratitude. Though the novel says that Ivanhoe had a happy life with Rowena, Scott allows that "Rebecca's beauty and magnanimity [might have recurred] to his mind more frequently than the fair descendant of Alfred might altogether have approved." Knowing that her racial difference makes a relationship with Ivanhoe impossible, Rebecca resolves to dedicate her life to serving her people in Spain.[45]

Written over two centuries after Marlowe and Shakespeare's plays, Bulwer-Lytton's *Leila* employs many of the same stereotypes of the Jewess. Lytton situates his tragedy of the *belle juive* in 1491 during Spain's siege of Granada. In this novel, the Jewish father, Almamen, is consumed not by his fortune, but by his political interests. Like Marlowe's Abigail, Almamen's daughter, Leila, becomes an object of trade in her father's political maneuverings. Seeking political freedom for his people, Almamen declares, "I demand for the people of Israel . . . free trade and abide within the city." He also insists that the Jews be "subjected only to the same laws and the same imposts as the Christian population." Almamen hates the Moors and leaves Leila with King Ferdinand and Queen Isabel as a hostage to prove his loyalty to Spain. He promises that he will "obtainest the exile or death of Muza," the Moorish prince whom Leila loves, and bring the "chief councillors of Granada, the written treaty of the capitulation, and the keys of the city" to the king.[46]

In his construction of Leila as an object of exchange, Bulwer-Lytton also emphasizes the ambiguity of Jewish racial identity: Leila believes that she is a Moor, not a Jew. Raised in isolation, Lelia does not even know her father's name. But when Almamen fears that a Moor has claimed his daughter's heart, he quickly reveals the secret of her identity to invoke racial difference between his daughter and her lover: "Daughter of the great Hebrew race, arise and curse the Moorish task-master and spoiler."[47] Fearing that in her love for the Moorish prince Leila has been influenced by the "lascivious arts of the Moorish maidens . . . their harlot songs, and their dances of lewd delight," Almamen unsheathes his poniard and considers killing Leila. Instead he tosses the knife on the ground where she kneels before him, telling her, "If thou hast admitted to thy heart one unworthy thought towards a Moorish infidel, dig deep and root it out, even with the knife, and to the death—so wilt thou save this hand from that degrading task."[48]

Because the "chief charm of [her] exquisite countenance was in an expression of softness and purity, and intellectual sentiment, that . . . was wholly foreign to the voluptuous and dreamy langour of the Moorish maidens," Leila poses an even stronger sexual threat than the most wanton woman in a Moorish harem.[49] The Jewess is more threatening because her sexuality is coupled with intellect, and thus, as Spain's royal family views it, connivance and manipulation. The king and queen of

Spain fear that Leila's "wanton beauty" will seduce their son and make him a supporter of the Jewish people: "The arts that seduced Solomon are employed against thy son. The beauty of the strange woman captivates his senses; so that through the future sovereign of Spain, the counsels of Jewish craft may establish a domination of Jewish ambition. . . . [H]ow knowest thou but what the next step might have been thy secret assassination, so that the victim of witchcraft, the minion of the Jewess, might reign in the stead of the mighty and unconquerable Ferdinand."[50] These anxious sentiments are spoken by a Dominican friar who is so taken with Leila's "delicate limbs" that, immediately after leaving her, he must flagellate himself to discipline the desire she has inspired. The friar convinces the Spanish king that through "wanton beauty" and cleverness, the prince will be entrapped "into a passion for a Jewish maiden." Although the friar and king view Leila as a sexual threat to the prince, the queen believes that the Jewess "is more sinned against than sinning."[51] She arranges for Leila to be taken to a convent where she eventually converts to Christianity.

But, as in *The Jew of Malta*, becoming a nun is more fatal to the Jewess than if she married a Christian suitor, for conversion is conceived as a mode of self-betrayal or the denial of a "truer" racial self. Indeed, the *belle juive*'s sexuality was such a valuable commodity that becoming a nun, as Marlowe's Abigail and Bulwer-Lytton's Leila do, was often seen by their fathers as a more dangerous transgression than if they had run away and married a Gentile lover, as Jessica does in *The Merchant of Venice*. While conversion was a repudiation of both religious faith and racial ancestry, becoming a novice was a repression of sexuality, which was typically construed as woman's leading attribute. As Leila is about to take her vows, her father reclaims her. Wilting in her father's arms under his raised dagger, Leila's murder is staged as a spectacle: "Almamen . . . stood with his daughter in his arms, on the first step of the consecrated platform. But not a foot stirred—not a hand was raised. . . . [T]hey would have sooner rushed upon a tiger in his lair, than on the lifted dagger and savage aspect of that grim stranger." With Leila kneeling before him, Almamen declares: "Thy beauty is desecrated; thy form is but unhallowed clay. . . . Thus—thus—thus—Almamen the Jew delivers the last of his house from the curse of Galilee." The repetition of "thus" as Almamen's dagger penetrates his daughter's breast has a sexual import: "Thrice the blade of the Hebrew had passed through that innocent breast; thrice was it reddened with that virgin blood."[52] Leila is in effect defiled by her own father. The "virgin blood" not only emphasizes

Leila's innocence, but also her ineradicable Jewishness. In killing his daughter, Almamen affirms that Israel has triumphed over both the Moorish prince's and Christianity's attempts to claim his daughter's sexuality. Like Abigail's murder in Marlowe's play, Leila's death by her father's hand seems less a deliverance from the curse of Galilee than from the curse of celibacy. By imprisoning the tyrannical Hebrew father in the role of "Christ-killer" as he murders his own daughter, Marlowe and Bulwer-Lytton not only depict the Beautiful Jewess as a tragic spectacle of race, but they also construct a female figure whose identity, like that of the Tragic Mulatta, is determined by her sexuality.

As in the Renaissance dramas in which the *belle juive* either dies (Marlowe's Abigail), converts to marry a Christian (Shakespeare's Jessica), or goes into self-exile (Racine's Berenice), the Jewess does not survive the nineteenth-century narratives of Edgeworth, Scott, and Bulwer-Lytton. Jewish identity is eradicated from these texts because the heroine is actually a Christian, chooses self-exile, or is murdered by her father. For the Tragic Muse, however, Jewishness is a crucial part of the spectacular self she presents on the stage. While the *belle juive* was more victim than victimizer in the nineteenth-century imagination, her literary sister, the Tragic Muse, embodied both artistic power and the dangerous magnetism of the femme fatale. Like the Tragic Mulatta and the Beautiful Jewess, the Tragic Muse was a raced figure of exchange, but one that operated from a position of autonomy and self-commodification, traits typically attributed to the prostitute. Severing her ties to Jewish patriarchy, the Tragic Muse named herself and reveled in the power she exerted over her spectators and lovers. The next section explores how literary representations of Rachel reinvented nineteenth-century culture's conception of the Tragic Muse by revising the tragic narrative of the Beautiful Jewess.

## A "Beautiful Devil"

Both the Tragic Mulatta and Beautiful Jewess were private women whose conspicuous racialized bodies rendered them public spectacles. The Tragic Muse, on the other hand, courted public attention. Actively seeking to place her image and talent before her spectators, the Tragic Muse gained a power that the mixed-race slave on the auction block and the socially outcast *belle juive* did not possess. The American actress Anna Cora Mowatt described this power in her *Autobiography of an Actress* (1854): "The power of swaying the emotion of a crowd is one of the most thrilling sensations I have ever experienced." The sensation of power felt by the actress was also described in Geraldine Jewsbury's novel *The Half Sisters* (1848), in which Bianca explains: "You do not know the sense of power there is in seeing hundreds of men and women congregated together and to know that I can make all that assembled multitude laugh, weep, or experience any emotion I please to excite:—there is positive intoxication in it, and I would not change that real power to become a queen."[53]

As Sarah Siddons and Rachel proved, part of the actress's power came from her ability to captivate an audience and return their gaze (fig. 15). Describing one of Rachel's performances, Adam Badeau, an American writer and soldier, said: "She struck you with awe or horror, but she felt none herself; she moved you, but it was in spite of yourself. . . . When I saw the shivering, I knew she was about to move me, but I could not sit unmoved for all that knowledge. Her influence was akin to that of a sorceress. . . . You were as completely in her power, as if you had fallen in unawares. . . . [Y]ou were only the puppet to be worked upon."[54] Power also came from the actress's ability to transform herself into any character both on- and offstage. A comparison of the reception of Sarah Siddons and Rachel in the private drawing rooms they visited reflects the way racial and class differences impacted the refashioning of the Tragic Muse figure in the mid-nineteenth century. The British Tragic Muse, Sarah Siddons, used her stature on the stage to transform herself into a queen in the drawing room. As Kerry Powell explains: "Sarah Siddons provides a vivid example of the ways in which the actress could actively participate in the reconstruction of herself as somehow gentrified or even 'queenly.' She was known for a regal demeanor both on and off the stage."[55] Siddons refashioned herself so that her demeanor matched that of her aristocratic supporters. Whereas Siddons was respected for her majestic deportment, Rachel's demeanor in aristocratic circles, particularly her nonchalance and refusal to be dazzled by her aristocratic surroundings, raised questions about whether class traits were inherent. After all, how could a "vulgar little Jewish actress . . . assume the appearance of a young woman of good family" so easily? When a marquis proposed marriage, Rachel rejected the opportunity to become a marquise because she "could be a princess every evening" onstage at the Théâtre-Français.[56] Because of her ability to circulate in social gatherings from which she would be excluded if not for her talent and fame, Rachel's power was labeled "monstrous" by anxious spectators and social acquaintances who feared how far the "vulgar" Jewish actress would rise without the proper

FIGURE 15. E. E. Amaury-Duval, *La Tragédie*, 1854. (© Collections de la Comédie-Française.)

title or blood. When it came to class distinctions, Rachel was as liminal as the mixed-race slave.

As a "public woman," the Tragic Muse was able to float between her stereotypically lower-class or merchant-class heritage to the drawing rooms and salons of the upper class. Her experience on the stage enabled her to "act" the part of the "lady" in society since her racial difference was thought to make it impossible for a Jewess to possess the qualities of a lady. This social dexterity caused anxiety. Nina Auerbach explains that "by the very transgressive act of becoming someone else, of finding within herself other selves to become" the actress was a dangerous being. Describing the actress as a social danger, Faye E. Dudden asserts: "Whenever a woman enacts a part she implicitly threatens the prevailing definition of womanhood: she knows she can become someone else and make you believe it. The very project the actress engages in undermines assumptions about the fixity of identity."[57]

Rachel's representation in the visual culture of the period, however, undercuts the independence described in written accounts. She was depicted as a cultural commodity caught in struggles between men fighting for ownership of her: her biological father; her first teacher, Samson, who said that he "made" her; and her lovers, such as Jules Janin. Several contemporary cartoons depicted this predicament: she is caught between her lover, Dr. Louis Véron, and the director of the Théâtre-Français, Arsène Houssaye, or she is walking off with one man while a robed and heavily bearded figure reaches over a balcony to get her back. But perhaps the most telling caricature is Pruche's 1841 drawing of Rachel being sold to the British by her family (fig. 16). Rachel stands on the balcony in a white toga, the figure of Greek tragedy, while her mother stands obsequiously behind her and her father leans over the balcony, telling the fervent crowd of British men below: "People of England!! We are infinitely touched by the warm welcome! . . . what . . . who . . . at last there you are! but all this is not a reason for you to bother going to all this excess! I have already told you that you are great admirers of talent! so, pay! and keep quiet! otherwise there are some people who think that all this enthusiasm is a burden." The Tragic Muse put up for sale by her father resonates with the Tragic Mulatta put on the auction block. However, the Tragic Muse is not a victim of the market but a participant in it; she sells her talent as the prostitute sells her body.

Rachel's self-commodification is most evident in her decision to tour the United States in 1855. Writing to her friend Louise de Saigneville, Rachel exclaims, "I am making myself commercial, I take and I pile up the

FIGURE 16. Pruche, *People of England,* 1841. (Bibliothèque nationale de France.)

dollars."[58] Rachel's brother, Raphael Félix, managed the American tour rigorously, seeking to market Rachel not as a tragedienne, but as a popular entertainer as P. T. Barnum had done with Jenny Lind. Under her brother's management, Rachel began to feel her autonomy undermined. Identifying with American slaves during her trip to New York for her American tour, Rachel writes home: "Well, my mother, is it too much to pay by the labor of seven months in working like a negro? It is necessary the whites take the work, since the blacks refuse the service."[59] To her French countrymen, traveling the long distance to the United States was an opportunistic and ill-advised adventure for an actress who had played to monarchs. Janin denounced her American tour because "by virtue of the art she practices and the masterpieces she performs, she belongs to all that a Republic or a Monarchy can have of elegance and courtesy, of the elevated, the aristocratic, the refined," all of which were virtues that America was believed by Europeans to lack.[60] In addition, French critics did not think Americans would have a critical appreciation of French tragedy. However, as one review of her performance as Adrienne Lecouvreur observes: "The audience was well distributed, and filled amphitheatre, boxes and gallery. A succession of such houses will leave Mdlle. Rachel but little cause to repent her trip across the Atlantic."[61] In fact, Harriet Beecher Stowe, who attended Rachel's performances in Boston, was so impressed by the tragedienne that in her essay "Sojourner Truth, the Libyan Sybil" (1863), she compares the African lecturer to the French actress: "It is said that Rachel was wont to chant the Marseillaise in a manner that made her seem, for the time, the very spirit and impersonation of the gaunt, wild, hungry, avenging mob which rose against aristocratic oppression; and in like manner Sojourner, singing this hymn, seemed to impersonate the fervor of Ethiopia, savage, hunted of all nations."[62] By the end of her American tour, Rachel could also include Henry Wadsworth Longfellow and Ralph Waldo Emerson among her American admirers.

Writing home from Boston, Rachel declared that "she had carried her name as far as she could."[63] With her body succumbing to tuberculosis, Rachel would not live much longer to spread her name and fame throughout the world. As a woman who had declared, "I am *free*, and mean to remain *free*," and once brazenly remarked, "I will have renters, but not owners," Rachel's financial independence and sexual autonomy gave added significance to her death from consumption. Rachel Brownstein observes that tuberculosis "seemed to signify both 'consumption' by sexual desire, and punishment for desiring. . . . [T]uberculosis seemed to attest to [Rachel's] noble consuming spirit and 'male talent,' and also her corrupt female body . . . her unwomanly ambition and willfulness."[64] Even before her collapse in Charleston, South Carolina, and her subsequent retirement from the stage, Rachel was immortalized in the literature of contemporaries who had either witnessed her performances personally or had heard of her from others.

Rachel's reception and representation as a raced figure of womanhood informs Disraeli's *Tancred*, a political novel in which the eponymous hero gives up his place in Parliament to go on a pilgrimage to Jerusalem. His guide, Sidonia, tells him about the young actress Josephine Baroni, who is a tribute to Rachel, France, and Judaism. "Strikingly handsome, very slender, and dark as night," Josephine becomes the "glory of the French stage." Sidonia explains that "the spirit of French tragedy has risen from the imperial couch on which it had long slumbered, since her appearance," which "at once charmed and commanded the most refined audience in Europe."[65] Throughout the story of the Baroni family's rise from poverty to international celebrity, Tancred believes that an Italian family has achieved this acclaim for France. After Josephine has been glorified as a daughter of France, Tancred learns that the renowned family of performers is in fact Jewish. By revealing this detail at the end of the story, Disraeli echoes Sidonia's speech in *Coningsby* (1844): "Little do your men of fashion, your muscadins of Paris, and your dandies of London, as they thrill into raptures at the notes of a Pasta or a Grisi, little do they suspect that they are offering their homage to 'the sweet singers of Israel!'"[66]

Disraeli's novel offers the most enthusiastic and hopeful representation of the Tragic Muse as a respected daughter of Judaism and France. In other narratives, the Tragic Muse casts off the delicate femininity attributed to the mixed-race slave and the *belle juive*. She is a "public woman" whose body and private life are consumed by spectators. The Tragic Muse was a sexual commodity, but like her fellow public woman, the prostitute, she sold herself willingly. Walter Benjamin's description of the prostitute as "the saleswoman and wares in one" also applies to the Tragic Muse.[67] Theater historians such as Tracy Davis and Dudden offer detailed accounts of the conflation of the actress and the prostitute in nineteenth-century society. Explaining this link between the actress and the prostitute, Dudden describes acting as an "embodied art. . . . To act you must be present in the body, available to be seen. The woman who acts is thus inherently liable, whatever her own intent, to become the object of male sexual fantasy and voyeuristic pleasure."[68] Even though the spectator did not pay for sexual contact with the actress, the female performer was "delivered to her audience as a commodity to whom each spectator ostensibly [had] an unmediated relationship." In this relationship, Dudden observes, the "male gaze could render [the actress], without her consent, an object of sexual fantasy."[69]

Perhaps inspired by stories of Rachel's liaison with Count Alexandre Colonna Walewski, the son of Napoleon and the Polish countess Marie Walewska, Balzac conflates the figure of the Jewish actress with the courtesan in *Cousin Bette* (1846), depicting the Tragic Muse as a woman driven by material and sexual consumption.[70] The novel, which details the demise of the Hulot family due to the patriarch's profligate ways, introduces the character of Josépha, a famous opera singer who "wants to be rich, very rich. . . . She tried her claws on Hulot, and she has plucked him clean—oh, plucked isn't the word, you can call it *skinned*!" Josépha's presence in the novel is juxtaposed to Baroness Hulot, who is twice confronted with the prospect of prostituting her body to regain her daughter's dowry and to save her husband from political scandal. Unlike Brontë and Eliot, Balzac never places his Tragic Muse on the stage. Her performances are relegated to her drawing room, or, as the dissolute Hulot describes it, a "gold-and-pearl-bedecked den of wickedness."[71] Though she is described as a "bloodsucker" and compared to Cristofano Allori's 1615 painting *Judith with the Head of Holofernes*, Balzac's Josépha is not the femme fatale of the novel, a role that Balzac gives to the pernicious Madame Marneffe. Unlike the malicious courtesan Madame Marneffe, who consumes the fortunes of men until they have no money left to support her, Josépha is not a "man-eater."[72] In fact, the opera singer later helps to reunite the desperate baroness with her morally and financially ruined husband. Josépha replaces Baron Hulot with a duke who presents her with "the papers for a thirty-thousand-franc annuity in a white paper bag full of sugared almonds." Explaining her decision to cut her ties with the baron, Josépha generously says, "I'm leaving you just when if I stayed I might easily be helping you to squander your wife's future, and your daughter's dowry." In a description that clearly alludes to public opinion of Rachel, Balzac describes how "good bourgeois folk . . . take talented people for some kind of monster, eating and drinking, walking and speaking, quite differently from other human beings."[73]

In the works of Balzac, Brontë, Braddon, and Eliot, the Rachel figure is both awe-inspiring and terrifying in her artistic power, sexuality, and material consumption. As G. H. Lewes describes Rachel in *On Actors and the Art of Acting* (1875), the Tragic Muse has "little tenderness, no womanly caressing softness, no gaiety, no heartiness. She was so graceful and so powerful that her air of dignity was incomparable; but somehow you always felt in her presence an indefinable suggestion of latent wickedness . . . a beautiful devil."[74] While the Tragic Muse in *Cousin Bette* is represented as an avaricious courtesan, Charlotte Brontë's representation of Rachel focuses on the raced actress as a demonic being. Rachel appears in several of the letters Brontë wrote while visiting London in 1851, and the response is consistent: Rachel is a demon and not human. Brontë writes: "She will come to me in sleepless nights again and yet again. Fiends can hate, scorn, rave, wreathe, and *agonize* as she does, not mere men and women." In another letter, written after she had returned to Haworth, Brontë declares: "Rachel's acting transfixed me with wonder, enchained me with interest, and thrilled me with horror. . . . It is scarcely human nature that she shows you; it is something wilder and worse; the feelings and fury of a fiend."[75] However, Brontë does not confine the Tragic Muse figure to the role of monstrous woman. In *Villette*, Vashti is more than "Hate and Murder and Madness incarnate."[76]

Vashti is clearly an ironic name: the biblical Vashti was banished from her husband's kingdom for refusing to become a spectacle and display her beauty before her husband's guests. But though the Vashti in *Villette* displays herself, she appears on her own terms: "Suffering had struck that stage empress; and she stood before her audience neither yielding to, nor enduring, nor in finite measure, resenting it: she stood locked in struggle, rigid in resistance."[77] The Tragic Muse that Brontë describes refuses to yield to her spectators' gazes; she is rigid and immovable. Like the slave on the auction block, the Tragic Muse could not control the gaze of her spectators or the ways in which her body was sexualized in the fantasies of her audience. But the actress did have the power of self-commodification and, to borrow Susan A. Glenn's term, "self-spectacle." Glenn observes that as an "assertive self-spectacle," the actress was able to employ "theatrical spectacle as a vehicle for achieving a greater voice in culture and politics." Although managers "made a spectacle of women, positioning them as passive objects for audience consumption," the actress frequently used the theater as a political and cultural forum.[78] As can be seen in Badeau's description of Rachel, and in the autobiographies of Mowatt and the Italian tragedienne Adelaide Ristori, the actress was more active than passive, exulting in the powers she had to move her spectators to terror, laughter, or tears.

Vashti's presence in *Villette* crystallizes a larger interest in the role of the spectator and the forms in which female desire finds expression. As Lucy Snowe sits next to Dr. Graham, she looks at the pale figure on the stage and says: "I thought it was only a woman. . . . By-and-by I recognized my mistake. Behold! I found upon her something neither of woman nor of man: in each of her eyes sat a devil." Lucy attributes the actress's talent to "evil forces [that] bore her through the tragedy." In Brontë's description of Vashti, we see the attraction and anxiety that Vashti produces in Lucy, who is struggling to find ways to express her own sexual desire in the novel. Lucy says: "It was a marvellous sight: a mighty revelation. It was a spectacle low, horrible, immoral." The emotions that the Tragic Muse exhibits onstage reveal a range of emotions and experiences alien to the proper, bourgeois world of Lucy Snowe. At the same time that she admits that this experience is "marvellous" and "mighty," Lucy must also denounce the spectacle as "low, horrible, immoral," though she cannot stop looking.[79]

Lucy is slowly wrapped in the Jewess's spell as she contemplates and analyzes the performance of the figure writhing on the stage: "Wicked, perhaps, she is, but also she is strong; and her strength has conquered Beauty, has overcome Grace." As the chapter progresses, Lucy not only begins to distance herself from attacks on the actress; she begins to identify with her. The Tragic Muse even produces physical sensations in Lucy, whose desire, represented by the image of a sunflower turning toward the sun, is awakened as she watches the emotions performed onstage: "The strong magnetism of genius drew my heart out of its wonted orbit; the sunflower turned from the south to a fierce light, not solar—a rushing, red, cometary light—hot on vision and to sensation."[80] It is as though Lucy has been transported to another solar system. Arguing that Vashti's performance helps Lucy to "reimagine the spectator's role," Lynn M. Voskuil observes: "In contrast to the novel's earlier scenes of restrained emotion—scenes Lucy could observe dispassionately—Vashti compels Lucy to participate both emotionally and bodily. The images are at once psychological and sexual."[81]

Several chapters earlier, Lucy was chastised by Monsieur Paul for looking at another spectacle of raced femininity, Cleopatra. But the painting of the queen reclining on a couch in "inefficient raiment" does not captivate Lucy in the same way that Vashti does. To Lucy, the "huge, dark-complexioned gipsy-queen" is vulgar and the painting "on the whole an enormous piece of claptrap." Despite the crudeness of the sensual portrait, however, Lucy believes that she has the right to view it, an opinion which Monsieur Paul does not share: "How dare you, a young person, sit coolly down, with the self-possession of a garçon, and look at *that* picture?"[82] As a young lady, Lucy cannot be exposed to the indecency of Cleopatra. Though Lucy is criticized for viewing the painting, in pondering her own desires, as they are gratified vicariously through spectatorship, she's acting like a man. Indeed, the Tragic Muse and Cleopatra were unsettling figures of womanhood because while their sexuality was feminine, their self-possession was disturbingly masculine.

The male spectator can gaze at the queen with admiration and fascination, as Monsieur Paul does, saying that she has "des formes de Junon," but that he would not want this "femme superbe" for a wife, daughter, or sister. The dashing Colonel de Hamal diminishes the queen to a mere representation of wanton sexuality as he holds "a glass to one of his optics" and "tittered and whispered" in response to the "dusk and portly Venus of the Nile." And the cool Briton, Dr. Graham, sees only Cleopatra's racial otherness: "'Le voluptueux' is little to my liking.

Compare that mulatto with Ginevra."[83] Ginevra Fanshawe is a spectacle of Victorian womanhood who revels in mirrors and self-display as much as Gwendolen Harleth in *Daniel Deronda*. But unlike Cleopatra and Vashti, her display is confined to the private sphere. Because of Vashti's performance, Lucy opens herself up to desire and begins to feel the emotions that no proper woman should express. Her responsiveness is starkly contrasted to that of her companion, Dr. Graham, who at this point in the novel is deeply attractive to Lucy, but who Lucy discovers "was watching that sinister and sovereign Vashti, not with wonder, nor worship, nor yet dismay, but simply with intense curiosity." This "cool young Briton!" as Lucy calls him, cannot acknowledge his own fascination: when Lucy asks how he liked Vashti, he can only respond to the actress's violations of conventional womanhood: "Such a strange smile went wandering round his lips, a smile so critical, so almost callous! . . . [H]e judged her as a woman, not an artist: it was a branding judgment."[84] Lucy feels implicated in the doctor's critical reaction to Vashti, but his inability to appreciate Vashti makes him seem no longer worthy of Lucy's desire.

While the Tragic Muse in *Villette* advocates the public expression of female emotions, interiority, and desire, later literary incarnations of Rachel transform the Jewish actress into a sensation villain. Whereas the power of Brontë's Vashti is confined to the theater, in Braddon's sensation novel *Rupert Godwin*, the Tragic Muse's power becomes a dangerous weapon offstage. Possessing the sexual autonomy and unbreakable spirit of the Tragic Muse, the femme fatale Esther Vanberg is a reckless and violent figure. In addition to naming her Tragic Muse after the biblical Vashti's successor, Braddon borrows Brontë's language to describe her beautiful femme fatale as a "magnificent-looking woman—a woman who might have graced a throne; but there was something almost terrible in her beauty—something that sent a thrill of indefinable pain and terror through the heart of the thoughtful observer."[85] Through the villainy of Rupert Godwin, who is later revealed as Esther's father, Violet Westford and her family have been reduced to poverty and she has taken to the stage to make money. She becomes Esther's rival when she is chosen as the Queen of Beauty in a grand tableau. Desiring to be the "observed of all observers," Esther covets the role of Queen of Beauty, but the manager determines that he wants "a woman whose beauty should possess the charm of youth and innocence." Esther, mistress of the Duke of Harlingford, has a beauty that is "almost demonic in character—something which reflected the reckless wildness of her life and the violence of her temper."[86] Her violent passion leads her to become involved in Rupert Godwin's plot to ruin Violet's reputation.

With the exception of Balzac's Josépha, who continues to thrive as an actress and courtesan at the end of *Cousin Bette*, the narratives of Vashti and Esther Vanberg are disrupted with death or violence. In the nineteenth-century cultural imagination, tuberculosis was a disease that disciplined unruly female bodies. Female characters that loved and lived too passionately, such as the courtesans in Verdi's opera *La Traviata* and Alexandre Dumas *fils*'s *Camille*, were especially susceptible to the disease. In *Villette*, which was published five years before Rachel's death in 1858, Brontë presents a Tragic Muse who has death hanging upon her. In fact, Lucy Snowe describes the actress as if she had died before the story was narrated. Vashti's name "is hushed now: its once restless echoes are all still; she who bore it went years ago to her rest: night and oblivion long since closed above her." The actress's death scene, during which the "whole theatre was hushed . . . the vision of all eyes centered in one point," is interrupted by a fire in the theater. Despite her power and independence, the Tragic Muse's life was destined to be "quenched in a moment" if she chose to remain on the stage and continue the self-commodification of her body.[87] Writing almost a decade after Rachel's death from tuberculosis, Braddon imbues Esther Vanberg with the consuming sickness of the Tragic Muse: "Her dark eyes had an ominous lustre; there was a hectic bloom upon her oval cheek, and that cheek, perfect though its outline was, had a sunken look that presaged ill." Even though Braddon's Esther Vanberg has the hectic glow of consumption, her prostitution of her body as a courtesan calls for an even more violent death than the slow wasting away of her lungs. Against all advice, she buys Devilshoof, a dangerous horse that is deemed by its owner "unsafe for a lady to ride. He requires to be ridden by a man with a wrist of iron, and a temper as determined as his own."[88] In the end, Esther's back is broken during a fall from her horse and she soon dies, but not before she repents for her jealous revenge against Violet. Since horseback riding was often a metaphor for unrestrained female sexuality in nineteenth-century literature, Esther's death from a riding accident is punishment for her sinful life as a courtesan.

Despite her power and independence, the Tragic Muse could not write her own script. The fate of the Tragic Muses in *Villette* and *Rupert Godwin* was a common element in the "theatre fiction" that was published during the mid-nineteenth century. Powell observes that narratives of fire, disfigurement, and death "contributed to, as well as reflected, the anxiety with which Victorians regarded the actress, and were part of the disciplinary process by which the supposed excesses of theatre women could be moderated." Several works published during the period show the actress succumbing to the "patriarchal discipline" that called for either death or retirement to the domestic sphere.[89] In "Stella," one of the novellas in Mowatt's *Mimic Life; or, Before and Behind the Curtain* (1856), the stage ruins Stella's health. Her acting teacher warns her of the dangers of public life: "You do not know the difficulty of representing in public that which is easy to feel, or simulate, in private."[90] She eventually dies from a brain fever after playing Ophelia, a role which becomes "painfully real," so much so that when she returns home she is still playing her Shakespearean character: "She had removed her straw garland, and was tearing it into bits. She offered . . . a fragment, repeating: 'There's *rue* for *you*, and here is some for *me!*'" Stella's career is successful because of her remarkable "self-forgetfulness," but in the end, the constant shift of identities and characters that she must play results in insanity and death.[91] Like Stella, Bianca, the actress heroine of Jewsbury's *The Half Sisters*, is intoxicated by the power of public performance, but she eventually retires from the stage to preserve her health. Bianca's physician concludes that her public life has caused such "an alarming debility and general prostration that the worst results may follow. . . . [I]t is a moral influence alone that can be of any benefit. . . . [S]he must be removed immediately, or I will not answer for the consequences."[92] Bianca is promptly taken to the country, where she eventually marries.[93] In *Daniel Deronda*, however, Eliot questions whether there is a place in England's domestic sphere for the Jewish actress who wishes to retreat from public life.

## George Eliot's "Girl Tragedies"

In a journal entry dated December 1, 1876, George Eliot comments on recent reviews of *Daniel Deronda:* "Since we came home at the beginning of September I have been made aware of much repugnance or else indifference towards the Jewish part of *Deronda*, and of some hostile as well as adverse reviewing. On the other hand there have been the strongest expressions of interest—some persons adhering to the opinion, stated during the early numbers, that the book is my best—delighted letters have here and there been sent to me, and the sale both in America and in England has been an unmistakable guarantee that the public has been touched."[94] As Eliot's journal reflects, reviewers were fiercely divided over *Daniel Deronda*, a novel composed of two narratives—one that follows the efforts of the eponymous hero to reconcile his English identity with the discovery of his Jewish identity and another that follows the courtship and marriage of Gwendolen Harleth to Henleigh Grandcourt. Because of the seeming lack of synthesis between Gwendolen and Deronda's narratives, many of Eliot's contemporaries deemed the work a failure. While some proclaimed that "the part of Gwendolen Harleth is throughout an overwhelming success," others, such as one reviewer from the *Saturday Review*, argued that "when a young man of English training and Eton and University education, and, up to manhood, of assumed English birth, so obliging also as to entertain Christian sympathies, finishes off with his wedding in a Jewish synagogue . . . the most confiding reader leaves off with a sense of bewilderment and affront."[95] In addition to being unsettled by the novel's focus on England's Jewish community, many readers were also puzzled by the form of the narrative, several reviewers even accusing Eliot of abandoning realism for the genre of sensation fiction. As a reviewer from *Gentleman's Magazine* observed, "*Daniel Deronda* is essentially, both in conception and in form, a Romance: and George Eliot has not only never written a romance before, but is herself, by the uncompromising realism of her former works, a main cause for the disesteem into which romantic fiction has fallen." In fact, Henry James's satirical review in *Atlantic Monthly* goes so far as to declare that "the Jewish element in *Deronda* . . . [is] a very fine idea; it's a noble subject. Wilkie Collins and Miss Braddon would not have thought of it, but that does not condemn it."[96] According to James, the Jewish plot of the novel is so contrived that the century's two most well-known authors of sensation fiction would not have produced it. As these reviews demonstrate, *Daniel Deronda* was a departure in subject and form for the celebrated author of *Middlemarch*.

Reading the novel as a panorama of nineteenth-century transatlantic culture, however, reveals a cohesiveness between the seemingly disparate narrative threads. Indeed, I suggest that both Deronda's and Gwendolen's narratives are informed by Eliot's appropriation of elements from American abolitionist and sensation fiction. Though published in 1876, the year of the American centennial, the action of the novel takes place between 1864 and 1866, years that not only correspond to the American Civil War, but also to the height of British sensation fiction, a genre that was informed by American abolitionist fiction. Eliot's use of conventions from sensation fiction is ironic because, as she expressed in a letter to her publisher, John Blackwood, she was frustrated by the popularity of such sensation authors as Mary Elizabeth Braddon: "And yet I sicken again with despondency under the sense that the most carefully written books lie, both outside and inside people's minds, deep undermost in a heap of trash. I suppose the reason my 6/- editions are never on the railway stalls is . . . [that they] are not so attractive to the majority as 'The Trail of the Serpent'; still a minority might sometimes buy them if they were there."[97] The sensational elements in *Daniel Deronda*, such as the hero's hidden identity, Mirah's search for her family, and Gwendolen's discovery of Lydia Glasher, as well as the overtones of violence in her marriage to Grandcourt, are not so much a reflection of Eliot's desire to increase her commercial popularity, but instead illustrate the ways in which her novel blurs the boundaries between nations, races, and genres.[98]

Although American abolitionist fiction, the Civil War, and such figures as the Tragic Mulatta inform the novel's structure, the characters of *Daniel Deronda* (with the exception of Deronda and Mirah) are unaware of the violence occurring on the other side of the Atlantic. Gwendolen is, in Eliot's words, "a girl, busy with her small inferences of the way in which she could make her life pleasant . . . in a time . . . when ideas were with fresh vigour making armies of themselves, and the universal kinship was declaring itself fiercely."[99] Gwendolen is blissfully ignorant of the war raging in America, but it is against this backdrop that Eliot represents her courtship with Grandcourt. For example, during a private interview with Grandcourt, Gwendolen brings her riding whip, a symbol of mastery, as they walk through a "knoll planted with American shrubs." Gwendolen's impulsive decision to bring her riding whip with her reflects her fear of being submissive to Grandcourt, who is planning to propose to her. As they discuss marriage, Eliot depicts Gwendolen "lightly whipping the rhododendron bush in front of her." As Gwendolen torments the azaleas and rhododendrons, both she and Grandcourt politely struggle for control and power over each other. By the end of this scene, Gwendolen is aware that marriage to Grandcourt would require the "subjection to a possible self, a self not to be absolutely predicted about, [which] cause[s] her some astonishment and terror."[100] In this way, Gwendolen was not so different from the "almost white" slave girls in American abolitionist fiction.

Inspired by Harriet Beecher Stowe's *Uncle Tom's Cabin*, Eliot saw *Daniel Deronda* as an opportunity to highlight the universal kinship between British, Jewish, and American cultures.[101] With references to American slavery and the Civil War, Eliot aligns her female characters, Gwendolen Harleth, Mirah Lapidoth, and Alcharisi with the mixed-race slaves she encountered in *Uncle Tom's Cabin*, as well as the figures of the Beautiful Jewess and the Tragic Muse, which she read about in the works of Scott and Brontë. She portrays Mirah as a traditional Beautiful Jewess who resists the public life that her father desires for her. Following the stereotype of "the Jew who confuses his ducats and his daughter," Mirah's relationship with her father evokes the buying and selling of female flesh in the American slave trade.[102] Though Mirah's sojourn in the American theater is short, images of slavery follow her when she and her father travel to Europe. On board the vessel bound for Germany, Mirah overhears a gentleman passenger remark, "'I wonder what market he means that daughter for'"—a comment that not only awakens in Mirah for the first time an awareness of her racial difference, but also prefigures her father's attempt to "sell" her to a Viennese count. Mr. Lapidoth views the concubinage of his daughter and the count as "a splendid offer" that she ought to accept.[103] Mirah's father not only compels her to prostitute her body and emotions on the stage, but also desires her to become the mistress of a nobleman—both options resulting in his profit.

Mirah's construction as a Beautiful Jewess recalls the Tragic Mulattas Eliot read about in Stowe's *Uncle Tom's Cabin*. In fact, in a letter to Stowe, Eliot professes an aim similar to Stowe's abolitionism: "I therefore felt urged to treat Jews with such sympathy and understanding as my nature and knowledge could attain to. . . . There is nothing I should care more to do, if it were possible, than to rouse the imagination of men and women to a vision of human claims in those races of their fellow-men who most differ from them in customs and beliefs."[104] Such exchanges suggest that Eliot's description of Mirah on the verge of suicide was influenced by Stowe's writing. When Deronda finds Mirah dipping her cloak in the river so that it will weigh her down, his "mind glanced over the girl-tragedies that are going on in the world, hidden, unheeded."[105] With her reference to these "girl-tragedies," Eliot alludes to the mistreatment of female slaves in the United States and aligns them with a broader sexual politics.

Even though Mirah has escaped the stage and a concubinage with the count, she is still reduced to a cultural commodity in her desire to become a private music teacher so that she can support herself. When Deronda introduces the songstress to his family circle, Lady Mallinger is the most accepting of Mirah, but even this is an overstatement: Mirah is "very pretty. . . . And she has very good manners. I'm sorry she is a bigoted Jewess. I should not like it for anything else, but it doesn't matter in singing." The only acceptable place for a Jewess is on the stage or singing in the drawing room. On the night of Mirah's performance in the Mallinger home, Lady Pentreath compliments Mirah's beauty and comments: "But where is her Jewish impudence? She looks as demure as a nun. I suppose she learned that on the stage." After hearing these comments mixing racism and praise, Deronda begins "to feel on Mirah's behalf . . . an indignant dislike to her being remarked on in a free and easy way, as if she were an imported commodity disdainfully paid for by the fashionable public. . . . [T]he name 'Jewess' was taken as a sort of stamp like the lettering of Chinese silk."[106] Mirah is a "public woman" even if she is performing in the private space of a drawing room because she is compelled to sell her talent—her "wares"—to prove her ability to give private lessons.

By novel's end, Mirah's marriage to Deronda affirms her domestic identity as an ideal of Victorian womanhood. The wedding feast, which cuts across class and ethnic lines to include Sir Hugo and Lady Malinger, the Meyricks, Mordecai, and the Cohens, seems to reflect Eliot's vision of an England in which the upper and middle classes have "conquer[ed] their prejudices." However, the newlyweds do not remain in England but instead travel East where, Deronda explains: "I am going . . . to become better acquainted with the condition of my race in various countries there. . . . The idea that I am possessed with is that of restoring a political existence to my people, making them a nation again, giving them a national centre, such as the English have."[107] Deronda's words echo those of George Harris in *Uncle Tom's Cabin*, who, after reuniting with his mother, Cassy, in Montreal and acquiring a formal education in France, decides to immigrate with his family to Liberia: "The desire and yearning of my soul is for an African *nationality*. I want a people that shall have a tangible separate existence of its own." In sending Deronda and Mirah on a nation-building mission in the East rather than leaving them to build upon the British-Jewish community gestured toward at their wedding-feast, Eliot seems to borrow from the sentiment Stowe expresses through George's statement that as a result of the "sufferings . . . distresses and struggles" experienced in America, "I have no wish to pass for an American, or to identify myself with them."[108]

While the Tragic Mulatta and Beautiful Jewess inform Eliot's representation of Mirah, her depiction of Deronda's mother, Alcharisi, is inspired by the Tragic Muse. Ironically, Eliot's letters indicate that she was more impressed by literary representations of Rachel as the Tragic Muse than she was by the actual actress: "We went to see Rachel again. . . . I have not yet seen the 'Vashti' of Currer Bell in Rachel, though there was some approach to it in Adrienne Lecouvreur."[109] Like Rachel and the literary characters she inspired, Alcharisi longs to be a "woman in the marketplace."[110] She also has a controlling father, but one who wants to keep her off the stage and to bind her in what she describes as the chains of traditional Judaism. She tells Deronda: "I had a right to be free. I had a right to seek my freedom from a bondage that I hated. . . . And the bondage that I hated for myself I wanted to keep you from. What better could the most loving mother have done? I relieved you from the bondage of having been born a Jew." Freed by the deaths of her father and husband, Leonora Charisi "came out as a singer" and changed her name to Alcharisi.[111] She consumes the Charisi name, taking the name of the father and husband for whom she felt no love and making it her own. As Catherine Gallagher explains, Alcharisi's desire to become an actress or "public woman" allows her "to escape the identity imposed by a father." Even though her weakening voice eventually forces Alcharisi to leave the stage, she "retains her commodity form" and remarkets herself as a woman in search of a husband. Her marriage to Prince Halm-Eberstein and the births of five children, however, mark Alcharisi's exit from the public realm of exchange and her entry into the "realm of 'natural' production."[112]

Even though Alcharisi has become a wife and mother, her desire to return to the stage makes her embodiment of Victorian womanhood seem a performance: "I made believe that I preferred being the wife of a Russian noble to being the greatest lyric actress of Europe; I made believe—I acted that part. It was because I felt my greatness sinking away from me, as I feel my life sinking now. I would not wait till men said, 'She had better go.'"[113] While the actresses in Brontë's, Jewsbury's, and Mowatt's texts risk death by staying on the stage, Eliot's narrative offers a different ending for Alcharisi. Rather than preserving her health, her retreat to the private sphere proves detrimental in its eradication of the power, sexual autonomy, and self-ownership she experienced as a Tragic Muse.[114]

# 5 / "After All, Living Is but to Play a Part": The Tragic Mulatta Plays the Tragic Muse

*I have made a step; do not call it a desperate one; do not blame me, for your blame I cannot bear; but I have gone on the stage. There was no other means of independence open to me; and I had a dream, I have it still, that there, if anywhere, I might do my work.*

CHARLES KINGSLEY, *TWO YEARS AGO* (1857)

Marie Lavington, the runaway octoroon slave in Charles Kingsley's little-read novel *Two Years Ago*, makes the above declaration of independence in a letter to Tom Thurnall, the novel's hero. Though Tom helped her escape to a Canadian Quaker community, Marie has tired of the "staid and sober" lifestyle of a Quakeress.[1] She reenters the public marketplace by refashioning herself into an Italian diva, La Cordifiamma. Marie's ascent to the stage as La Cordifiamma marks the construction of a new female body in the mid-nineteenth century: the Tragic Mulatta who becomes a Tragic Muse.

This may seem an unlikely transformation, but Kingsley was not alone. The American author Lydia Maria Child recounts the same refashioning in *A Romance of the Republic* (1867), narrating Rosa Royal's transformation from a slave into the opera prima donna La Senorita Rosita Campaneo. To be sure, the two novelists develop disparate emphases in their treatments, which in large part reflect their different cultural milieus. Child's concern, even after Emancipation, is simply to secure the fundamental humanity of the mixed-race slave, which entails emphasizing not only her vulnerability to subjection, but also the readiness with which she can be absorbed into domestic womanhood. Kingsley, on the other hand, is more engaged by the figure of the mixed-race woman as an embodiment of undisciplined desire, at once dangerous and deeply alluring to men. In Kingsley's England, the Tragic Mulatta is no longer exposed to the threat of slavery, but she feels a different vulnerability inasmuch as she identifies her ancestry with a compromising susceptibility to passion, which must be concealed. For Kingsley's heroine, this concealment is manifested in hidden psychic depths, above all as reservoirs of erotic desire, whereas Child's heroine has no hidden depths because her conflict is more thoroughly social—between herself and the law—and thus more readily externalized.

Both Kingsley and Child seem to recognize in the exiled Tragic Mulatta a powerful resemblance to the Tragic Muse. As we saw in chapter 4, the Tragic Muse exulted in her power to move spectators to terror, laughter, or tears. But the actress's powers of fascination often were not confined to mere seduction; they could be turned to engagement with larger social and political currents. This power of "self-spectacle," Susan A. Glenn explains, enables the Tragic Muse to employ "theatrical spectacle as a vehicle for achieving a greater voice in culture and politics." The actress's desire to use the theater as a forum for public affairs was often in tension with the theater managers, who "made a spectacle of women, positioning them as passive objects for audience consumption."[2] But though the theater potentially subjected its actresses to exploitation and the sexual fantasies of spectators, for many female performers the stage offered a voice, a profession, and financial freedom, as Florence Nightingale asserts in *Cassandra* (1860). In particular, the stage offered the slave on the auction block, who endured with downcast eyes the probing eyes and hands of potential buyers, an opportunity to return the gaze of her spectators. In Kingsley's novel, the stage also gives the runaway slave a voice. While a slave, Marie was whipped for "speaking as a woman should speak," but as La Cordifiamma, she intends to use the stage as a platform for abolitionism (1:125).

Of course, the very freedom that makes the Tragic Muse attractive as an emblem of autonomy makes her unsettling as well, because her sexuality seems undisciplined by conventional restraints. In Kingsley's and Child's novels, the fusion of the Tragic Mulatta and the Tragic Muse embodies a host of anxieties associated with middle-class femininity. Here, perhaps, in concert with the concerns to "fallenness" that proliferate the 1850s, as the Tragic Muse linked feminine autonomy, erotic spectacle, and material exchange, she incarnated forces seemingly inimical to domestic womanhood. Catherine Gallagher has suggested some of these in her influential article on the Jewish actress "George Eliot and *Daniel Deronda*: The Prostitute and the Jewish Question."[3] But the connection of the Tragic Muse to the Tragic Mulatta further complicates this web of associations, inasmuch as the mixed-race slave is born into a more radical subjection in which she is legally, and not merely figuratively, a form of property—a state, moreover, in which her exchange value is quite explicitly linked to the erotic allure of her body.

The link between the Tragic Mulatta and the Tragic Muse thus amplifies the pressures shaping nineteenth-century womanhood. On the one hand, the stage offers the prospect of an escape from subjection, both through the effacement of an earlier identity and in the sense of self-determination the successful actress may enjoy. At the same time, both Kingsley and Child insist on the costs of this effort, which not only denies the performer the more conventional satisfactions of marriage and motherhood, but also (so they suggest) ultimately entails an unwitting surrender of the self to a new subjection, that of the paying audience, which aligns the actress with the prostitute. Amanda Anderson has explored this theme as a preoccupation with what she calls "attenuated agency": commentators attribute to the fallen woman only "the minimal and paradoxical freedom of knowing that she cannot alter her character, for it is no longer her own."[4] As fallen figures, Kingsley's and Child's Tragic Mulattas display similar traits of self-consciousness and social determinism. But unlike the fallen figures in Charles Dickens's *Dombey and Son* (1846–47) and *David Copperfield* (1849–50) and in Elizabeth Gaskell's *Ruth* (1853), the Tragic Mulatta is born into her predicament—by virtue of the black blood in her veins, she is already fallen. While Child, as well as Harriet Beecher Stowe and William Wells Brown, use the Tragic Mulatta figure to show that mixed-race or black womanhood is not inherently fallen, Kingsley and his male spectators are drawn to Marie for the erotic spectacle her black blood promises. Marriage beckons as a relief from the pressures of public spectacle, and yet the domestication of the Tragic Mulatta reinforces a question raised by the allure of the Tragic Muse: Is marriage truly a refuge from exchange, or a refashioning of it, in which the actress surrenders her unruly desires in return for material security? The second half of the chapter examines a set of little-known works that transform the Tragic Mulatta from a spectacular victim into an exotic femme fatale who passes for white. Through the artistic, sexual, and entrepreneurial powers typically associated with the Tragic Muse, this former victim of sexual and racial peril is transformed into a villainess who passes into white society, where she preys upon the lover who spurned her. Though this section of the chapter examines relatively obscure texts, such as Nathaniel Hawthorne's *The Marble Faun* (1860), Alexandre Dumas *fils*'s *L'Étrangère*, or *The Stranger* (1876), and Florence Marryat's *Daughter of the Tropics* (1888), these narratives reflect how the Tragic

Mulatta–turned–femme fatale represents anxieties about raced bodies passing undetected into the domestic sphere.

## Marie Lavington, La Cordifiamma

Although Marie's ascent to the stage in Kingsley's novel reflects topical interest in American abolitionism, which was especially intense in the wake of *Uncle Tom's Cabin*, the character also reflects a fascination with the raced woman in general. This fascination runs throughout Kingsley's later career, from his enthusiasm for Tennyson's "Locksley Hall" (which pivots on a miscegenation fantasy) to Ayacanora, the Indian princess, in *Westward Ho!* (1855), as well as his extended, almost obsessive preoccupation with women of color in his 1871 travel narrative *At Last: A Christmas in the West Indies*.[5] Whereas some authors writing about miscegenation and slavery, such as Child, Stowe, and Brown, provide detailed genealogies for their Tragic Mulattas, Kingsley is more interested in how heroines of mixed race articulate psychological conflict, in particular the clash between erotic desire and its restraint. As James Eli Adams argues, mixed-race women in Kingsley's works are a "sign of the contest between desire and reason, impulse and self-restraint."[6] In *Two Years Ago*, Marie is an undisciplined body whose desire needs to be restrained.

Kingsley's representation of Marie shows how her impetuous nature is disciplined by *plaçage* and slavery. Although Marie is a slave when Tom rescues her, the few details Kingsley gives about her childhood reveal connections to *plaçage*. Marie is haunted by the image of her great-grandmother, "an ancient negress, white-haired, withered as the wrinkled ape," yet the denigration does not efface a hint of dignity conveyed by the phrase "old dame." Marie's mother, by contrast, is degraded by *plaçage*: she is a "gay quadroon woman, flaunting in finery which was the price of shame" (1:190). While her mother capitalized on the material goods gained from concubinage, Marie's liaison with a southern surgeon is imbued with issues of (sexual) domination and power. Whereas early Tragic Mulatta texts explain the mixed-race woman's devotion to her white suitor as a by-product of her white blood, which draws her away from men of her own race, Kingsley explains Marie's desire for the southern surgeon as a willing embrace of her subjection. To those who might think a woman of color belongs with a man of her race, Marie declares that until the male slaves rise up against their masters, "those who are the masters of their bodies, will be the masters of our hearts." Alluding to her liaison with the white surgeon, Marie says, "Was there not one . . . to hear whom call me slave would have been rapture; to whom I would have answered on my knees, Master, I have no will but yours!" (1:124).

Marie's unabashed allusion to her liaison with the surgeon is out of character for the Tragic Mulatta figure, who was typically an exemplar of true womanhood. While Child, Stowe, and Brown claim the Tragic Mulatta as a figure of true womanhood, Kingsley represents her as a desiring body lacking self-restraint. Marie's "lack of self-discipline . . . exert[s] a profound erotic attraction for the Kingsleyan male spectator," Adams argues, because it is interpreted as a sign of "insufficiently regulated desire."[7] Marie is desired by nearly every male character she encounters; even Tom, a skeptical doctor, is attracted to her. According to Marie, Tom struggles to restrain his desire for her when he helps her escape to Canada: "However tempted he may have been, and Heaven knows he was tempted, he could respect the honour of his friend, though that friend lay sleeping in a soldier's grave ten thousand miles away" (1:200–201). Tom first becomes acquainted with Marie through stories told by her white lover, whom he meets in the army in Circassia. The lover, Tom says, "used to go half mad about her sometimes . . . for fear she should have been sold—sent to the New Orleans market," where she would have been sold as a "fancy girl." Fulfilling the surgeon's dying wish, Tom travels to New Orleans and discovers that Marie has already been sold into slavery and has suffered the lashes of the scourge for "speaking as a woman should speak" (1:21, 125).

From the outset, Kingsley's depiction of Marie is heavily sexualized, and her mixed inheritance comes to figure a "strange double nature" (1:203). Although Kingsley invokes the Tragic Mulatta figure when Marie declares that Tom rescued her from "slavery, shame, suicide," we hear little of her actual experience of slavery itself. We learn only that when Marie "sobbed out . . . the story of her life," "What it was need not be told. A little common sense, and a little knowledge of human nature, will enable the reader to fill up for himself the story of a beautiful slave" (2:366, 1:201). In this passage, Kingsley invokes an archetypal male fantasy of "a beautiful slave," inviting the male reader to imagine precisely the sexual exploitation that the narrator refuses to specify. At the same time, however, Marie is not merely a passive victim. In a familiar association, her African ancestry is presumed to bring with it unruly sexual desires, whose force Marie pointedly feels when she escapes to a Quaker community in Canada. As a male fantasy of a "beautiful slave" Marie, despite her sexual exploitation and violent punishment in slavery, still longs for the expression of her erotic desire when she resides in the Quaker community. For Marie, being a Quakeress is as imprisoning as being a slave. She fears that the Quakers' austere lifestyle will deplete her "youth and vigour" as her "swift-vanishing Southern womanhood wrinkles itself up into despised old age." "Another such winter, and I shall die," she declares in her letter to Tom. "Let me take the evil with the good, and live my rich wild life through bliss and agony . . . instead of crystallizing slowly here into ice, amid countenances rigid with respectability" (1:126, 123). Unlike the mixed-race slaves in *Uncle Tom's Cabin* who use racial performance to find the refuge of generous Quaker communities, Marie uses her powers of performance to escape this haven.

In moving from a Quaker community to the stage, Marie traverses virtually the entire spectrum of Victorian eroticism. Though her reentrance into the public sphere as an actress is partly motivated by vanity and fear that her beauty and sexual desirability will wither among the Quakers, by refashioning herself into the Italian diva La Cordifiamma, Marie gains the independence and ownership of her body withheld from her by *plaçage* and slavery. As La Cordifiamma, Marie returns to the public marketplace in which actresses, as Kerry Powell observes, "cannot 'belong' absolutely to one man—their thoughts and feelings, as well as bodies, seem to be commodities in a free market of men at large."[8] However, when she disguises herself as La Cordifiamma, Marie demonstrates more self-discipline than she ever did as Marie Lavington, the former *placée* and slave. Unlike the stereotype of the actress as prostitute, Marie is "unapproachable . . . a very Zenobia, who keeps all animals of the other sex at an awful distance." This self-discipline is necessary for her disguise as La Cordifiamma because Marie's sexuality is the one racial feature that could expose her true identity. She must restrain the erotic desire that, in Kingsley's fantasy of the mixed-race woman, is a result of her African blood. She does so by harnessing that desire to the cause of abolition: when the dramatist, Stangrave, promises to compose republican dramas for her, Marie tells Tom of her hope that these plays will "give full vent to my passion, and hurl forth the eternal laws of liberty" (1:142, 127).

Yet Kingsley insists on the precariousness of her new identity and autonomy. The mere mention of Stangrave makes Tom fear that her independence might be compromised: "But who is this friend? Singing-master, scribbler, or political refugee? or perhaps all three together? A dark lot, those fellows. I must keep my eye on him" (1:128). To what extent is Marie, or the Tragic Muse generally, still a commodity? Is she in control of the marketing of her body on the stage, or is a manager or writer prostituting her talent in exchange for sexual favors?

Marie, however, rejects the suspicion that she is a helpless ingénue: as she tells Stangrave: "After you found me, or rather I found you—you the critic, the arbiter of the green-room, the highly-organized do-nothing . . . the would-be Göthe who must, for the sake of his own self-development, try experiments on every weak woman whom he met. And I, the new phenomenon, whom you must appreciate to show your own taste, patronize to show your own liberality, develop to show your own insight into character." With the regal condescension of the Tragic Muse, Marie boldly declares that she discovered Stangrave, and she proceeds to tell him how she has manipulated him into carrying out her political aspirations: "You had attempted to play with the tigress—and behold she had talons; to angle for the silly fish—and behold the fish was the better angler, and caught you." Here is the sexual power and threat of violence that separates the Tragic Muse from the mere actress. Like Rachel and Charlotte Brontë's Vashti, Marie, with her "dreadful beauty," crosses into the realm of the femme fatale: "I may scorch you, kindle you, madden you, to do my work" (1:187). Although she secretly loves Stangrave, she refuses to acknowledge this love until he joins the abolitionist cause.

By sublimating desire into activism, Marie becomes a moral figure for her male spectators. Lord Scoutbush, an admirer with a reputation for a "shy and secret generosity" toward his lovers, certainly admires La Cordifiamma out of more than lust: "It's not her beauty merely; but there is something so noble in her face . . . and when she is acting, if she has to say anything grand, or generous . . . she brings it out with such a voice, and such a look, from the very bottom of her heart,—it makes me shudder. . . . I am sure she is [a hero or a martyr], or she could not look and speak the way she does" (1:140, 157). In Scoutbush's description, La Cordifiamma's power to make men shudder is moral as well as erotic. Although Scoutbush entered her home with fantasies of possessing this erotic spectacle, of "taking a viscountess from off the stage," he leaves with a renewed commitment to his military career (1:182).

Such theatrical self-possession, however, is at odds with a typically feminine vulnerability, and Marie's susceptibility to romantic love is signaled, tellingly, by a breakdown in her poise. When Marie begins to lose her poise, her theatricality becomes more overtly defensive: she constantly looks in the mirror to see if evidence of her true racial heritage might betray her. She rehearses lines "standing by the fireplace in a splendid pose, her arm resting on the chimney-piece, the book from which she had been reciting in one hand, the other playing in her black curls, as her eyes glanced back ever and anon at her own profile in the mirror." Such self-consciousness merges the conventional vanity of the actress with a more pointed anxiety of self-betrayal. Even though she has refashioned herself into the sexually disciplined La Cordifiamma, the desire produced by her African blood cannot be restrained in Stangrave's presence. As Marie looks in the mirror and thinks of the African blood in her veins and whether Stangrave will read the signs of her ancestry, her performative nature takes over and conjures up an African physiognomy: "Was it mere play of her excited fancy,—or did her eyelid slope more and more, her nostril shorten and curl, her lips enlarge, her mouth itself protrude? It was more than the play of fancy; for Stangrave saw it as well as she. Her actress's imagination, fixed on the African type with an intensity proportioned to her dread of seeing it in herself, had moulded her features, for the moment, into the very shape which it dreaded. And Stangrave saw it, and shuddered as he saw" (1:182, 189).[9] After a moment, Marie's "African" face fades away, but her ancestry lingers in her eyes. The dark, melancholy eyes of the Tragic Mulatta are the last trace of her compromised heritage. Marie's face then transforms into that of the great-grandmother she describes as a "wrinkled ape" (1:190). When she shakes off the spell, she believes that she sees recognition in Stangrave's eyes and bursts into a hysterical fit. Even though she has refashioned herself into a Tragic Muse, the Tragic Mulatta figure reclaims her.

While Scoutbush shudders at the power of the Tragic Muse, Stangrave shudders at the Tragic Mulatta that lurks behind the Muse's mask. However, once the spell passes, Stangrave's "loveblinded eye could see nothing in that face but the refined and yet rich beauty of the Italian." Although Lord Scoutbush describes her acting, Kingsley does not show Marie performing on the stage. We witness only her performance of African ancestry in front of the mirror. As she molds herself into the image that frightens her most, she even has a captive audience. Marie does not have the heart to tell Stangrave that the woman he is in love with carries the blood of slaves in her veins. She instead uses the mirror and the power of facial expressions as a way of performing her hidden secret: "Instinctively she had looked round at the mirror—for might he not, if he had eyes, discover the secret for himself?" (1:190, 189). Marie performs her secret for Stangrave, silently asking him to interpret the images she enacts for him. She not only dares him to love the mixed-race body beneath La Cordifiamma's mask, but also to accept the sexual experience that is requisite in Kingsley's archetype of the "beautiful slave."

In previous Tragic Mulatta narratives, such as "The Quadroons," *Uncle Tom's Cabin,* and *Clotel,* the refined beauty and demeanor of the mixed-race slave or *placée* had been treated as inherent traits of her (white) blood. She is a disciplined body that white men misread as sexually undisciplined. Marie, however, does not demonstrate the moral refinement typically embodied by Xarifa, Cassy, and Clotel until after she has refashioned herself into La Cordifiamma. But even this refinement and emotional placidity is unstable. At moments La Cordifiamma's mask slips and her black blood seems to take over, causing her to resemble the disruptive West Indian figure as embodied by Bertha Rochester. Unlike her literary predecessors, whose mixed blood possessed a resilient whiteness, Marie's allure is focused in a blending of blood in which the black blood refuses to be subdued by the white. Characterizing this allure, Kingsley describes her nature as a mixture of "deep feeling, ambition, energy . . . instability, inconsistency, hasty passion, love of present enjoyment . . . a tendency to untruth," which are traits that Marie's male spectators interpret as signs of her unruly desire (1:203).

When Stangrave proposes marriage, the offer is not only an attempt to neutralize the power of the Tragic Muse, La Cordifiamma, but also a way to control the unstable racial and sexual identities of Marie Lavington, the Tragic Mulatta. Stangrave responds to Marie's performance and the hysterics that follow by saying, "You excite yourself till you know not what you say, or what you are." Even though Marie murmurs that she knows what she is, Stangrave does not listen. Her identity is so much a by-product of performance that he believes he can mold her into the image he desires. Looking at his muse, Stangrave sees the image of his future wife. Holding her captive in his arms and overlooking the secret that was just revealed to him, Stangrave imposes his own desire on hers: "You are my wife, and you alone! And he held her so firmly, and gazed down upon her with such strong manhood, that her woman's heart quailed" (1:190, 191). Stangrave's "strong manhood" is affirmed through the patriarchal power to call her his wife. Yet, Marie rejects Stangrave's proposal; he is in love with a fantasy, La Cordifiamma rather than Marie Lavington, the former slave.[10]

But in Kingsley's novel, even the runaway slave becomes a fantasy. When Scoutbush vows to "fetch and carry for [her] like a negro slave" during their second meeting, she tells him that he directs his lovelorn pleas to a runaway slave (1:281). She expects him to reject her, but Lord Scoutbush tells her, "You will have all London at your feet after a season or two, and all the more if they know your story." When Scoutbush and, later, Stangrave discover that their beloved La Cordifiamma is a runaway slave, they sentimentalize her and render her a sympathetic figure incapable of sexual agency. They have written an abolitionist narrative in which the virtue of the former slave is reinstated and she is free to live and love at will in England. This beautiful slave retains more sexual agency than the stereotypical Tragic Mulatta: Marie does not regret her liaison with the surgeon. However, Scoutbush and Stangrave understand her purely as a victim of exploitation. Although Marie sees that "her origin formed no bar whatever to her marrying a nobleman," she does not believe that she is worthy to become a viscountess because she is tainted by more than her racial heritage. She sees herself as a concubine, a fallen woman, telling her persistent suitor: "I cannot tell you all.—You must not do yourself and yours such an injustice" (1:283). Although Scoutbush knows the secret of her race, he has not fathomed the secret of her sexual life.

In her predicament, Marie might seem to epitomize Anderson's account of "attenuated agency." The early Tragic Mulatta figures in the texts of Child and Brown reflect this narrative imprisonment wherein they are fallen women perceived by other characters as texts that are "already written rather than as . . . agent[s] capable of dialogical interaction."[11] However, Cassy in *Uncle Tom's Cabin* and Marie Lavington both exemplify the Tragic Mulatta disrupting her story through performance. The theatricality of Cassy performing as the ghost of Simon Legree's mother and Marie Lavington's transformation into La Cordifiamma show the Tragic Mulatta changing the conventional narrative—her "script," as it were—to escape the social structures that enslave and abuse her. Unlike Cassy, who escapes to Canada and regains her role as mother, Marie has escaped into another paradigm of fallenness—the stage. And that world takes its toll. Sabina notices the enervating effect of Marie's nightly performances: "That white cheek had been fading more and more to a wax-like paleness; those black eyes glittered with fierce unhealthy light; and dark rings round them told, not merely of late hours and excitement, but of wild passion and midnight tears." She comes to verge on a stereotype of overstimulated exhaustion: "I am beginning to long for brandy and water . . . to nerve me up for the excitement of acting, and then for morphine to make me sleep after it" (1:286). Blaming her "wild Tropic blood" for her addictive habits, Marie confesses to Sabina, "I feel at times that I could sink so low—that I could be so wicked, so utterly wicked, if I once began!" Her African ancestry is clearly coded as a realm of impulsive desire: in Stangrave's absence, Marie experiences the loss of self-control, presumably a surrender to sexual impulses, and the "hasty passion" and "love of present enjoyment" that Kingsley attributes to her "strange double-nature" (1:287, 203).

Ultimately she is redeemed, however, through marriage. Although Marie, the Tragic Mulatta passing as the Tragic Muse, is aligned with the disruptive bodies of the slave, prostitute, and actress, she still becomes Stangrave's wife. Stangrave "had heard enough in the last ten minutes to bewilder any brain" when Marie reveals her past, but he proposes marriage because, to him, her status as a "beautiful slave" guarantees her a form of innocence. She could not prevent her own exploitation. The former concubine and slave enters the cult of domesticity in which, as Hazel Carby and Claudia Tate have argued, true womanhood was defined against the unregulated bodies of the slave (2:366).[12] At this crucial junction, even though Marie has entered the cult of true womanhood, Kingsley tellingly still evokes the undisciplined strains of her sexuality. Upon accepting Stangrave's proposal, Marie's "theatric passionateness had passed:—'Nothing was left of her, / Now, but pure womanly.'" The quoted phrase echoes Thomas Hood's famous poem "The Bridge of Sighs," which exhorts,

> Think . . .
> Not of the stains of her,
> All that remains of her
> Now is pure womanly.[13]

In a radical and deeply unsettling ambiguity, Kingsley would reclaim Marie's womanhood by likening her to a dead prostitute. Evidently the stain of her sexuality is difficult to efface. But unlike Hood's homeless "unfortunate," Marie's disruptive body is absorbed into the private realm. She is no longer a slave or an actress, but a wife. Kingsley thus domesticates the Tragic Mulatta narrative, changing it from a narrative of seduction to one of courtship and marriage—the only means by which Marie's troubling desire can be safely mastered.[14]

Has Marie really escaped slavery through marriage? In the United States, a crucial issue in abolitionism was the commodification of white women on the marriage market. Activists such as Elizabeth Cady Stanton, who declared that women were "given in marriage like an article of merchandize" and that "the rights of humanity are more grossly betrayed at the altar than at the auction block of the slaveholder," wondered whether freedwomen would receive self-ownership or become the property of their husbands.[15] Kingsley acknowledges such interpretations in passing references to eligible young women being "sold" into marriage for their property.[16] Coming from a history of *plaçage* and slavery in which the female body is only a sexual commodity, Marie becomes a different sort of commodity when she refashions herself into La Cordifiamma. She sells herself on the stage, but there's a level of self-ownership in her self-merchandizing.

When she enters the cult of true womanhood, however, Marie surrenders her self-ownership. Both her exploitation and the sexual agency that she demonstrated during her liaison with the surgeon are erased when Stangrave removes her "fair, pure, noble flesh" to the domestic sphere (2:369). Despite Tom's misgivings that Stangrave will tire of Marie's temper and flightiness—signs of her unruly black blood—once her beauty goes, Marie becomes the ideal of Victorian womanhood, bearing Stangrave two children. When the novel ends with everyone greeting Tom after he returns from the Crimean War, Marie is absent. She and the children have not made the trip from London, which may be a sign that she has lost not only the theatric passions of the Tragic Muse, but also the mobility. Even though Marie has become a mother and has exchanged the stage for domesticity, she carries the scars of slavery into her marriage. The scars from her past cannot be erased, but entrance into the private sphere has defused Marie's dreams of social revolution. Stangrave now carries out the quest alone: as Marie settles into the private sphere of home and children, the violence and political struggle of the public sphere are no longer her concern.

## Rosa Royal, La Senorita Rosita Campaneo

Published after Emancipation, Child's *A Romance of the Republic* also revised the Tragic Mulatta's narrative by allowing her to marry. While the stories she published in the *Liberty Bell*, such as "The Quadroons" and "Slavery's Pleasant Homes," narrated the tragic deaths of mixed-race slaves, her 1867 novel *A Romance of the Republic* offered a different ending, revising the Tragic Mulatta's narrative by allowing her to marry. The mixed-race heroine, Rosa Royal, is an admirable exemplar of true womanhood, but in the wake of Emancipation, the interracial marriages that Child celebrates in her novel were deeply suspect. While Kingsley is more interested in the erotic dynamics of the interracial marriage plot, Child is invested in interracial marriage as a form of universalism in which racial, class, and cultural differences are erased and everyone is united under one nation, a theme that she explored with Native Americans in *Hobomok* (1824) and "Willie Wharton" (1863). As Deborah Clifford explains, Child believed that miscegenation would reduce racism and "diminish the amount of crime and violence in the world."[17] Child's depiction of the Tragic Mulatta is also a reaction against the rigid roles and expectations prescribed for (true) women. *A Romance of the Republic*, Carolyn L. Karcher argues, explores the question of "whether a woman has the right to seek another chance at happiness after a sexual misalliance, be it an illicit affair or an unhappy marriage."[18]

For Child, the Tragic Mulatta playing a Tragic Muse not only embodies the fantasy of a woman surviving a sexual fall, but also represents a dream of self-fashioning that anyone—regardless of sex, race, or culture—could distinguish and support themselves if they had talent. In *Woman's Journal*, Child enters the debate on the equality of women by declaring, "All I ask is perfect liberty to choose our own spheres of action, and a fair, open chance to do whatsoever we can do well."[19] She extends these sentiments to African Americans when Child predicts in an earlier essay their impact on American theater and music. In "A Chat with the Editor of the Standard," an article published in the *National Anti-Slavery Standard* in 1865, Child writes that before long, "operas will embody the romantic adventures of beautiful fugitive slaves; and the *prima donna* will not need to represent an Octoroon, for men will come to admire the dark, glowing beauty of tropical flora, as much as the violets and lilies of the North."[20] Transforming the Tragic Mulatta into a prima donna in *A Romance of the Republic* reflects Child's belief that mixed-race women would one day sing in opera houses to audiences who admired their virtuosity rather than the price their bodies brought on the auction block.

Before the octoroon heroine of Child's novel ascends the stage, she must first escape from *plaçage* and slavery, systems that commodify and sexually exploit her raced body. Rosa and her sister, Flora, are the daughters of Mr. Royal and Eulalia, a "Spanish" lady. Most of Mr. Royal's acquaintances assume that Eulalia was a *placée*. After their father suddenly dies, leaving behind several large debts, the sisters discover that their mother was actually a slave and that they are now property that can be sold to pay off their father's debts. Although Rosa refuses to escape with her suitor, Gerald Fitzgerald, until after he has married her, she soon learns that their marriage was not legal—when Fitzgerald shockingly brings a new wife, Lily Bell, to his plantation. Like the typical Tragic Mulatta, Rosa is nearly destroyed by this discovery, and by the further revelation that she is Gerald's slave. After hearing this news, Rosa undergoes a familiar transformation, as suffering brings out her white ancestry. When Gerald next sees her, "the warm coloring had entirely faded from her cheeks, leaving only that faintest reflection of gold which she inherited from her mother; and the thinness and pallor of her face made her large eyes seem larger and darker."[21] As in Boucicault's *The Octoroon*, suffering not only makes the mulatta whiter, but the "faintest reflection of gold" in her skin underscores another inheritance from her mother: she is a commodity that can be sold on the slave market.

Learning that she is not Gerald's wife but his slave not only places Rosa outside the boundaries of true womanhood; it also denaturalizes her relationship to her child. She has given birth to property. With this recognition, Rosa slips into a momentary insanity in which she rebels against the reproductive role that slavery has prescribed for her. When she learns that she and her son have been sold, Rosa's demeanor becomes "wild and strange": "The wild, hard look came into her eyes. Such a tempest was raging in her soul that she felt as though she could kill [Gerald] if he stood before her. This savage paroxysm of revenge was followed by thoughts of suicide. She was about to rise, but hearing the approach of Tulee, she closed her eyes and remained still" (198). In similar situations, Rosa's tragic predecessors are driven to suicide (Francilia in Braddon's *The Octoroon*) or infanticide (Cassy in *Uncle Tom's Cabin*). But the more resilient Rosa switches her newborn with Lily Bell's infant son when Chloe, a slave woman from Gerald's plantation who often visits Rosa's secluded cottage, brings Lily Bell's newborn during one of her visits. Although the reader does not learn until much later in her story that the children have been switched, the exchange occurs when Rosa succumbs to temporary insanity. After exchanging the half brothers, Rosa moves away from the Tragic Mulatta construct toward that of the Tragic Muse, who performs her despair onstage.

While Marie refashions herself into a Tragic Muse, Rosa's identity as La Senorita is constructed with the help of her former governess, Madame Guirlande, and her music teacher, Signor Papanti. Suffering from shock and exhaustion at the knowledge that Gerald was going to sell her and their son, Rosa is "whirled away, without time to think of anything," transported from Madame's house in New Orleans, to Philadelphia, New York, and finally to Marseilles (203). (Tulee and the baby, Lily Bell's son, have been left at the home of Madame's cousin.) Unlike Marie, who actively pursues the public stage, Rosa is a relatively passive figure: sexually fallen and in need of a way to support herself, she nonetheless remains closer to true womanhood because she does not actively seek a public career, but relies on her talents as a singer simply to survive.

Entering the public marketplace as an actress is a necessity that, however reluctant she may be, grants Rosa independence. By the time she premieres in Italy as La Senorita Rosita Campaneo, Rosa has already achieved success by singing at private parties of accomplished musicians in Paris and Queen Amelia has given her an enameled wreath. Unlike Marie, who views acting as a means to the revolutionary life she dreams of living, Rosa has difficulty acting or singing a part unless she truly feels it: "Again and again Rosa sang the familiar airs, trying to put soul into them, by imagining how she would feel if she were in Norma's position. Some of the emotions she knew by her own experience, and those she sang with her deepest feeling" (229).

Such identification helps to shield Rosa from suspicions of deception and theatricality. As the lead in Bellini's 1831 opera *Norma*, Rosa performs the part of a Druid high priestess who has been spurned by her Roman lover, Pollione. Though Rosa often performed arias from the opera on the island for Flora and at private parties after her transformation into La Senorita, the idea of singing "before an audience of entire strangers, filled her with dismay." While rehearsing in private before her premiere, Rosa wonders, "Will my heart pass into it there, before that crowd of strange faces, as it does here?" (227, 228). Unlike Marie, who can be "some one else for two hours every night," Rosa cannot inhabit the role fully unless she can identify with the emotions of the character she is playing (1:147).

Rosa's performance as Norma underscores her unease in a public role. When Rosa performs *Norma* for the first time on the stage, she does not embody the role until she sings "Casta Diva," a song that she often sang with Flora when they lived on the island with Gerald. The audience holds her in this moment of authenticity, crying "Bis! Bis!" until she has performed the memory from her past three times. Rosa's moment of authenticity is briefly disrupted during her duet with Adalgisa, her rival both on- and offstage, but when she notices Gerald and Lily Bell watching her from a box near the stage, her reaction to these specters from her past makes the audience believe that "her look, her attitude, her silence, her tremor, all [seem] inimitable acting." Ironically, she owes the authenticity and "theatrical genius" of the moment to Gerald's holding her in his gaze. While seeing Gerald and his wife watching her eagerly from their box evokes Rosa's Tragic Mulatta past, "a glance at the footlights and at the orchestra recalled the recollection of where she was": she is no longer Rosa Royal the slave, but La Senorita performing the tragedy of a betrayed lover (230–231). But Child is careful to emphasize that La Senorita's performance is successful because she is reliving on the public stage her private experience of betrayal. Unlike Marie, Rosa is more thoroughly an ideal woman because she is not performing, but expressing her feelings. At the same time, when she's onstage, she feels a certain kind of safety as well as danger: "the recollection of where she was" protects her from compromising her self-expression.

Like other Tragic Muse figures, Rosa's virtuosity is presumed to draw on forms of experience and emotion beyond those of "respectable" bourgeois women, such as George Eliot's Gwendolen Harleth and Brontë's Lucy Snowe. As La Senorita, Rosa is associated with an aura of transgression or forbidden experience. But unlike the femmes fatales, such as Rachel and Eliot's Alcharisi, or the prostituted actress or chorus girl, Rosa's experience was attained through passive victimization. As the Tragic Mulatta, she has experienced what her spectators have not, but if not for slavery and anti-interracial marriage laws, she would be an ideal model of Victorian womanhood. Rosa shares the values of her "respectable" spectators even though she is a fallen woman. However, her popularity onstage suggests the desire of the audience to enjoy vicariously the pleasures of her transgression.

To create a female fantasy of true womanhood regained, however, Child distinguishes Rosa from skilled actresses, such as Rachel and La Cordifiamma, who artfully appropriate the identities of their characters, reminding readers that La Senorita "had not yet learned to be an actress" and that any semblance of skill in her performance was a result of her tragic past. Rosa's true womanhood has not been erased by her public display on the stage. Indeed, in future performances, when Gerald is not present to elicit fear, anger, and desire for revenge, Rosa tries to summon her feelings from the opening night's performance, but to no avail. Unlike La Cordifiamma and Rachel, who can easily transform themselves into their characters, Rosa struggles and has to leave much of her stage presence to "the inspiration of the moment" (230, 239). Despite her initial reluctance to perform onstage and resistance to her public identity as La Senorita, Rosa is not entirely immune to the audience applauding her: "When the wave of her own excitement was subsiding, the magnetism of an admiring audience began to affect her strongly" (232). But the praise of the audience does not diminish the consequences of Rosa performing her private pain on the public stage for all to witness. Making her private emotions public takes a physical toll on Rosa's health. She is pale when she leaves the stage and has to be lifted into the carriage.

Whereas Marie uses performance to escape her Tragic Mulatta narrative, Rosa is more akin to Gaskell's Ruth and Dickens's fallen women Alice Marwood, Emily, and Martha Endell, who are controlled by the stories of their falls. Though La Senorita has escaped to the public stage and refashioned a new identity for herself, her role in *Norma* requires her to perform her tragic past each night. La Senorita retells her story each time she performs an aria from *Norma*, but she cannot change her narrative. After making the story of her fall public through her performance in *Norma*, Rosa seems to be transformed: "The glossy dark hair rippled over her forehead in soft waves, and the massive braids behind were intertwisted with a narrow band of crimson velvet, that glowed like rubies where the sunlight fell upon it. Her morning wrapper of fine crimson merino, embroidered with gold-colored silk, was singularly becoming to her complexion, softened as the contact was by a white lace collar fastened at the throat with a golden pin. But though she was seated before the mirror, and though her own Spanish taste had chosen the strong contrast in bright colors, she took no notice of the effect produced." The description of Rosa as the Tragic Muse contrasts with her faded appearance when she is ill and pregnant. No longer "lying on the bed, in a loose white robe," Rosa is dressed in the regal colors of crimson and gold (233–234, 173). Though Child attributes Rosa's choice of colors and fabrics to her Spanish taste, her dress reflects the crimson and gold-embroidered clothing worn by Melpomene, the Tragic Muse in Greek mythology: "Her gown and petticoat are crimson, the gown turned up with lace and ermine, the petticoat ornamented with gold fringe and embroidery."[22] Unlike Marie, who constantly looks in the mirror, Rosa ignores her reflection because she has no hidden depths to reveal. Rosa possesses the transparency of ideal womanhood and is not besieged by the anxiety of self-betrayal reflected in Marie's experience in front of the mirror. At the same time, her obliviousness hints at the jaded sensibility of a kept woman. She is dressed as La Senorita, but this Tragic Muse still feels herself enslaved; instead of being kept or enslaved by a man, however, she is kept by the stage.

Rosa takes no joy in her regal appearance because she sees herself as playing another part. Though she is uncomfortable as a public spectacle, her career on the stage has afforded her financial autonomy. But despite her mobility and financial freedom, La Senorita is unable to escape her Tragic Mulatta origins; these are reclaimed when Gerald visits her the day after her premiere in *Norma*. When Signor Papanti, Rosa's music teacher and manager, asks the intruder to leave the dressing room, Gerald disparages Rosa's character by declaring that Signor Papanti is her sexual "protector": "So *you* are installed as her protector. . . . You are not the first gallant I have known to screen himself behind his years" (236). Gerald's insults remap the history of *plaçage* onto Rosa's body. Since she did not die in childbirth or commit suicide, the only way she could survive Gerald's treachery would be to find a new "protector" and continue her role as concubine. Because they are both nonwhite, Rosa and Signor are incapable of forcing Gerald to leave the house. The only person who can do this is Alfred King, a friend of Rosa's father and Gerald's social equal. For a moment, Rosa melts away into the passive existence of the Tragic Mulatta while the three men argue over their sexual and legal claims to her.

Unable to escape her Tragic Mulatta past and transform herself completely into a Tragic Muse, Rosa admits to Alfred: "I hardly know myself as La Senorita Campaneo. It all seems to me so strange and unreal, that, if it were not for a few visible links with the past, I should feel as if I had died and passed into another world." During this pivotal conversation in which Rosa both decides the future of her career and accepts Alfred's marriage proposal, she indeed "passes into another world," deciding to enter the domestic sphere as Alfred's wife. With marriage, the Tragic Mulatta gains entrance to the cult of true womanhood, and the fallen woman gains a second chance at happiness. Marriage to Alfred removes Rosa from the marketplace. When Alfred suggests that Rosa's "romantic story" of slavery would make her a "great lioness" in England, Rosa responds: "I should dislike that sort of attention. . . . Do not suppose, however, that I am ashamed of my dear mother, or of her lineage; but I wish to have any interest I excite founded on my own merits, not on any extraneous circumstance." By keeping her history "strictly confidential," Rosa prevents her story from becoming another product for public consumption, retaining control over the way in which her body will circulate in the private sphere as Mrs. King (248, 252).

Still, Rosa's past as an object of public exchange follows her into the private sphere. The white baby that Rosa left behind with Tulee in Louisiana and the "black" baby whom Lily Bell has raised as her own are the hidden signs of difference that plague Rosa in the same way that Marie is haunted by her scars and her great-grandmother's African physiognomy. Rosa's final act as the Tragic Mulatta creates treacherous consequences within the private sphere through a tangled web of plot complications. On the night of her premiere in *Norma*, Rosa receives a letter informing her that Tulee and the white baby (only Rosa knows this is Lily Bell's son) died of yellow fever, but the baby has in fact survived (and will grow up to call himself George Falkner), only to be sold into and later escape from slavery. While Lily Bell's white son escapes slavery by passing as a white gentleman aboard the ship *The King Cotton*, Rosa's mixed-race son, Gerald Fitzgerald, has been raised as a white gentleman in a family whose fortune came from the cotton industry.[23] The young Gerald Fitzgerald is not only evidence of Rosa's sexual fall, but since he has been raised as Lily Bell's son, he is a reminder of Rosa's alienated motherhood in slavery.

The emergence of this past threatens Rosa's marriage. When Rosa is staggered at a ball by the sight of her son, Gerald, Alfred presumes she has seen a former lover, and the novel begins to veer from sentimental romance into sensation fiction. Alfred fears infidelity while Child's readers fear incest, since young Fitzgerald is "entirely devoted to the queen of the evening." As an intimacy arises between Fitzgerald and Eulalia, Rosa's daughter and his half sister, Rosa attempts to distract Gerald, but thereby arouses Alfred's jealous suspicion that "his modest and dignified wife was in love with this stripling." Rosa finally unburdens her heart when her husband suggests that she is the victim of "an unworthy passion" (299. 349, 350). To reclaim her character from her husband's erroneous assumption, Rosa finally confesses that she switched her child with Lily Bell's and that their daughter is being courted by her half brother.

This confession markedly alters the dynamics of power in Rosa and Alfred's marriage. Whereas before their marriage Alfred wished to "leave her in perfect freedom" to decide whether to retire from the stage, when Rosa blanches at the thought of informing her son of his true heritage, Alfred gently takes control of matters and assumes the role of the confident patriarch: "You have wisely chosen me for your confessor, and if I recommend penance I trust you will think it best to follow my advice" (252, 355). After resolving to tell young Fitzgerald the truth about his past, Alfred informs Rosa that she "ought to make a full confession to Mrs. Fitzgerald," to which Rosa responds, "It will be a severe penance . . . but I will do whatever you think is right." After tying up the various loose ends—Gerald is killed in the Civil War, Alfred settles George Falkner in business in Marseilles—Rosa's past deeds as the Tragic Mulatta have been confessed and righted, and she thereby attains the "pure womanliness" of Marie Stangrave. She tells her husband: "I should never have found my way out of that wretched entanglement if it had not been for you. You have really acted toward me the part of Divine Providence" (356, 439). The Tragic Muse is subsumed in a celebration of husband and country.

While Marie is presented as a passive victim of slavery, Rosa is a sinner whom her husband must redeem. As Alfred tells her at the end of the novel, "I think you may now have a tranquil mind; for I believe things have been so arranged that no one is very seriously injured by that act of frenzy which has caused you so much suffering." With young Gerald's death and George Falkner's immigration to Europe, evidence of Rosa's sins have indeed been erased. No longer a Tragic Mulatta or a Tragic Muse, Rosa fades into the background as a true woman. The novel concludes with a celebration of husband and country when a patriotic tableau featuring Eulalia bedecked in red, white, and blue ribbons and crowned with a circle of stars is revealed in honor of Alfred's birthday (438, 440).

Marie Stangrave's and Rosa King's entries into the domestic sphere allow them to escape the violent death that typically ends the Tragic Mulatta's narrative and the exhausting public display and self-commodification of the Tragic Muse. But in becoming "true women," Marie and Rosa experience a different demise as they lose their independence, individuality, and most notably, their racial identities. At the end of *Two Years Ago*, Marie is merely "as beautiful as ever" (2:383). Whereas Kingsley never explains whether Marie and her children are passing, Child explains that Rosa and Flora have decided not to reveal the truth of their racial lineage to their children "till time and experience had matured their characters and views of life" (287). Though Kingsley and Child's fantasies rescue the mixed-race woman from sexual exploitation and public exposure, in doing so her racial identity is erased. Despite Marie and Rosa's entries into the domestic sphere, the cult of true womanhood remains a realm where only "white" women may tread.

## From Tragic Muse to Villainess

While the white skin of Kingsley's and Child's mixed-race heroines allows them to attain the privacy and protection of the domestic sphere, in texts such as Hawthorne's *Marble Faun*, Dumas's *L'Étrangère*, and Marryat's *Daughter of the Tropics,* the mixed-race femme fatale's ability to pass for white enables her to exact revenge upon her enemies. Unlike the virtuous and victimized Tragic Mulattas from the early nineteenth century, these mixed-race protagonists are worldly, aggressive adventuresses. They desire wealth and class status, as well as the (sexual) attention of the white hero who is seemingly indifferent to their "exotic" beauty and charm. Whereas the Tragic Mulatta of the antebellum period was exposed on the auction block, fin de siècle reenvisionings of this figure show her exposing the secrets of white characters. In these texts, white femininity is victimized by the mixed-race femme fatale eager to enact her revenge. Combining the artistic, entrepreneurial, and sexual power of the Tragic Muse, the Tragic Mulattas in these texts evolve into adventuresses or exotic femmes fatales seeking to escape narratives that seem to insist on their social exile or destruction. However, unlike the villainous sensation heroines that preceded them, such as Lydia Gwilt and Lady Audley, the mixed-race femmes fatales are pitied for how their lives have been shaped by the abuses and treacheries of slavery and the resulting commodification and sexual exploitation.

Miriam, the ambiguously raced heroine in Hawthorne's *Marble Faun,* is an early figuring of the Tragic Mulatta as femme fatale. She is not an actress, but her artistic talent as a painter and sexual agency evoke the power of the Tragic Muse. Hawthorne's text centers around four friends: Hilda, Kenyon, and Miriam are American expatriates studying art in Rome, and Donatello is an Italian count. Donatello, who embodies youthful innocence, falls in love with the mysterious Miriam, and eventually kills a man from her past who has been stalking her. The novel focuses on the repercussions Dontaello's violent act has on the lives of the four friends. Although she's positioned as a victim in the narrative, Miriam's presence and influence inadvertently corrupt the moral and physical constitution of Donatello.

Miriam is a figure closely akin to the heroines of *Berenice, Leila,* and *Ivanhoe,* who are believed to possess the power to bewitch reluctant or unwitting lovers. Early in the novel, Kenyon, the sculptor, teases her: "You have bewitched the poor lad [Donatello]. . . . You have a faculty of bewitching people, and it is providing you with a singular train of followers."[24] Miriam's unknown origins add to her allure: "There was an ambiguity about this young lady, which, though it did not necessarily imply anything wrong, would have operated unfavourably as regarded her reception in society, anywhere but in Rome." In describing various conjectures about Miriam's origins, Hawthorne unites the Jewess with the mixed-race American slave. Writing during a time when American literature was pervaded by the Tragic Mulatta, Hawthorne explains: "It was said . . . that Miriam was the daughter and heiress of a great Jewish banker, (an idea perhaps suggested by a certain rich Oriental character in her face), and had fled from her paternal home to escape a union with a cousin. . . . Another story hinted, that she was a German princess. . . . According to a third statement, she was the offspring of a

Southern American planter, who had given her an elaborate education and endowed her with his wealth; but the one burning drop of African blood in her veins so affected her with a sense of ignominy, that she relinquished all, and fled her country" (18, 20).[25] She was also said to be the lady of an English nobleman whose love of art had led her to toss away title to pursue her love in a Roman studio. Hawthorne's comic passage emphasizes the protean character of "otherness" grounded in little more than a darker complexion. In making Miriam's features so ambiguous—she could literally be anything from a Jewish heiress to a German princess to a mixed-race American slave—Hawthorne suggests how subtle racial distinctions can be.

Miriam's sketches of biblical heroines associate her with women both Jewish and fatal. Visiting her studio, Donatello sees her sketches of "Jael, driving the nail through the temples of Sisera," Judith, and Salome "receiving the head of John the Baptist in a charger." These sketches of Jewish women "acting the part of a revengeful mischief towards man" deeply unsettle Donatello: "He gave a shudder; his face assumed a look of trouble, fear, and disgust; he snatched up one sketch after another, as if about to tear it in pieces. Finally, shoving away the pile of drawings, he shrank back from the table and clasped his hands over his eyes" (36, 37). Noticing the effect her work has had on the count, Miriam explains that the "ugly phantoms" are not things that she created, but things that haunt her. Although Miriam herself has displayed no violent inclinations, Hawthorne likens her to Jael, explaining that the sketch was "dashed off with remarkable power . . . as if she herself were Jael, and felt irresistibly impelled to make her bloody confession, in this guise" (37, 36).

Hawthorne never fully explains what crime or tragedy haunts Miriam, but throughout the novel he connects her with deadly women. Even in her self-portrait, the young woman represented could be either Rachel, Jacob's beautiful and devoted wife, or the murderous Judith, who "vanquished Holofernes with her beauty, and slew him for too much adoring it" (40). Unlike the true femme fatale for whom innocence is a thin veneer, Miriam inhabits an ambiguous middle ground in which she is a good character surrounded by an air of danger that affects everyone she loves. Hawthorne emphasizes her ambiguous moral character when she views Hilda's copy of Guido's painting *Portrait of Beatrice Cenci*. Miriam wishes that she could enter the consciousness of Beatrice, who was beheaded in 1599 for plotting to kill her father, who had molested her: "If I could but clasp Beatrice Cenci's ghost, and draw her to myself! I would give my life to know whether she thought herself innocent, or the one great criminal since time began!" While Miriam speaks, Hilda notices that "her friend's expression had become almost exactly that of the portrait." Telling her friend not to look so forlorn, Hilda exclaims: "What an actress you are! And I never guessed it before." This reference to Miriam as an actress, when paired with her ambiguous racial identity, reflects how racial differences could be exploited by an adept performer, as is evinced by Kingsley's Marie Lavington and Child's Rosa Royal.

Miriam's attraction to the image of Beatrice hints at the troubles that plague the mysterious artist. An event has occurred in Miriam's past that, like Beatrice's sin, might have been "no sin at all, but the best virtue possible in the circumstances." The words with which Hilda describes her copy of Beatrice might also be applied to Miriam: "She is a fallen angel, fallen, and yet sinless" (53). Several chapters before the conclusion of the novel, we learn that Miriam fled to Rome to escape marrying an older gentleman—a gesture that is explained by her ancestry: "There was something in Miriam's blood, in her mixed race . . . which had given her freedom of thought, and force of will, and made this pre-arranged connection odious to her." But Miriam is not simply an icon of freedom. In addition to spurning marriage to this man, whom Miriam says suffered from an "insanity which often develops itself in old, close-kept breeds of men, when long unmixed with newer blood," the tragic heroine is also involved in an unnamed crime (341).

Miriam's association with crime reinforces her resemblance to a sensation heroine. Even though Miriam has "flung herself upon the world, and speedily created a new sphere," someone who knows her involvement in the crime has followed her to Rome. Her friends refer to this person as "the Model" because his face appears in many of the sketches of men being murdered by Jewesses. Miriam encounters the Model several times during the story, and eventually Donatello murders him because he believes that in doing so he is protecting Miriam. The novel, however, suggests that much of the responsibility is Miriam's. Echoing stereotypes of the Tragic Muse as a bewitching seductress, Donatello is led into the crime by Miriam's eyes. Donatello's crime is a form of sexual initiation, which is emphasized in the way that Miriam presses him close to her bosom and they both experience a "kind of rapture" when the Model is cast from their lives (342, 139).[26] The criminal bond that now unites them "was closer than a marriage-bond." Yet, in a further alignment of Miriam with the femme fatale, she goes unpunished. While Donatello suffers in prison, his Beautiful Jewess is free since "her crime lay merely in a glance; she did no murder" (364, 369).

Whereas Hawthorne's Miriam seems to be a victim in need of protection, the mixed-race femmes fatales in Marryat's and Dumas's texts seek revenge, specifically against white women. Unlike the early Tragic Mulattas and the villainous British sensation heroines that followed, the mixed-race femme fatale of the fin de siècle fashioned a respectable public identity for herself. However, she has trouble securing a proper place for herself in the white domestic sphere and must resort to blackmail and manipulation to insinuate herself there. For example, in Dumas's *L'Étrangère*, the mixed-race femme fatale Mrs. Clarkson is a successful businesswoman, but though she "received all of the most elegant, most noble, most distinguished men there were . . . she never calls on any lady."[27] Mrs. Clarkson, who is reminiscent of one of Balzac's manipulative courtesans or perhaps Henry James's Madame Merle, helped arrange the marriage of Catherine, the daughter of a wealthy merchant, to the morally corrupt and bankrupt Duke de Septmonts. As in the earlier Tragic Mulatta narratives of Boucicault and Braddon, as well as Child's *Romance of the Republic*, the commodification of the mixed-race slave is juxtaposed to a white woman being sold off on the marriage market. However, in Dumas's novel, Mrs. Clarkson has aided in the commodification of Catherine, who has been forced by her father to marry for money and title rather than for love. The women in the play are critical of Mrs. Clarkson and skeptical of her wealth: "The money which she wins at play, I know well whence it comes," they say, insinuating that she is a courtesan. The women are surprised to learn that she is married: "What, has she a real husband? What was it they said—that she had only other people's husbands."[28]

In 1876, Sarah Bernhardt participated in a read-through of Dumas's *L'Étrangère* at the Comédie-Française, where she performed the role of the Duchess de Septmonts. But when the parts were assigned, she was given the role of Mrs. Clarkson, the mixed-race "stranger" of the play's title. Reflecting on this unexpected reassignment, Bernhardt writes, "I burst out into irrepressible laughter, which surprised everybody present," and when asked why "I was laughing like that, I exclaimed: 'At all of you . . . who are in the plot, and who are all a little afraid of the result of your cowardice. Well, you need not alarm yourselves. I was delighted to play the *Duchess de Septmonts*, but I shall be ten times more delighted to play the *Stranger*. And this time, my dear Sophie, I make no account of you . . . for you have played me a little trick which was quite unworthy of our friendship!"[29] No explanation is given for why she was assigned the part of the "stranger," but perhaps like Rachel, who was asked to play the role of a *mulâtresse* in Alphonse Lamartine's *Toussaint Louverture*, producers of the play saw an affinity between Bernhardt's Jewish identity and that of the quadroon adventuress she was asked to play. Although Dumas's play has faded into obscurity, it was described by James as "the event of the winter." However, James goes on to criticize the drama, explaining: "I confess that "*L'Étrangère* strikes me as a rather desperate piece of floundering in the dramatic sea. . . . Suffice it that the 'Foreigner' who gives its title to the piece, and who is played by that very interesting actress, Mme. Sarah Bernhardt, is a daughter of our own democracy, Mrs. Clarkson by name. She explains, in the second act, by a mortal harangue—the longest, by the watch, I have ever listened to—that she is the daughter of a mulatto slave-girl and a Carolina planter." James, and several of his contemporaries, didn't see the point of having Miss Clarkson in the play at all: "She is out of time with all her companions. She is, on Dumas's part, an incredible error of taste" with "her beauty, her diamonds, her sinister reputation, her innumerable conquests, and her total absence of female friends."[30]

Though Mrs. Clarkson may seem a courtesan, she is in fact a chaste divorcee and businesswoman. Revealing her racial secret and history to Catherine, Mrs. Clarkson tells her later in the play: "I am the daughter and grand-daughter of slaves. . . . My mother was a mulatto, in other words, my grandmother had married or loved a negro."[31] Before she and her mother are separated at a slave auction, her mother urges: "Recollect, forever, the name of the man who has put us up for sale and who has separated us; and, if you live, avenge us. Any means are good." Mrs. Clarkson escapes slavery with her virtue intact, travels to Boston, where she works as a servant in a hotel and later marries Mr. Clarkson, "who had returned from the mines with nearly twenty thousand dollars. I was seventeen or eighteen years old. He fell in love with me. That was all I could hope for the better, so as to commence what I had to do."[32] By marrying her off before her revenge has begun, Dumas sets up a dichotomy in which Mrs. Clarkson plays the part of a vengeful adventuress while maintaining her status as a chaste wife. Marriage protects her from sexual aspersions cast against her character and emphasizes Dumas's point that sexual fallenness is not the reason for her moral depravity. Mrs. Clarkson does not rely on her husband for money. Her revenge allows her to possess the plantation where she was once property. She goes to Charleston to seek revenge upon her father, but since he's dead, she carries out her vengeance on her half brothers. She says: "I had but to step between them to make them mortal enemies, and, three months after my arrival, the elder killed the younger with a knife. The victim, who loved me madly, had been careful enough to make his will, and left me all he possessed, about a hundred thousand dollars. That was the commencement of my fortune."

Mrs. Clarkson gains both financial security and pleasure from preying on men, reversing the typical narrative of the victimized Tragic Mulatta. Called "the virgin of evil" by one of her victims, Mrs. Clarkson declares that she "had drawn from the stupidity of these men all they could produce, I sent them back to what they had so well merited—to prison, madness, dishonor, murder, or suicide. If other women would be, like myself, conscious of their force and power, man would be a pretty small affair."[33] There is no hint of domestic sentiment: of her relationship with her husband, she explains: "I have business capacities; we are no longer man and wife, we are partners; it is no longer his name that I bear, it is that of the house of Clarkson and Company—one of the most important in the States." In taking the name of a company, she becomes "industry" or "business" in a metaphorical sense. She says that she doesn't want to marry again because she "preferred my liberty and my fortune." But Dumas does not entirely surrender the older narrative: "In the midst of all these false men on whom I avenged myself, who served my purpose, or of whom I made sport, I met one who was truly great in mind and heart. . . . He is the only one who has not submitted to my rule, and I have felt at once that I should perhaps submit to his." Like other Tragic Mulattas, Mrs. Clarkson is fated to love a man, Gerard, who does not return her desire: "This man . . . will be everything to me, or he shall be nothing to anybody, and somebody will die of it; perhaps he, perhaps you, perhaps myself."[34]

Unlike Mrs. Clarkson, Marryat's Lola Arlington has managed to create a respectable position for herself in the white domestic sphere. Marryat's novel, *Daughter of the Tropics*, tells the story of Lola, an octoroon from Haiti who is now working in London as a housekeeper and secretary for Mark Kerrison, a bachelor and playwright. Lola, whose name conjures images of the infamous courtesan Lola Montez, is in love with Mark, but he is repulsed by her tainted bloodline.[35] As he tells Colonel Escott, who saw "many wives with that flaw in their composition" during his time in India: "It is never purged from the system! The taint remains for ever!"[36] Rejecting Lola's amorous declaration, Mark instead marries a woman with a compromised past. Lola attempts to break up the marriage by staging a play based on the sexual past of Mark's wife; however, when the play fails to destroy the couple's union, Lola accidentally poisons Mark with a draught intended for his wife. The vengeful deeds of this exotic seductress eventually result in her self-destruction. Rather than wait for the authorities to discover her crime, Lola drowns herself.

While the previous Tragic Mulattas were "white women" with a fatal stain, Lola's otherness goes beyond her West Indian ancestry; her otherness or racial difference is more dangerous. She has links to revolution, voodoo, cannibalism, and a Jewish husband, whom she poisoned. Like Boucicault's Zoe, Lola exhibits self-loathing, wishing to forget her ties to her mother and grandmother: "She hated and despised them! She hated herself sometimes for having sprung from so unworthy a beginning, and almost wished she had been born a veritable negress than endued with blood that had a taint upon it" (1:64). Her mother resisted letting her daughter become a *placée* and instead insisted upon marriage: "Did I not marry you to Agar? Aye—*marry* you hard and fast in the church! I had a battle to do it, I can tell you, Lola! The man offered me hundreds of pounds—enough to make me comfortable for life—to let him off. But I was firm. I was determined that my beautiful daughter should be a lady, and have her own fortune, and so I forced him to give in to my wishes and make you his wife." Lola responds: "You sold me as a child of fifteen to a horrible old Jew with the worst of characters, who initiated me into every sort of crime. He only wanted me as a decoy-duck to his gambling-saloon" (1:49–50). By marrying her to a Jewish merchant, Marryat taps into the anti-Semitic stereotype of Shylock, which emphasizes Lola's commodification and her moral corruption.

Lola's marriage to a Jewish moneylender places her in the role of victim and commodity sold off by her Haitian mother. As Agar's wife, she is placed in the public sphere; however, after poisoning him, she seeks a respectable situation for herself in the domestic sphere by becoming Mark's housekeeper. But despite escaping to the private sphere, she still bears the markings of a public woman, performing as a singer whose voice is "melodious, low, rich, and sweet; and her songs were the wildest, most bewitching carols Escott had ever heard" (1:44). Though Marryat aligns Lola with public display and performance, she keeps her securely within the private sphere. She's not actually on the stage or even writing dramas or literature under her own name, but she is still depicted as a "public" woman. It is almost as though her black blood insists on her public exposure.

Lola is eager to escape her "public" past by becoming Mark's wife. As one character explains: "She rules Kerrison with a rod of iron; he daren't say his soul is his own, without asking her permission first. . . . She not only orders his household affairs for him; she regulates his expenditure, and writes half his plays. . . . O, the fair Lola is a very clever woman, you may take my word for it. Matrimony is the stake she plays for, and I'll back her to win." However, Mark is too repulsed by Lola's blood even to be attracted to her, let alone consider making her his wife. While Escott is attracted by Lola's exotic appearance, Mark detests her black blood: "I have such a horror of it that I would rather marry a woman 'with a history!' . . . But the blood is well diluted. I believe she's an octoroon—seven parts white. Still, it's *there*, and I should never forget it" (1:39, 49).[37] Whereas Mark is depicted as a racist, the men who do desire Lola are racially marked themselves—Agar is a Jew and Escott's Englishness is compromised by his time in India.

Although Mark would never consider marrying Lola, his creative livelihood depends upon her. In this text, it's not the Tragic Mulatta's body that is desirable or the commodity, but her mind. Escott, who wishes that he could replace Lola and be the one to help Mark, learns: "There's no doubt his plays have been twice as successful since she associated herself with his work. . . . It's a woman's wit he needs—a woman's touch to round off his ragged edges—a woman's fancy to give his love-passages reality. Kerrison couldn't afford to part with Lola Arlington now, even if he wished it." Like the "housekeepers" in the West Indian travel narratives examined in chapter 1, Lola's position in Mark's house is one of exchange. However, though Mark treats Lola as he would a mistress, he exploits her creative abilities rather than her body. When Lola confesses her desire to Mark, she says, "I am everything in the library . . . but out of it I am *nothing*—nobody—only the *housekeeper!*" Instead of promoting her to the role of wife, Mark changes her title from housekeeper to "lady-secretary," explaining, "This will place you at once in your proper position with the ladies who may chance to honour me by dining here" (1:42, 117, 133).[38]

Whereas the mid-nineteenth-century Tragic Mulatta narratives discussed in chapter 3 show the mixed-race heroines being exposed on the auction block, these later Tragic Mulatta narratives show the raced femmes fatales exposing someone else's secrets. Indeed, in both Dumas's play and Marryat's novel, Mrs. Clarkson and Mrs. Arlington have the power to ruin their white female rivals, whose reputations have been compromised in some way. In these narratives, the Tragic Mulatta exacts revenge on white femininity. In Dumas's play, for example, she who has been commodified and sold as a slave has a hand in selling a white woman on the marriage market. Initially, Catherine refuses to visit Mrs.

Clarkson, explaining: "That woman has sold me, yes, sold me to the duke; the bargain was made in her house, between my father and M. de Septmonts. That is how I came to be a duchess."[39] Knowing that Catherine is in love with Gerard, Mrs. Clarkson exposes the duchess to her husband by making sure he finds a letter in which she declares her love for Gerard.

In Marryat's novel, the "dark" woman has achieved the status of lady while her fair rival, Lily Powers, was born a lady but must turn to the stage to make a living because she gave her love to a man who spurned her in order to keep his mother's fortune. No sexual fall occurred, but Lily lost her reputation. Even though the fair woman becomes the "public" woman, Mark only sees Lily as an ideal of Victorian womanhood: "With her delicately-chiselled features, her luminous eyes, her pale gold hair, and her alabaster skin, she looked like the incarnation of purity. No one, to see her, would ever have imagined she could feel the force of a consuming passion. . . . There are some men for whom such statuesque temperaments express the ideal of womanhood, and Mark Kerrison was one of them." However, Lily is a "woman with a history" (1:181, 49). Marryat places Lola in the position of being able to look down on Lily as a public woman who has taken to the stage. Despite her mixed bloodline and her manipulative nature, Lola fulfills the duties of the angel of the house. As she tells Colonel Escott: "But she is no companion for him. It is *I* to whom he looks for conversation and amusement. *I* who assist him in his work, and keep him a comfortable and happy home" (2:48).[40] Lola seeks revenge by using the stage to expose Lily's past. Revealing that the play she composed is based on Lily's life, Lola tells Mark, "I resolved that you too should know the story of her antecedents," which is a statement that parallels the moment in the Tragic Mulatta's narrative in which the auction block becomes the stage upon which the white slave's black antecedents are made public. Though Mark says he would rather marry a woman with a history than a woman with African ancestry, finding out the truth about Lily taints her in his mind: "Kerrison would never reproach Lily for the story she had told him. He would never, probably, allude to it again. But he would not forget it nevertheless" (2:162, 184).

Dumas's and Marryat's femme fatale narratives end with the mixed-race villainess's exile or self-destruction. Ironically, after Lola accidentally poisons Mark in her attempt to kill his wife, the colonel helps her escape by booking her passage on a ship bound for Australia, even though he knows she killed his friend. Though she committed murder, he cannot bear the thought of her being exposed on the gallows. Instead of the auction block, Colonel Escott "pictured to himself those glorious charms, on which he had so delighted to dwell, dragged to a felon's cell—exposed to the gaze of a deriding multitude in the prisoner's dock—and finally led forth to undergo the most terrible execution ever devised by man" (2:259). In a moment of madness brought on by guilt and fear that her crime will be detected, Lola throws herself overboard before the ship departs. In Dumas, however, the villainous mulatta does not die or destroy herself; she moves on to another city. After Mr. Clarkson kills the duke in a duel, Mrs. Clarkson tells Catherine, "It was through me your marriage was brought about, it is through me that it is undone." With that statement, Mrs. Clarkson's reign of revenge ends and she reunites with her husband, telling him: "You are a good and a brave fellow. I shall leave with you. I have had enough of Europe; it is too small. Do you understand that I am going to be loving? Come, let us depart, I suffocate."[41] Now that Europe is too small for her, she and Clarkson plan to conquer the East with their American gold. Describing her financial power earlier in the text, Mrs. Clarkson declares: "This power I proclaim to be the first in the world. It aids in the possession of all you desire, and in not regretting what cannot be had. I wished for this power, I have it; I desire it still greater. Well, then, make us rich, Clarkson, very rich, and perhaps, one of these days, when I shall be completely tired of their European civilization which sometimes appears to me rather narrow and constrained, perhaps I shall give you a rendezvous upon some ocean, so we may go away to India or Africa, have ourselves proclaimed king and queen, or god and goddess, that, if the throne does not suffice for me, I may have a temple."[42] Although Mrs. Clarkson and Lola Arlington exhibit a powerful agency produced by a potent blend of ingenuity and desire, in the end, Dumas and Marryat do not permit the mixed-race femmes fatales to claim a proper place within the white domestic sphere.

# Conclusion: "I Know What I Am": Race and the Triumphant "New Woman"

*We are in, and of, England . . . charity, and filial piety, and reverence, and amiability are our natural virtues. All those hateful habits that novelists ascribe to us are untrue, and dismally failing as jests.*

EMILY HARRIS, *ESTELLE* (1878)

*I am not unhappy, and I am a mulatto. I just enjoy my life, and I don't want to die before my time comes, either. There are lots of good things left on earth to be enjoyed even by mulattoes, and I want my share.*

PAULINE HOPKINS, *CONTENDING FORCES* (1900)

Although Charles Kingsley and Lydia Maria Child redefine Victorian womanhood so that it encompasses nonwhite women who previously circulated as commodities in the public sphere, their texts conclude with the mixed-race heroines passing, or at the very least, evading questions about their racial origins. However, Henry James and his Jewish and African American contemporaries Emily Harris, Frances Harper, and Pauline Hopkins do not conceal the racial identities of their heroines, and thereby dramatize relations between race and domesticity, and between race and the public sphere. While the Jewish and African American heroines in Harris's *Estelle* (1878), James's *The Tragic Muse* (1890), Harper's *Iola Leroy* (1892), and Hopkins's *Contending Forces* (1900) make no effort to conceal their racial heritages, they struggle to resist narratives that insist on seeing them as tragic or sexually imperiled. Borrowing from representations of the Tragic Mulatta, Beautiful Jewess, and Tragic Muse examined in the previous chapters, the Jewish and African American "New Woman" narratives examined in this conclusion, as well as the heroines themselves, refuse easy categorization. As Dora Smith declares in Hopkins's *Contending Forces*, she is not a Tragic Mulatta, but a mixed-race woman who wants her share.

Dora's desire for her "share" was an issue taken up in discussions about civil rights, as well as debates about the Woman Question. What share did women deserve? Could they pursue a vocation or their artistic talents outside the home? Was marriage and motherhood the only option, or were these choices a woman had the right to make for herself? Unlike Kingsley's Marie and Child's Rosa, who left the stage to become wives and mothers, Harris's Estelle Hofer, James's Miriam Rooth, Harper's Iola Leroy, and Hopkins's Sappho Clark want to continue the work they pursued as single women in the public sphere. In following their attempts to redefine true womanhood so that it encompasses their professional desires and racial origins, this conclusion argues that these raced heroines were contemporaries of the infamous "New Woman" figure that populated the fiction, newspaper articles, and medical treatises of the 1880s and 1890s.

Several sources have been suggested for the origins of the New Woman. Henry James's Henrietta Stackpole, Isabel Archer's journalist friend in *The Portrait of a Lady* (1881), and Olive Chancellor in *The Bostonians* (1886) are harbingers of the female spectacle who would dominate both the British and American cultural imaginaries at the end of the century. Though versions of the New Woman circulated in *Punch* and the works of authors from Sarah Grand to Thomas Hardy, the figure was a liminal presence that represented different values to different groups. To some, she was physically degenerate, a bespectacled figure without womanly curves who sacrificed her femininity, particularly her ability to reproduce, to further her education. While the New Woman sometimes was unsexed and boyish, other representations, particularly in the 1890s, depicted her as sexually voracious; she was a degenerate femme fatale with the ability to contaminate the world with diseased offspring. Conflicting portrayals of the New Woman as unsexed or an oversexed believer in free love, hyperphysical or physically enervated, emphasize the fundamental indeterminacy of this figure in popular fantasy, where above all she was an affront to domestic womanhood. British writers, including Sarah Grand, Mona Caird, Ouida, Olive Schreiner, Thomas Hardy, and George Gissing, were generally thought of as New Woman writers, or, as Margaret Oliphant denounced them, writers of "The Anti-Marriage League." Though this spectacle of unnatural femininity is generally thought of as a figure growing out of British literature and sexual treatises of the fin de siècle, the New Woman also had an impact on the American side of the Atlantic. In the 1890s, Grand lectured in the United States and enjoyed an American best seller in *The Heavenly Twins.*[1] Indeed, the American literary imagination also had its share of New Women characters who rebelled against the expectations and restrictions of ideal Victorian womanhood: Henrietta Stackpole in *The Portrait of a Lady,* Olive Chancellor in *The Bostonians,* Edna Pontellier in Kate Chopin's *The Awakening* (1899), the unnamed narrator in Charlotte Perkins Gilman's *The Yellow Wallpaper* (1899), and, in the early twentieth century, Lily Bart in Edith Wharton's *The House of Mirth* (1905) and Undine Spragg in *The Custom of the Country* (1913).[2] Recent scholarship has also treated Hopkins's *Contending Forces* as a New Woman text, but for the most part, New Women were traditionally spectacles of improper white femininity.[3]

This is not to say that questions of race did not enter into the New Woman debate. As a construction of imperial culture, the British New Woman was linked to questions of race, eugenics, and empire. Though some viewed her as unsexed or a sexual degenerate, the New Woman in the works of George Egerton, Grand, Caird, and Schreiner saw herself as preserving the British race by choosing a healthy marriage partner for herself. Many New Women, both fictional and historical, believed that men at the end of the century were sexually degenerate, weak, ruined, or contaminated by lust, and they felt they had the right to choose a biologically desirable partner (even if that meant crossing class lines) so that they would have healthy offspring to keep up the British race. Anxieties over the vitality of imperial rule directed attention to strengthening the British "race." As Rebecca Stott explains: "One of the primary areas of shared concern between feminists and those who championed imperialism were questions of racial superiority, racial purity, and racial motherhood. . . . [M]any New Women were actively campaigning for the continuance of the 'race' through the championing of motherhood, support of the empire and purity campaigns."[4] The New Woman's concern with purifying the British race, as Angelique Richardson describes it, was a "eugenic feminism" in which the "central goal . . . was the construction of civic motherhood, which sought political recognition for reproductive labour; in the wake of new biological knowledge they argued that their contribution to nation and empire might be expanded if they assumed responsibility for the rational selection of reproductive partners."[5] Darwin's theories of natural selection and inheritance are reflected in New Women texts in which questions of origins and heredity are explored. Like the Tragic Mulatta, the Beautiful Jewess, and the Tragic Muse, the New Woman was a spectacle of sexuality upon which writers and readers mapped their anxieties about how and in what way physical and emotional characteristics were passed on to offspring.

Because domesticity is coded as white, the New Women who distort or escape its pull are presumed to be white as well.[6] Yet the New Woman in fiction nonetheless conjured up racial differences as she was distinguished from norms of domestic womanhood. Before the raced women in *Estelle, The Tragic Muse, Iola Leroy,* and *Contending Forces* could redefine ideal womanhood, they first had to establish a claim to true womanhood by demonstrating their sexual purity and morality. After proving their virtue, Estelle Hofer, Miriam Rooth, Iola Leroy, and Sappho Clark challenge domesticity from within by resisting and eventually redefining marriage (gender roles) so that they retain the professional interests—painting, acting, teaching, and stenography—that they passionately pursued as single women. With the exception of Harris's Estelle, who chooses not to marry, marriage provides a safe way for these women to pursue their professional interests because as wives, they lack the unsettling autonomy of the New Woman. Though becoming a wife tempers their professional pursuits in some cases, it does not erase them completely, as was the case in Kingsley's *Two Years Ago* and Child's *A Romance of the Republic.*

## The New Jewish Woman

Described by Nadia Valman as "the first feminist novel by an Anglo-Jewish writer," Harris's *Estelle* examines the eponymous heroine's attempt to pursue a career as a painter while upholding the standards of ideal femininity decreed by her father.[7] Published two years after George Eliot's *Daniel Deronda*, Harris's text attempts to recover the image of the Jewish woman from representations of the Beautiful Jewess and Tragic Muse in previous novels. Critiquing the stereotypical depiction of Jews in such novels as Sir Walter Scott's *Ivanhoe* (1819) and Charles Dickens's *Oliver Twist* (1837–39) and *Our Mutual Friend* (1864–65), Estelle declares: "We are in and of England. . . . charity, and filial piety, and reverence, and amiability are our natural virtues. All those hateful habits that novelists ascribe to us are untrue, and dismally failing as jests." Harris underscores the English identities of the Hofer sisters by subtly eliciting comparisons between the contradictory dispositions of her Jewish heroines and those of Elinor and Marianne Dashwood in Jane Austen's *Sense and Sensibility* (1811). Like the Dashwood sisters, Estelle and Alexina (who is affectionately known within her family as Lexie) grow up on an estate in the English countryside. The Hofer sisters have limited interactions with their Christian neighbors and almost no contact at all with others of their faith. Lexie laments: "Is it not very hard that we do not go to concerts and balls and pay visits, as other girls do in the world? Papa wants to bury us, Estelle, before we are actually grown up."[8] Indeed, the Hofer sisters are not allowed to read novels, they have never visited London, and the family's circle of friends does not extend beyond their cousin Philip and their gentile neighbors, the invalid Edith Craven and the Hayes family. They do not meet another Jewish acquaintance or relative until their stepmother's uncle arrives to advise them on how to handle their affairs after their father's death. Like Eliot's Mirah Lapidoth, whose social interactions are limited to Daniel Deronda, her brother, Mordecai, and the Merryick family, the Hofer sisters do not become acquainted with other Jews until the loss of income after their father's death forces them to relocate with their stepmother and younger siblings to London.

Harris's depiction of the relationship between the Hofer sisters and the Hayes family serves as a microcosm of the relationship between bourgeois Jews and Christians in late-nineteenth-century England. Jewishness is represented as a spectacle, a curiosity to be explored and examined. Indeed, Cecil Hayes describes Estelle, Lexie, and their cousin Philip as "exotics, brought by chance to an English balcony. How the cold air would chill and pale them! how, in the keen wind of a strange experience they would languish and tremble!" He observes that "trouble surely lay in wait" for Estelle "unless she continued her secluded existence, and dwelt for ever apart from the throng of the world" (1:187–88). When Estelle notices Cecil watching her as she teaches her younger siblings Hebrew, she asks: "Are you interested in Hebrew. . . . Or, perhaps it is only because you find the Jewish race fashionable just now. Like other ancient articles, our value has increased lately. We have become precious, like old china, or lace, as regards our customs, and take our turn at public appreciation the same as pre-Raffaelite art." Estelle's comment not only represents Jewishness as a cultural commodity, but her reference to Pre-Raphaelite art points to stereotypical representations of Jewish women as either virtuous victims, such as Sir John Everett Millais's *Ophelia* (1851–52), or femmes fatales, such as Dante Gabriel Rossetti's *Lady Lilith* (1868). As Lexie later declares, "We are very interesting to everybody; it is a sort of reaction after being hated without reason" (1:36–37, 170).

As figures of curiosity, Estelle and Lexie must define themselves against romanticized representations of Jews in such novels as *Ivanhoe* and *Our Mutual Friend*. Scott's Rebecca and Dickens's Riah are, as Estelle says, "like nobody on earth" (1:108). Harris's work demonstrates the role that literary genres such as the travel narrative and the novel play in defining racial difference. Cecil's sisters, Gertrude and Helen, refer to both the account of their cousin Gerard Holden, who has toured the Jewish Quarter in London and traveled to Syria and Jerusalem, and Scott's

*Ivanhoe* to explain their brother's interest in Estelle: "Gerard told me that the attraction exercised by a Jewish girl over a Christian youth is by no means infrequent. Since Ivanhoe's days—perhaps much before that period—such things have happened." Helen, however, reassures her sister by reminding her, "Ivanhoe did not marry Rebecca," leaving Gertrude to conclude, "Cecil shall not wed Estelle." Whereas Cecil describes Estelle and her family as "well-bred, educated, and with just that freshness of idea, and peculiarity of principle, and firmness of faith, that heightened their charm, and added piquancy," his sisters sexualize Jewish womanhood by using the word "attracted" to describe his relationship with Estelle, while using the word "admire" to describe Cecil's attitude toward Juliet Fairfax, the woman they would like him to marry (2:119, 1:60).

Although Estelle and Lexie are compared to Rebecca, as well as to the "graceful, dreamy, dark-eyed maidens of the eastern regions" Gerard has visited, they distinguish themselves from images of the Beautiful Jewess, actively working to disappoint "pre-conceived notions of Jews, who, according to . . . belief, were distinctly eastern in taste, and traits, and training, very bigoted, lazy, and uncultivated, but from a picturesque point of view extremely attractive." Because they have separated themselves from the stereotypical signifiers of Jewish identity, Gerard does not recognize Estelle and Lexie as Jewish when he first meets them. Although Helen contends that Estelle's face reveals her "eastern origin," Gerard responds: "But that is what I could not determine. . . . I should never have believed her to be Jewish." The Hofer sisters are rendered spectacles because, as Gertrude observes: "They do not wear turbans, nor speak in Hebrew, nor are they loaded with jewels. They are quite Anglicized, and just as civilized as any one else" (1:105, 60, 113), "Wilful little Lexie," as Gertrude describes her, dresses to be "fashionable and conventional, to mortify Gertrude and Helen, who should not display her as an oriental guest." As she explains to Estelle: "Strangers wish to make us more distinctly and peculiarly peculiar. Now, when we go to Haye Place on Thursday, I feel sure that Miss Haye will expect to see us attired like Sir Walter Scott's 'Rebecca'" (1:61, 85, 76), Resisting the position of "oriental" objet d'art, Lexie declares to Estelle, "Do not let us, either of us, be gorgeous, but English." For Lexie, both Englishness and Jewishness are roles that can be performed. Indeed, she tells Cecil that she imagines Estelle using her as a model for Shakespeare's Jessica in *The Merchant of Venice* and ponders how her father "would look as Shylock, dressed in the yellow conical cap. . . . We might have a charade, which would be entirely in keeping with us, and amuse Miss Haye and Helen." In fact, Lexie's erroneous description of Jessica's filial obedience reveals her unfamiliarity with the play and that the stereotypes it constructs are "beyond or beside [her] own actual experience of [her] mode of life" (1:88, 216, 215).

Through her representation of the Hofer sisters, Harris interrogates how Jewish women negotiate both their racial and artistic identities within the public and private spheres. Harris's novel, as Valman observes, is in many ways a response to Eliot's *Daniel Deronda*, which offers two images of the Jewish woman as artist. As discussed in chapter 4, Mirah Lapidoth, who is forced onto the stage and circulated as a commodity by her father, prefers to relegate her talent to the domestic sphere, where she gives private lessons to affluent women such as Gwendolen Harleth. Conversely, Alcharisi eschews the private sphere to develop her talent on the public stage. Whereas Mirah remains devoted to her Jewish faith and ideal womanhood, Alcharisi severs her ties to Judaism, going so far as to conceal her son's heritage, thereby securing Deronda's identity as an English gentleman. Although Estelle remains firmly tied to her Jewish identity, Harris's novel places her heroine within the debate generated by many New Woman novels.[9] Through her representation of Estelle, Harris explores the following questions: Can a Jewish woman pursue her artistic talent without severing ties to her Jewish faith and her father who wants her to remain within the protection of the private sphere? Can she maintain her domestic identity while pursuing her talent in the public realm?

Estelle tries to follow her stepmother's request that she "try to be domestic." While Lexie's talent as a singer is praised as a female accomplishment, Estelle's desire to become a painter does not fit within the domestic ideology of the Hofer household. She pursues her craft in secret, leaving her stepmother to anxiously wonder why she has pinned images of the Virgin Mary to her bedroom walls. "If you were ill," Mrs. Hofer admonishes, "you would set everybody conjecturing, surmising, speculating of your faith, your convictions. . . . Suppose you were ill, Estelle, and a doctor came; of what would those pictures convince him?" (1:3, 7). Estelle, however, is not questioning her faith but is instead using images of the Virgin Mary as a model for painting scenes relating to the Jewish faith.[10] Although Estelle keeps her talent for painting hidden from her family, she reveals her secret during a picnic organized by Cecil and his sisters. Miss Charteris, the Hayes' aunt who chaperones the outing, inquires about Estelle's accomplishments, observing, "I read ambition in your eyes, child, and sure it echoes in your voice." This prompts Estelle to confess: "I tell this to you, a stranger. I have studied drawing by myself ever since I can remember. . . . I wish, I want, to assure myself if it be self-deceit or presumption that causes me to hope I have found some channel wherein my own true thoughts and hopes may flow" (1:125, 126). Miss Charteris asks to see Estelle's drawings when she and her nieces and nephew visit the Hofers' home later in the novel. At Miss Charteris's request, Lexie proudly displays her sister's paintings to the astonishment of their stepmother, who initially "resented this sudden surprise, and felt hurt that the knowledge of her step-daughter's talent should come upon her in the presence of comparative strangers." While her family is proud yet astonished by the talent that Estelle has silently cultivated in her garret without their knowledge, her cousin Philip chastises her for revealing her secret to the Hayeses first: "You have not been appreciated, but your parents will feel your power as a punishment, coming so suddenly upon them" (1:192, 200). Harris's representation of Estelle's artistic power and the effect it has on her family associates the young Jewish painter with the Tragic Muse. Helen observes: "Why, Miss Hofer, you must have a turn for the stage, I do think. This scene is so dramatic. Every member of your family has been more or less in ignorance of the genius that has flourished beneath this roof; and now it is displayed and positively amazes us. . . . I do think, Miss Hofer, among your other unknown accomplishments, you number that of dramatic representation. Would not you like to have gone on the stage?" Estelle, who has "scarcely ever been inside a theatre," shocks her family and friends with her avowal that she would have liked to be an actress. While Helen's comment alludes to descriptions of the Jewess as dissembling or cunning, Cecil's description of the power of the actress invokes the Tragic Muse who acts as "a sort of key that unlocks a hundred doors of sympathy. The belief that one is appealing to a mixed assembly—that by one voice, one inspiration, hundreds can be moved, touched, soothed, elevated, is and must be an immense goal to that sort of ambition. . . . [of] one of those gifted creatures who can put self side and represent trouble, trial, and pain surmounted, and act the finest lessons, and play as if she were inspired by some acute instinct that never deceives nor daunts. Good acting is the perfection of a certain creative power" (1:201–203). Estelle's "creative power," like that of the Tragic Muse, cannot be confined to the domestic sphere.

The revelation of Estelle's artistic talent disrupts the Hofers' home. Although her father declares her "a true artist" when he sees her sketches of her younger siblings and a portrait of the family's Sabbath celebration, he does not want Estelle to accept Miss Charteris's offer to take her on a Grand Tour of Europe to begin her formal education as an artist.

In the same way that they cultivate and encourage Lexie's singing talent, Estelle's parents would support her desire to be an artist, but only so long as it does not require her to leave the protection of their home. Dr. Hofer, who upholds Edith Craven, an "uncomplaining and resigned" invalid, as a model of ideal womanhood, believes that "Home was, or should be, sufficient to girls" (1:252, 84). He tells Estelle: "You are too young to travel with aliens. You could not possibly preserve your own particular belief. You are too timid, and too ignorant." He is also concerned about the growing friendship between Estelle and Cecil, "that young man at Haye Place—agreeable, clever, and amiable; you would see him, you would see many like him. What Jews would you meet?" (1:271, 273). Dr. Hofer does not forbid Estelle to go, but tells her to take the week of Passover to consider her request: "When you have well thought over it, you shall tell me if you wish to leave us for a year, and if you can trust yourself to overcome the temptations of life apart from our guardianship. In the mean time, I shall not refuse, and your own choice shall guide you" (1:275–276). Estelle's father does not outright forbid her to go, but he does hope her sense of filial loyalty will help her make the sensible choice. Estelle recognizes that "if her father persisted in his object, [she] must relinquish her wish. Dr. Hofer forbore positive refusal, because he was beginning to comprehend the affectionate temperament that would not struggle and could not dispute, and was withal wholly unfitted to wrest its favours of fate by excessive demonstration of any sort. Thus, by leaving the decision to his daughter, he had nearly gained his point." Lexie, who declares earlier in the novel, "We have progressed," begins to question this belief as she observes the battle of wills between her father and sister. She rejects Philip's proposal, exclaiming: "Marry you . . . to be tutored, and disciplined, and lectured forever! No, Philip. . . . you do not require a wife—it is a docile disciple, an awe-struck pupil that you want" (2:4, 1:243–244).[11] Rejecting Philip's proposal and hearing about the various adventures Estelle will experience on her trip abroad leads Lexie, who has become restless and dissatisfied with her life in the countryside, to beg her parents to move to London.

Ultimately, Dr. Hofer's sudden death increases filial obligation instead of freedom for his daughters. Not only does Estelle turn down Cecil's marriage proposal, but the resulting loss of income after her father's death forces her family to relocate to London, where she supports her stepmother and younger siblings by giving drawing lessons. Because they do not have the money to pursue the pleasures of London, Lexie retreats into the domestic sphere, quitting her job as a singing tutor after only a week. Estelle, however, eventually takes drawing classes and travels abroad with the Freunds, a cosmopolitan Jewish family whose children, Victoria and Albert, she tutors. By the end of the novel, Lexie marries Philip and returns to the countryside to her childhood home, which he has purchased for her. Although Lexie invites Estelle to return home, she remains with the Freunds in London, where her career flourishes. Although she eventually achieves artistic fame, she mourns the union she might have had with Cecil. As she told Cecil when she rejected his proposal, "We have each something to forego, some sacrifice to make, something less brilliant than both hoped for to encounter." While she has achieved the artistic success she dreamed of, Estelle, who never marries, sacrifices her desire for Cecil. Harris writes: "Fame and affectionate attention were hers; and if other love were denied her, some are designed for suffering, some set apart for isolation. . . . She had been firm, she had been loyal. Rectitude could not reward, but it must suffice; and she knew where to turn in woe, when the well-known solemn words came to her in loneliness of spirit, 'Aus der Tiefe rufe ich dich, Herr Gott,'" or "From the depths I cry, O God" (2:140–141, 293–294). In these final words of the novel, which are taken from Psalm 130, and were also her father's dying words, Estelle pledges herself to her faith and her father.

Whereas Estelle's loyalty to Judaism and the memory of her father leads her not to marry, Miriam Rooth in James's *The Tragic Muse* refuses to choose marriage over professional glory. When Peter Sherringham, a British diplomat, tells her, "Give it up and I'll marry you to-morrow," Miriam, an actress determined to become the English Rachel, responds to his insistence that she give up her theater career to become his wife by demanding, "Don't you think I'm important?"[12] This question, which resonates with both female and male characters in *The Tragic Muse*, echoes debates about the Woman Question and whether a woman could pursue her professional ambitions and ask her husband to share her glory, as Miriam asks Peter in this passage, without being accused of selfishness or self-absorption. Beginning with his novella *Daisy Miller* (1878), Henry James portrayed women whose desire leads them outside the bounds of ideal womanhood. His early heroines, Daisy Miller and Isabel Archer in *The Portrait of a Lady*, suffer for their independence—Daisy by her compromised reputation and death, Isabel by entrapment in marriage with a cold, domineering husband. As Osmond's wife, Isabel loses not only her independence, but also her identity. Ralph remarks upon Isabel's transformation after her marriage to Osmond: "If she wore a mask, it completely covered her face. There was something fixed and mechanical in the serenity painted upon it; this was not an expression . . . it was a representation."[13] While Isabel's blank mask keeps up appearances, Miriam's face, as well as Verena Tarrant's in *The Bostonians*, is naturally blank, which allows her to be more successful in moving between social spheres.

Before demonstrating how his Tragic Muse moves between the public and private spheres, James uses racial stereotypes to construct her identity. We first see Miriam Rooth and her mother through the eyes of Biddy Dormer. Biddy is an English lady, but unlike her mother, Lady Agnes, who is firmly rooted in the old regime of true womanhood, Biddy's work as an artist's model places her on the margins of proper femininity, which is reflected in the way her mother warns her repeatedly, "Don't be vulgar." When Biddy sees Miriam and her mother with their companion Gabriel Nash, she immediately classifies Gabriel as a gentleman despite his foreign appearance, but she sees the mother and daughter as "people whom in any country, from China to Peru, you would immediately have taken for natives" (22, 28), Here is the racial liminality of the Jewess, which figures so prominently in nineteenth-century literature. Whatever their race, Miriam and her mother are clearly not Biddy's social equals. In fact, her encounter with them recalls European encounters with the "native" in *Oroonoko* (1688), but here the "other" returns the English gaze with a "pair of largely-gazing eyes." The effect is disconcerting: Biddy notes that Miriam's eyes were "resting at this moment for a time—it struck Biddy as very long—on her own." Unlike most racialized others, the Tragic Muse has the power to look back at her spectators. Unsettled by Miriam's bold gaze, Biddy tries to calm herself by reading the Jewess's body to place her socially. Noting touches of impropriety in the clothing of Miriam and her mother, Biddy observes, "These ladies were clad in light thin scant gowns, giving an impression of flowered figures and odd transparencies, and in low shoes which showed a great deal of stocking." Biddy reads their clothing as a sign that they are "connected possibly with the old-fashioned exhibition of the shawl-dance" (29). Though she has encountered these women in France, she automatically places them in the Orient. In Biddy's reaction to Miriam and her mother, James emphasizes the power of stereotypes in keeping the unfamiliar at a distance, placing and framing difference so that it doesn't seem to impinge upon one. However, when Miriam returns the gaze, Biddy's security is breached. In the presence of these women who embody exoticism and inappropriate public display, Biddy "feared she would pass with this easy cosmopolite for a stiff scared English girl" (30).

Miriam's exoticism also ruffles male observers. Nick Dormer, Biddy's brother and a friend of Gabriel Nash, doesn't introduce his sister to either Nash or his exotic female companions, which heightens the feeling that Nash and his female companions are inappropriate company for an English girl. When Biddy encounters the women again and is finally introduced, she learns that Miriam is "more than half Jewess," which causes her to ask Gabriel whether the aspiring actress is a lady, to which Gabriel responds: "Oh tremendous! The great ones of the earth on the mother's side. On the father's, on the other hand, I imagine, only a Jew stockbroker in the City" (49, 51). Biddy responds to Miriam's "mixed" heritage by exclaiming, "A Jewish stockbroker, a dealer in curiosities: what an odd person to marry—for a person who was well born!" The relationship of Miriam's parents is reminiscent of the "misalliance" of Herr Klesmer and Catherine Arrowpoint in *Daniel Deronda*. Before Miriam's father became a stockbroker, he "was very versatile and, like most of his species, not unacquainted with the practice of music. He had been employed to teach the harmonium to Miss Neville-Nugent [Miriam's mother] and she profited by his lessons." Here, once again, is the pairing of artistic genius with sexual and racial danger in the construction of the Jew: Rudolf Roth was "darkly and dangerously handsome" (52).

While Englishwomen tend to see her as a spectacle of vulgarity, owing to her Jewishness, Miriam is pleased to be a spectacle, an actress, for whom Jewishness is just one facet of her identity. While calling herself Miriam Rooth would give her the benefit of aligning herself with Jewish artisans, like Rachel whom she aspires to be, the young actress slips between different stage names—Maud Vavasour, Edith Temple, and Gladys Vane—before finally settling on Miriam Rooth. Like Oscar Wilde's Sybil Vane, who is never herself, Miriam moves between racial and national identities, telling Peter, "I can act just like an Italian." As for her Jewish identity, Miriam sees it as another costume that she can appropriate to further her career. In response to Peter's summation, "You're a Jewess—I'm sure of that"—Miriam "jumped at this, as he was destined to see later she would ever jump at anything that might make her more interesting or striking; even at things that grotesquely contradicted or excluded each other." Exclaiming that she wants to be the "English Rachel," she seems to echo Gwendolen Harleth in *Daniel Deronda,* whose "waking dreams and cogitations as to how she would manage her destiny sometimes turned on the question whether she should become an actress like Rachel, since she was more beautiful than that thin Jewess" (135).[14]

To Peter, the English Rachel is an oxymoron: an Englishwoman would never have the virtuosity of a Jewess ("I'd rather you acted like an Englishwoman if an Englishwoman would only act"), and a Jewish woman is never entirely English. Miriam is as detached from her Jewish identity as an Englishwoman (like Gwendolen Harleth) might be. Miriam does not see her Jewish ancestry as automatically placing her in Rachel's company. She even distances herself from her Jewish name, explaining, "My name's Jewish . . . but it was that of my grandmother, my father's mother," to which Peter responds, "Put all that together and it makes you very sufficiently of Rachel's tribe." Miriam responds: "I don't care if I'm of her tribe artistically. I'm of the family of the artists—je me fiche of any other! I'm in the same style as that woman—I know it" (135). Though she receives Peter's declaration that she is Jewish as an insult, Miriam claims not to be bothered about being Jewish—her more important affiliation with Rachel is artistic. Miriam's attitude recalls that of Alcharisi in *Daniel Deronda,* whose choice of acting as a surrogate "tribe" reflects her resistance to being reduced to her ancestry.

Miriam distances herself from Rachel's tribe, eventually moving beyond her desire to become the English Rachel by becoming a star in her own right. But as the Tragic Muse, she is an erotic spectacle of Jewish womanhood slipping between racial and class identities. Describing his love for Miriam from the viewpoint of his profession as a diplomat, Peter concludes: "Miriam Rooth was neither fish nor flesh: one had with her neither the guarantees of one's own class nor the immunities of hers. What was hers if one came to that? A rare ambiguity on this point was part of the fascination she had ended by throwing over him." Although she is an actress, Peter does not place her in the category of coquines or dishonorable young women. Yet Miriam does not have the unequivocal gentility of someone like Biddy, whom Peter can look at and know exactly what kind of wife she would be. As a Jewess from "the Continent," Miriam is a mysterious entity, and Peter, who feels obligated to choose as his ambassadress a wife who would, along with himself, "be a representative of the greatness of his country," is unable to see this "dark" Jewish actress as a "full-blown lily of the future" (202, 203).

The worry over conventional femininity is underscored by Miriam's anxious mother. Though Miriam is oblivious to class and propriety, she avoids aspersions by staying just inside the margins of "proper" femininity. As Peter observes, Miriam had "a large profanity, an absence of ceremony as to her social relations" because she had a "good-humoured inattention to detail—all detail save that of her work, to which she was ready to sacrifice holocausts of feelings when the feelings were other people's." This point is emphasized in her encounter with Julia Dallow, Nick's fiancée, who comes upon the young actress when Nick is painting her portrait in his studio: Miriam "had done nothing at all, which was precisely what was embarrassing; she only stared at the intruder, motionless and superb" (218, 270).

Despite Miriam's oblivion to social decorum, her mother insists anxiously at every turn, "We're very, very respectable," this in itself being, for James, rather vulgar in its overinsistence. Mrs. Rooth echoes the voice of insular Englishness, only to be confounded by her daughter's louche attitude toward class and propriety. Her mother repeats several times, "Ah what's the best acting compared with the position of a true English lady?" (88, 207–208), Miriam, who thinks such anxiety about class status is ridiculous, responds to her mother's flurried concern over respectability by saying: "She wants me to be some sort of tremendous creature—all her ideas are reducible to that. What makes the muddle is that she isn't clear about the creature she wants most. A great actress or a great lady . . . but on the whole persuading herself that a great actress, if she'll cultivate the right people, may be a great lady." James emphasizes this point in the actor Basil Dashwood's critique of Mademoiselle Voisin, who teaches femmes du monde, or society women, how to be "ladylike": "See how I walk, see how I sit, see how quiet I am and how I have le geste rare. Now can you say I ain't a lady?" (385, 223). According to Dashwood, Voisin performs as if she were teaching a class, and the irony is that the society women who attend the theater are picking up behavior cues from an actress whom they would never entertain in their drawing rooms. Though James acknowledges that people can be taught to perform social class, Dashwood's remark mocks such self-fashioning, and thus implicitly conjures up "ladylike" as an innate, essential quality.

To Mrs. Rooth, Biddy Dormer is the ideal that Miriam should live up to, one that mingles racial purity and upper-class status. Mrs. Rooth says that Biddy "comes of a beautiful Norman race—the finest purest strain" and "is a lovely girl—such an aristocratic type!" (406, 415). Mrs. Rooth, of course, cannot say the same of her own daughter. Before marrying Rudolf Roth, Mrs. Rooth came from the best of families, having the "high lineage" of a Neville-Nugent of Castle Nugent. She longs for the class status (and perhaps even the racial purity) that she gave up when she married Rudolf Roth and was reduced to selling secondhand items, "various pictures, tapestries, enamels, porcelains and similar gewgaws," to support herself and child after her husband's death (52, 51), When Miriam scoffs at her mother's desires for her to become a lady, Mrs. Rooth tells her "poor perverse passionate child," "Once a lady always a lady—all the footlights in the world, turn them up as high as you will, make no difference there." Unlike her mother, who is constantly self-deprecating but also always seeking out associations with the Dormers, Miriam has a more jaded view of social status, which goes along with her disdain for social delicacies. While Mrs. Rooth encourages Biddy to visit them "if some day you found courage . . . you might find it pleasant, though very different of course from the circle in which you habitually move," Miriam thinks, "It seems to me rather a social muddle, this rubbing shoulders of 'nice girls' and filles de théâtre: I shouldn't think it would do your poor young things much good" (416, 406, 415), Though Miriam says, "I'm awfully conservative and I know what respectability is . . . I know also what it isn't—it isn't the sweet union of well-bred little girls ('carefully-nurtured,' don't they call them?) and painted she-mummers." She concludes, to her mother's chagrin, that if she were in the position of Biddy, "I should never look at the likes of us!" (415–416).

Mrs. Rooth's relationship with Miriam resembles the relationship between Verena Tarrant and her mother in *The Bostonians*. Like Miriam, Verena is oblivious to social expectations while her mother desires her to have the social connections that she herself gave up when she married the mesmerist Selah Tarrant. Though not of aristocratic lineage like Mrs. Rooth, Mrs. Tarrant had "passed her youth in the first Abolitionist circles" as the daughter of Mr. Greenstreet. Her family and associates disapproved of her marriage to Selah, whose name elicits associations with Jewishness, because "even in a society much occupied with the effacement of prejudice there had been certain dim presumptions against this versatile being." Despite the "free love" climate of the Cayuga community to which Selah belonged, Mrs. Tarrant's greatest disappointment in her husband was that "he didn't know how to speak. . . . He couldn't hold the attention of an audience, he was not acceptable as a lecturer."[15] Mrs. Tarrant, like Mrs. Rooth, wants her daughter to mingle with Boston's beau monde, wishing for her to have "a little more of the fragrance of Beacon Street," where Olive Chancellor and her upper-class associates live. When Olive condescends to a visit with Verena's parents, Mrs. Tarrant "endeavored to keep the conversation in a channel which would enable her to ask sudden incoherent questions of Olive, mainly as to whether she knew the principal ladies (the expression was Mrs.

Tarrant's), not only in Boston, but in the other cities, which, in her nomadic course, she herself had visited."[16] The irony, of course, is that Olive is virtually a misanthrope except when it comes to Verena Tarrant.

Both Verena and Miriam are public women. Verena, however, does not have the ambition of Miriam. Her public presence has "an air of artless enthusiasm, of personal purity. If she was theatrical, she was naturally theatrical."[17] Unlike Miriam, who has to practice and hone her skills, Verena possesses a natural gift, almost like a "talent" in the biblical sense. To Basil Ransom, however, this woman on display is an exotic spectacle: "She had the sweetest, most unworldly face, and yet, with it, an air of being on exhibition, or belonging to a troupe, of living in the gaslight. . . . If she had produced a pair of castanets or a tambourine, he felt that such accessories would have been quite in keeping." Though Verena is "very pale," Basil says that there was "something rich in the fairness of this young lady," which is a telling comment coming from a young southerner who grew up around the "rich" whiteness of mixed-race slaves on his father's plantation. Likening Verena to the gypsy girl Esmeralda in *The Hunchback of Notre Dame,* Basil "would have thought she looked like an Oriental, if it were not that Orientals are dark." By comparing Verena's complexion to the "rich" whiteness of both America's mixed-race slaves and "Orientals," James suggests that putting oneself on display has a racializing quality.[18]

Though Verena is a "public" woman exhibiting herself before the crowd, Basil sees her as a victim of a father who wants to use her for his commercial gain. James's description of Verena's father, a mesmerist who "sells" Verena to Olive, is reminiscent of the relationship between Mirah and her father in *Daniel Deronda.* Viewing Selah Tarrant as a "confidence man" who openly exploits his daughter, Basil reacts to Tarrant's method of drawing Verena out and preparing her for the spirit of elocution as a form of violation: he believes her father is debasing her in a vaguely sexual way. As Tarrant "stroked and soothed his daughter," whom Basil describes as a "moving statue," the southerner becomes incensed with "Tarrant's grotesque manipulations, which he resented as much as if he himself had felt their touch, and which seemed a dishonour to the passive maiden. They made him nervous, they made him angry."[19] Olive, like her distant cousin Basil, wants to "rescue the girl from the danger of vulgar exploitation," but she does so by buying the girl herself. She tells Verena's father, "Leave us alone—entirely alone—for a year, and then I will write you another" check.[20] Olive becomes Verena's keeper, and though she insists that the young elocutionist is her own person,

Olive prizes and seeks to protect Verena's chastity, even making Verena promise that she will never marry. Basil believes Olive's ownership of Verena is as base and exploitative as Tarrant's and seeks to carry Verena into the private sphere.

Agency is a central question in *The Bostonians* and *The Tragic Muse.* Olive and Verena both insist that the young star is free to form social connections and move about however she wants, but Olive monitors Verena's social activities to such a degree that the young girl must lie or keep secrets to obtain any freedom. Indeed, Verena never really owns herself—she goes from one owner or protector to the next. Miriam is the freest character in *The Tragic Muse* because she doesn't feel constrained by her racial and class status. But for Nick Dormer, who struggles between artistic and professional life, maintaining one's freedom proves difficult. While he is campaigning for the parliamentary seat his father held, he feels that his freedom is slipping away: "The sense so pressed upon him that these were the last moments of his freedom" (67). Without a father or his father's money, Nick has become beholden to a kind benefactor and to his widowed cousin Julia Dallow, each of whom has conditions for the financial support that they would like to bestow upon him. When his mother urges him to marry Julia, Nick responds: "I love my freedom. I set it above everything." His mother fires back: "Your freedom? What freedom is there in being poor? . . . Talk of that when Julia puts everything she possesses at your feet!" (161). Nick is torn between the responsibility to maintain his mother and sisters in the lifestyle to which they are accustomed and his desire to pursue his artistic talent. After winning the seat, Nick ultimately resigns and decides to pursue his passion, leaving his mother to fret about how the aesthetic life he has chosen to pursue instead of politics is "a horrible insidious foreign disease . . . eating the healthy core out of English life." Miriam, however, is a woman on the margins of acceptable society, who must make her own way—"So much depends—really everything! . . . It's either this . . . or it's I don't know what!" (361, 84). Miriam's use of the imperative implies that there is a constraint on her agency, yet she's in some sense freer than Nick because of her social marginality.

In both *The Bostonians* and *The Tragic Muse,* women threaten to surpass men in professional ambition.[21] Indeed, both Basil Ransom and Peter Sherringham are distracted by romance, while the women they pursue continue on their paths (until, of course, Basil kidnaps Verena). Miriam's ambition is almost a necessity since she and her mother are trying to escape the other career choice of unmarried girls without social connections—governess. Miriam will do almost anything to pursue her dream of being a famous actress, even declaring to her mother and Peter: "I want to act—that's what I want to do. . . . I can look out for myself—I'm all right! . . . As for doing the [bad women in the plays] I'm not afraid of that" (110). Miriam is eager to tackle even morally compromised characters if they will further her career. In fact, in an earlier discussion, Miriam fades into the background as her acting coach, Madame Carré, Mrs. Rooth, Gabriel Nash, and Peter discuss how best the young girl should preserve her "personal integrity" in the questionable moral atmosphere of the theater. But even though Madame Carré alludes to the role of sexual exchange in the theater—"When they're handsome they always succeed—in one way or another"—Miriam manages to become famous without compromising her virtue (90, 94).

Despite Verena and Miriam's success, men are constantly imploring them to retreat from the public world in order to be absorbed back into private life, into the domesticity that they resist. Basil even explicitly states that as his wife, Verena will not have a "place in public. My plan is to keep you home and have a better time with you there than ever."[22] Basil's desire to marry Verena is coded in a rhetoric of violence: "If he should become her husband he should know a way to strike her dumb"; he wants to "take possession"; and he knows that "however she might turn and twist in his grasp he held her fast."[23] With an urgency that is echoed in Peter's pursuit of Miriam, Basil resolves to kidnap Verena before she experiences the sensation of being "widely popular" with the public.[24] With her complicity, he wrenches her away from the Music Hall on the night of her public debut: "Ransom . . . thrust the hood of Verena's long cloak over her head, to conceal her face and her identity." With no identity, Verena is now ready to enter the cult of domesticity in which her elocutionist skills will make her a brilliant conversationalist. Though Verena's final words in the novel are, "Ah, now I am glad!" which she breathes once Basil rescues her from the Music Hall, James does not allow his readers to see her "live happily ever after" with her southern pauper prince.[25] Instead, Verena's tears are a sign that her marriage will bring more tears. The conventional woman tries to be a New Woman in *The Bostonians* only to end up in an unhappy marriage.

Just as Basil accuses Verena of not believing in the ideals she espouses, Peter believes that Miriam does not know who she really is. Echoing criticism of Rachel, he describes Miriam's liminal identity and public displays as monstrous: "She was always acting . . . before the perpetual mirror of some curiosity or admiration or wonder—some spectatorship that she perceived or imagined in the people about her. . . . [S]he had no moral privacy, as he phrased it to himself, but lived in a high wind of exhibition, of figuration—such a woman was a kind of monster in whom of necessity there would be nothing to 'be fond' of, because there would be nothing to take hold of. . . . [S]he positively had no countenance of her own, but only the countenance of the occasion, a sequence, a variety." At several moments in the text Peter refers to Miriam's monstrosity: "I'd rather see you as a Medusa crowned with serpents. That's what you look like when you look best" (126, 363).[26] Miriam's unnatural desire for public life threatens Victorian masculinity, which is emphasized when Peter jokingly calls her a "devouring demon" (383). Miriam is a monster because she seeks public adulation. And like Basil, Peter seeks to wrestle Miriam off the stage before she becomes a renowned public persona: "The last thing he expected the future ambassadress to have been was a *fille de théâtre*. The answer to this objection was of course that Miriam was not yet so much of one but that he could easily, by a handsome 'worldly' offer, arrest her development." Telling Miriam, "I want you for myself—not for others," Peter soon realizes that "she had crossed the line and sold herself to the vulgar, making him indeed only one of an equalized multitude" (202, 234, 312).

Unlike Basil Ransom, Peter has the wealth and attractive political position that would still allow Miriam to maintain a high profile in the public sphere as an ambassadress. However, Miriam does not desire the power or position that one man can give her—she seeks self-fulfillment through power over a large audience. When Peter tells her that she has "no nature of your own," Miriam responds, "I know what I am" (138, 139). Unlike Kingsley's La Cordifiamma, she does not shy away from her racial or social origins: "Her greatest idea must always be to show herself, and fortunately she has a great quantity to show. I think of her absolutely as a real producer, but as a producer whose production is her own person" (352). This self-commodification, this willingness to circulate her body in the public, makes her monstrous to a man like Peter, who wants her to belong only to himself. Miriam isn't against marriage, and unlike Verena and Olive, she doesn't see marriage itself as restricting a woman's freedom. Laughing at Peter's inquiry about whether she plans to marry her fellow actor Dashwood, Miriam says: "Mercy, how you chatter about marrying! . . . *C'est la maladie anglaise*—you've all got it on the brain." Miriam is more focused on her career, and though Peter assures her that she will be "a great diplomatist's wife," Miriam knows that there are elements of her nature that he would want to eradicate before he married her: "And the demon, the devil, the devourer and destroyer, that you are so fond of talking about: what, in such a position, do you do with that element of my nature?" (384, 385). Though Peter promises to "bribe," "amuse," and "gorge [her nature] with earthly grandeurs," Miriam believes that he is asking her to give up too much in proposing marriage: "He expects others—me, for instance—to make all the sacrifices" (385, 418). Peter makes his final marriage proposal to Miriam on the night of her grand debut; she is "still painted and bedizened, in the splendid dress of her climax, so that she seemed protected and alienated by the character she had been acting." In having Miriam appear before Peter in full costume, James makes clear that Peter must take as his wife the actress, not the woman. When Peter offers to manage her, only to explain that he will be managing her in the global theater of diplomacy, which is "a bigger theatre than any of those places in the Strand," Miriam offers a different solution: "Stay on *my* stage. Come off your own" (430, 432, 433).

Miriam resists Peter's effort to fold her into a securely private realm of domesticity because she believes marriage must offer some profit or benefit to her: "I go in for closeness of union, for identity of interest. A true marriage, as they call it, must do one a lot of good!" For Miriam, this means that marriage must boost rather than inhibit her career. Peter considers her proposal, telling her that he will take a year to decide (or to reconcile himself) to giving up "everything, my prospects, my studies . . . my emoluments, my past and my future, the service of my country and the ambition of my life, and engage to take up instead the business of watching your interests so far as I may learn how and ministering to your triumphs so far as may in me lie" (440, 442). However, when he returns from his diplomatic assignment in Central America to make good on his promise, he discovers that she has married Dashwood, who is now her manager. Miriam was in love with Peter, but she refuses the narrative of George Eliot's Tragic Muse, Alcharisi, who surrenders herself to the domestic sphere. In Dashwood, Miriam has with certainty a husband who would always promote her professional interests.

## The New African American Woman

Like Harris and James, Harper and Hopkins show their mixed-race heroines seeking professional and financial independence instead of marriage. In *Iola Leroy*, the eponymous heroine resolves to "join the great rank of bread-winners" by seeking a position as a saleswoman. However, Iola soon discovers that the public sphere is a "white" space where people of her race are not welcome. She obtains several positions, but as soon as her fellow employees discover her secret, her position is terminated. Iola is not intimidated by the prejudice she encounters; she resolves "to win for myself a place in the fields of labor." Though her uncle advises her not to reveal her race, Iola declares that though she will not volunteer the information, she will never deny it: "The best blood in my veins is African blood, and I am not ashamed of it."[27] Iola eventually finds work as a nurse to an invalid girl of fifteen whose father gives her a position in his store once his daughter's health is restored, telling his employees that if "any one objected to working with [Iola], he or she could step to the cashier's desk and receive what was due" (211). In *Contending Forces*, Hopkins's Sappho Clark also has difficulty finding a place for herself as a professional in Boston's public sphere. Although during her leisure time "in the free air of New England's freest city, Sappho drank great draughts of freedom's subtle elixir," she faces the same racism as Iola when she tries to find employment. After several rejections, Sappho eventually finds work as a stenographer but only because, as she explains to Dora Smith, "I do not interfere with the other help, because I take my work home; many of the other clerks have never seen me, and so the proprietor runs no risk of being bothered with complaints from them."[28] In the same way that Iola's work as a nurse parlays into a job as a shopgirl, Sappho's and Dora's occupations show that economic power for mixed-race women in these texts comes from a merging of the private and public spheres.

The boardinghouse run by Dora's mother becomes an emblem of mixed-race women transforming their domestic skills into business opportunities. Upon graduating from high school, Dora took over the managing of the boardinghouse, "proving herself to be a woman of ability and the best of managers, husbanding their small income to the best advantage" (86). Because they've become financially independent, Iola, Sappho, and Dora do not feel compelled to marry for the sake of security. In fact, Dora, who is engaged to John Langley, tells Sappho she feels "*unsexed*" because, as she explains: "Now I tell John P. that I'm busy, or something like that, and I'm rid of him; but once you marry a man, he's on your hands for good and all. . . . I dread to think of being tied to John for good and all; I know I'll be sick of him inside of a week" (121–122).[29] Although Harper's and Hopkins's mixed-race heroines redefine ideal womanhood and the domestic sphere so that it encompasses their mixed-race identities, as well as their professional pursuits, they cannot fully embody the autonomy of the New Woman until they exorcise the history of violence and violation that links them to the Tragic Mulatta.

Like Harris's Estelle Hofer and James's Miriam Rooth, who must differentiate themselves from the images of the Beautiful Jewess and the Tragic Muse in such texts as *The Merchant of Venice*, *Ivanhoe*, *Villette*, and *Daniel Deronda*, the mixed-race heroines in Harper's and Hopkins's novels must distinguish themselves from the images of the Tragic Mulatta that had been circulating in British and American travel narratives and novels since the late eighteenth century. Whereas Harris's and James's narratives of the new Jewish woman are set during the late nineteenth century, Harper's novel opens during the Civil War while Hopkins's begins in Bermuda in the winter of 1790. The opening chapters of both *Iola Leroy* and *Contending Forces* reconstruct the narratives of the Tragic Mulatta examined in the previous chapters of this work. Readers are first introduced to Iola Leroy, who is described as "a reg'lar spitfire; dey can't lead nor dribe her," when the Union army arrives in North Carolina. Tom Anderson, a former slave who has joined the Union ranks, applies to the army commander for Iola's release from her master, who bought her to be his "housekeeper" but expected her to be his concubine. Upon seeing Iola's "beautiful long hair . . . [and] putty blue eyes," the general cannot imagine that this "young and beautiful girl had been a chattel, with no power to protect herself from the highest insults that lawless brutality could inflict upon innocent and defenseless womanhood" (38, 39). The commander's description of Iola evokes images of the "almost white" slaves in abolitionist texts, such as *Uncle Tom's Cabin*, *Clotel*, and *A Romance of the Republic*, which did not question the virtue of its mixed-race heroines, but instead showed how her virtue and body were imperiled by men in slaveholding society.

*Iola Leroy*, however, takes a different approach with its female characters: the Tragic Mulatta was not necessarily virtuous. In fact, before Harper introduces readers to Iola, she shows a slave talking about how his wife left him to be a slave trader's mistress: "I used to love Mirandy as I love my life. . . . But she fooled me all over the face and eyes, and took up with that hell-hound of a trader, Lukens; an' he gave her a chance to live easy, to wear fine clothes, an' be waited on like a lady" (30). While Stowe's Cassy and Emmeline, Brown's Clotel, and Child's Rosa were figures of ideal womanhood, the female slaves in Harper's novel are corrupted by their desire to become fine "white" ladies. Indeed, Harper depicts some of the mixed-race women as opportunists who use their bodies to improve their social stations: "What has come over you? Talking of the virtue of these quadroon girls! . . . I think from the airs that some of them put on when they get a chance, that they are very willing victims." In Harper's novel, the complicity of slave women can be bought with fine things: "If she is managed right she will soon get over it. Give her plenty of jewelry, fine clothes, and an easy time" (70, 101–102).

Unlike previous Tragic Mulattas, Iola must establish her virtue and claim to true womanhood. After she is rescued from her master, Iola works as a nurse to Dr. Gresham, who is tending the wounded during the Civil War. The doctor, however, does not know that his assistant is black, although he is fascinated by her: "She is one of the most refined and lady-like women I ever saw. . . . She is self-respecting without being supercilious; quiet, without being dull. . . . I cannot understand how a Southern lady, whose education and manners stamp her as a woman of fine culture and good breeding, could consent to occupy the position she so faithfully holds" (38, 57). Before he knows her race, Dr. Gresham sees Iola as a refined and virtuous woman who has a curious relationship with the black soldiers at the camp. Upon learning of her ancestry, Dr. Gresham assumes that as a raced woman, Iola was sexually tempted by her masters. Correcting Dr. Gresham's assumption, Iola says: "Tried, but not tempted. . . . I was never tempted. I was sold from State to State as an article of merchandise. I had outrages heaped on me which might well crimson the cheek of honest womanhood with shame, but I never fell into the clutches of an owner for whom I did not feel the utmost loathing and intensest horror" (115).

In her construction of Iola's history, which the heroine reveals when Dr. Gresham proposes marriage, Harper borrows from the conventions of the sentimental and sensation genres that typically shaped the Tragic Mulatta's narrative. Indeed, like Van Buren Denslow's Julia and Mary Elizabeth Braddon's Cora, Iola grows up believing she is white, even going so far as to tell her parents that she "would hate to be colored. 'It is so hard be looked down on for what one cannot help,'" when she relates the story of a "colored girl" who was removed from her northern boarding school (91). She discovers her black ancestry after her father dies from yellow fever and his avaricious cousin has her parents' marriage voided so that her father's white relatives will inherit his estate. Hopkins's *Contending Forces* also uses elements of the sensation genre to construct Dora Smith and Sappho Clark's ancestry. But unlike Harper's novel, in which Iola and her mother are imperiled but escape violation, Hopkins's narrative reveals the physical and sexual violence endured by mixed-race women from the West Indies and New Orleans. In fact, as much as she wishes to distance herself from the Tragic Mulatta figure, Dora's full name, Dora Grace Montfort Smith, provides a permanent connection to the tragic history of her great-grandmother, who leaves her native Bermuda to move with her husband to a plantation in North Carolina. Underscoring the ambiguous racial identities of Creole women in the West Indies, Hopkins describes Grace as "a dream of beauty even among beautiful women. . . . Her complexion was creamy in its whiteness, of the tint of the camellia." Her opaque complexion leads one character to observe, "Thar's too much cream color in the face and too little blud seen under the skin fer a genooine white 'ooman" (41). Once in America, Grace is imperiled by her ambiguous racial identity. Rumors circulating about "the suspicion of Negro blood in the veins of Mrs. Montfort," as well as her husband's plan to free their slaves, result in several of their neighbors banding together to raid the Montfort plantation in order to "rid a peaceful neighborhood of sech a disturbin' critter as Montfort." Charles is killed, and Grace, whose lily-like limbs . . . had never known aught but the touch of love," is brutally whipped. Hopkins blends images of both sexual and physical violence, showing readers a white woman tied to a whipping post where her garments are torn from her body and she is whipped until "the blood stood in a pool about her feet" (64, 68, 69). Grace drowns herself before a lascivious planter claims her as his property.

Whereas Grace Montfort embodies the history of white and mixed-race West Indian women, Hopkins's representation of Sappho Clark's violation invokes the history of free women of color in New Orleans. In her depictions of both Grace and Sappho, Hopkins shifts away from romanticized representations of mixed-race womanhood in travel narratives and abolitionist fiction and instead offers a graphic account of physical and sexual violation within the institution of slavery. During a school vacation, the fourteen-year-old Mabelle Beaubean is raped by her white uncle, who then abandons her in a New Orleans brothel, leaving her "a poor, ruined, half-crazed creature." Hopkins traces Mabelle's violation back to the *plaçage* between her grandparents that resulted in her father's inheriting part of his white father's estate. Monsieur Beaubean's white half brother mocks this tradition of *plaçage* when he claims Mabelle for himself, telling her father: "Your child is no better than her mother or her grandmother. What does a woman of mixed blood, or any Negress, for that matter, know of virtue? It is my belief that that they were a direct creation by God to be the pleasant companions of men of my race. Now, I am willing to give you a thousand dollars and call it square" (260, 261). Taken by a friend of her family to a convent for women of color, Mabelle was believed to have died in childbirth. Although she and her son survived, Mabelle leaves her child under her grandmother's care and constructs a new identity for herself as Sappho Clark.

Harper's and Hopkins's texts show that denying one's racial identity or, in the case of Sappho Clark, concealing sexual violation, perpetuates the violence and subjugation of slavery. In order to become New Women, Iola Leroy and Sappho Clark reject passing, thereby creating a dramatic shift in the Tragic Mulatta's narrative. Whereas passing is a compelling choice for Kingsley's Marie and Child's Rosa, Iola refuses to distance herself from her African American heritage, which means sacrificing her desire for Dr. Gresham, who proposes marriage, deciding that Iola was "his ideal of the woman whom he was willing to marry" (59). In the passages leading up to the proposal, Harper shows that Iola also desires Dr. Gresham: "When he held her hand in his a tell-tale flush rose to her cheek, a look of grateful surprise beamed from her eye, but it was almost immediately succeeded by an air of inexpressible sadness, a drooping of her eyelids, and an increasing pallor of her cheek." When she assists him while they care for wounded soldiers, "he would drop a few words at which her heart would beat quicker and her cheek flush more vividly. . . . She knew . . . that he had power to call forth the warmest affection of her soul; but she fought with her own heart and repressed its rising love" (109, 111). But like Harris's Estelle, Iola sacrifices her own desire out of loyalty to her race. She refuses to pass into white society: "I have too much self-respect to enter your home under the veil of concealment." She believes "the time will come when the civilization of the negro will assume a better phase than you Anglo-Saxons possess" (117, 116). By refusing to pass, Iola escapes the Tragic Mulatta's narrative and becomes a New Woman intent on attaining her "share."

Sappho, however, has much more to overcome when it comes to moving past the Tragic Mulatta stereotype. Hopkins constructs Sappho's sexual past as a passing narrative.[30] Although she has fashioned a new identity for herself, she cannot escape her identity as Mabelle Beaubean. Whereas Iola chooses not to pass, Sappho, who desires "self-forgetfulness," is forced to confront her past when Dora's fiancé, John Langley, discovers her secret and tries to blackmail her into being his mistress (182). Sappho has become engaged to Dora's brother, Will, and believes that she is close to leaving behind her past as the violated Mabelle Beaubean. But when John calls her by her former name, Sappho gasps, "Not that name—not that name," and pleads for his mercy because, "I was a victim! An innocent child!" Telling her that Will would never marry a woman with her past, John tries to compel Sappho to be his mistress because "ambitious men do not marry women with stories like yours!" (318–319, 320). After this encounter, Sappho returns to New Orleans, where she reclaims the child that was the product of her violation. By returning to New Orleans, Sappho is released from the Tragic Mulatta narrative. She eventually reunites with Will and learns that although she was robbed of her innocence, she is a virtuous woman who has every right to the "happiness of home and love" (182).

In releasing Iola and Sappho from the Tragic Mulatta's narrative, both Harper's and Hopkins's novels show the role that public meetings within the African American community play in revising the discourse of race and ideal womanhood. At meetings where women and men have an equal voice and speaking time, Iola speaks about the race question and the uplift of her brothers and sisters. After presenting a paper titled the "Education of Mother," Iola and her neighbors discuss whether women should focus their energy on the public or private sphere. Though Harper emphasizes throughout the novel Iola's desire to work in the public sphere to support herself, the discussion of motherhood places emphasis on women working within their homes to better society: "There is a field of Christian endeavor which lies between the school-house and the pulpit, which needs the hand of a woman more in private than in public." Iola responds, "If we would have the prisons empty we must make the homes more attractive," insisting that young women must be self-reliant and self-supporting, but at the same time make every effort to be angels of their homes to instill their husbands and children with morality (253, 254).

Similarly, in Hopkins's text, the "sewing-circle" that assembles in Ma Smith's private quarters in the boardinghouse offers a forum in which "the evolution of true womanhood" is discussed (146). Mrs. Willis, "the brilliant widow of a bright Negro politician" who is described as being "shrewd in business matters," has transported her elocutionary talent from the drawing rooms of white philanthropists to the parlors of African American women such as Ma Smith (143, 144). Speaking to a group of young women that includes Dora and Sappho about the virtue of African American women, specifically former slaves, Mrs. Willis declares, "It will rest with you and your children to refute the charges brought against us as to our moral irresponsibility, and the low moral standard maintained by us in comparison with other races." Arguing that the "native African woman is impregnable in her virtue," Mrs. Willis explains that they will "not be held responsible for wrongs which we have unconsciously committed, or which we have committed under compulsion. We are virtuous or non-virtuous only when we have a choice under temptation" (149). Through the conversation led by Mrs. Willis during the "sewing-circle" and a meeting of the American Colored League during which one of the speakers shares the story of Mabelle Beaubean's rape and abandonment in a New Orleans brothel, Hopkins's novel does the important work of showing that women who were violated and exploited within the institution of slavery had every right to claim a place within the cult of true womanhood.[31]

Although true womanhood is not contingent upon marriage in Harper's and Hopkins's texts, Iola, Sappho, and Dora eventually marry. In Hopkins's novel, Sappho is reunited with Will and Dora, who breaks off her engagement to the villainous John Langley, eventually marries her childhood playmate, Dr. Lewis, and travels with him to "his far-off Southern home to assist him in the upbuilding of their race" (381).[32] Unlike the mixed-race women examined in the previous chapters, Iola, Sappho, and Dora choose to marry within their race and thereby redefine the new African American woman's narrative. By the end of Harper's novel, for example, Iola has gained a place in the public sphere as a shopgirl, she is reunited with her mother and brother, she has solid ties to her community, and most importantly, she has achieved all of this without hiding her racial identity. Dr. Gresham reappears and again proposes marriage, but Iola is resolute. Although Dr. Gresham urges her to think of herself as white because her "eyes are as blue and complexion as white as [his]," Iola responds, "I am not willing to live under a shadow of concealment which I thoroughly hate as if the blood in my veins were an undetected crime of my soul." Dr. Gresham urges her: "If you love your race, as you call it, work for it, live for it, suffer for it, and, if need be, die for it; but don't marry for it. Your education has unfitted you for social life among them" (232, 233, 235). However, in Dr. Latimer, whose "aristocratic ancestry" has bestowed blond hair and blue eyes upon him, Harper provides her heroine with an "almost white" mixed-race husband who is Dr. Gresham's equal (239). Although Harper has provided Iola with a companion who has sacrificed fortune and privilege in favor of his race, just as she sacrificed her desire, it is curious that she does not provide her heroine with an "unmixed" husband. In fact, when Iola's brother tells her about his future wife, proudly declaring that "neither hair nor complexion show the least hint of blood admixture," Iola responds: "I am glad of it. . . . Every person of unmixed blood who succeeds in any department of literature, art, or science is a living argument for the capability which is in the race" (199). But when Harper introduces readers to Dr.

Frank Latimer two chapters later, we learn that "generations of blood admixture had effaced all trace of his negro lineage." Harper explains that when given the opportunity to become his white grandmother's heir if "he would ignore his identity with the colored race," he refuses this offer and like Iola seeks to make his success as an African American man (239). Perhaps by giving Iola a husband who, like her, chose not to pass for white, Harper shows that a white identity is not necessary for professional success or ideal womanhood to be achieved.

## "A Houseless Shadow Evermore"

The works examined in this conclusion show African American and Jewish heroines struggling to define their identities as separate from the heritages proscribed by the narratives of the Tragic Mulatta, Beautiful Jewess, and Tragic Muse. Adah Menken's "Infelix," the final poem in her posthumous collection, *Infelicia*, represents the movement from "My Heritage" to "Myself" as a moment of self-exile:

> Myself! alas for theme so poor
> A theme but rich in Fear;
> I stand a wreck on Error's shore,
> A spectre not within the door,
> A houseless shadow evermore,
> An exile lingering here. [33]

For Menken, a New Orleans native whose sensational performances as Mazeppa took her across the Atlantic to London and finally to Paris, where she died in 1868, self-definition is described in terms of fear. Looking at the endings of *Estelle*, *The Tragic Muse*, *Iola Leroy*, and *Contending Forces*, it would also seem that the Jewish and African American heroines in these texts are "houseless shadows" whose redefinition of ideal womanhood has also changed the meaning of home. By redefining how their bodies circulate in the public and private spheres, these women are freed from the scripted narratives of the Tragic Mulatta, Beautiful Jewess, and Tragic Muse, but in doing so have they lost their domestic, and perhaps even their national homes?

Whereas the Beautiful Jewesses and Tragic Muses in Scott's *Ivanhoe* and Eliot's *Daniel Deronda* leave England, Harris's and James's Jewish heroines return to England at the end of their narratives. However, Harris's Estelle does not return to her family's home in the country where Lexie and Philip reside but instead remains in London with the cosmopolitan Freund family. Unlike Estelle, who remains unmarried, Miriam Rooth does wed at the end of James's novel, but instead of inviting her friends to visit her new home, she tells them about the box she's reserved for them at the new theater she and her husband are setting up. The concept of home is also redefined in Harper's and Hopkins's novels to reflect this intersection of the public and private spheres. In Harper's novel, Iola and Dr. Latimer have an egalitarian marriage in which they are also united in service for their race. Iola returns to North Carolina with her husband, where she decides to "teach in the Sunday-school, help in the church, hold mother's meetings to help these boys and girls to grow up to be good men and women." She's going to be the "enlightened mother" who works within the domestic sphere to uplift the race. Indeed, by devoting herself to working for her community, Iola is able to breach the divide between the public and private spheres. As Harper concludes, "In their desire to help the race . . . one grand and noble purpose was giving tone and color to their lives" (276, 266).

Hopkins's novel also ends by returning her characters to the South, where they reunite in New Orleans. Dora and Dr. Lewis, as well as Sappho and Will, resolve to "work together to bring joy to hearts crushed by despair." However, instead of showing her characters engaging in this work, Hopkins ends with a tableau of the couples, their children, and Ma Smith standing on the deck of a ship sailing for Europe, where they will visit Mr. Withington, the British cousin of Charles Montfort. In the last image of the novel, Sappho and Will "stood upon the deck that night long after the others had retired to their staterooms, watching the receding shores with hearts filled with emotion too deep for words" (401–402). Although the last image of the novel is of the New Orleans coast disappearing into the darkness, Sappho has not severed ties with her home. Harris, James, Harper, and Hopkins show that wherever their Jewish and African American heroines go—whether they are unmarried or married, working in public or private, traveling to the West Indies, America, England, or France—home, to borrow Ruskin's words, is always around them.[34]

# Notes

## Introduction: "I Thought That to Seem Was to Be": Spectacles of Race in the Nineteenth-Century Transatlantic Imaginary

1. Thomas Allston Brown, *A History of the New York Stage*, 3 vols. (New York: Dodd, Mead, 1903), 2:196.

2. Adah Isaacs Menken, "Some Notes of Her Life in Her Own Hand," *New York Times*, September 6, 1868.

3. Adah Isaacs Menken, *Infelicia and Other Writings*, ed. Gregory Eiselein (Peterborough, Ontario: Broadview, 2002), 48.

4. Ibid., 165.

5. For more scholarship on Menken in addition to Renée M. Sentilles's critical biography *Performing Menken: Adah Isaacs Menken and the Birth of American Celebrity* (New York: Cambridge University Press, 2003), see the chapter "Lincoln's Body" in Shirley Samuels's *Facing America: Iconography and the Civil War* (New York: Oxford University Press, 2004), as well as Daphne A. Brooks's *Bodies in Dissent: Performing Race, Gender, and Nation in the Trans-Atlantic Imaginary* (Durham, N.C.: Duke University Press, 2006).

6. Menken, *Infelicia*, 68, 69.

7. Sentilles, *Performing Menken*, 128.

8. Brooks, *Bodies in Dissent*, 145, 144.

9. Menken, "Some Notes of Her Life," *New York Times*, September 6, 1868.

10. Brooks, *Bodies in Dissent*, 146.

11. Menken, "Some Notes of Her Life," *New York Times*, September 6, 1868.

12. Gregory Eiselein's introduction to *Infelicia* offers a concise summary of the possible identities of Menken's parents.

13. Sentilles, *Performing Menken*, 34, 274. This section of Barclay's biography has become an archival mystery. As Daphne Brooks notes in *Bodies in Dissent*, "The twenty-two copies of this volume housed in contemporary libraries and archives do

not seem to have been printed with pages 25 and 26, the pages which Sentilles cites for this anecdote" (139). A complete copy of Barclay's *The Life and Career of Adah Isaacs Menken, the Celebrated Actress* (Philadelphia: Barclay & Co, 1868) has not yet been located.

14. Sentilles, *Performing Menken*, 283.

15. Ibid., 47.

16. See Josiah C. Nott's "The Mulatto a Hybrid—Probable Extermination of the Two Races If the Whites and Blacks Are Allowed to Intermarry," *American Journal of Medical Sciences* 6 (1843): 252–256; John Bailey, *The Lost German Slave Girl: The Extraordinary True Story of Sally Miller and Her Fight for Freedom in Old New Orleans* (New York: Atlantic Monthly Press, 2005); Carol Wilson, *The Two Lives of Sally Miller: A Case of Mistaken Racial Identity in Antebellum New Orleans* (New Brunswick, N. J.: Rutgers University Press, 2007); and, for more about Anastasie Desarzant, see Shirley Elizabeth Thompson's *Exiles at Home: The Struggle to Become American in Creole New Orleans* (Cambridge: Harvard University Press, 2009).

17. Sentilles, *Performing Menken*, 32.

18. Mark Twain, "The Menken—Written Especially for Gentlemen," *Virginia City (Nev.) Territorial Enterprise*, September 17, 1863, in Menken, *Infelicia and Other Writings*, 197, 198.

19. While critics such as Joseph Roach, Werner Sollors, and Jennifer Devere Brody have examined the transatlantic circulation of narratives about the Tragic Mulatta in the Anglo-American literary world, more recently Eve Allegra Raimon, Teresa Zackodnik, and Cherene Sherrard-Johnson have focused on American representations. In *Neither Black nor White Yet Both: Thematic Explorations of Interracial Literature* (New York: Oxford University Press, 1997). Werner Sollors, for example, examines Child's "Joanna," which many scholars cite as the first Tragic Mulatta narrative, as a retelling of John Gabriel Stedman's *Narrative of a Five Years Expedition against the Revolted Negros of Surinam* (1796). In her exploration of the construction of blackness and femininity in Victorian literature, Jennifer Devere Brody coins the term "mulattaroon" to underscore the status of the woman of color "as an unreal, impossible ideal whose corrupted and corrupting constitution inevitably causes conflicts" in Anglo-American narratives that "attempt to promote purity" (Brody, *Impossible Purities: Blackness, Femininity, and Victorian Culture* [Durham, N.C.: Duke University Press, 1998], 16). Both Zackodnik and Sherrard-Johnson carry the study of this figure into the Harlem Renaissance, where, as Sherrard-Johnson explains, the "mulatta emerges as an iconic figure at the cusp of the Harlem Renaissance, a period in which narratives of passing preoccupied black and white modernists, just as the legal designation of mulatto/a was disappearing." She considers the ways in which the mixed-race woman's "ambiguity and complexity enabled Harlem Renaissance writers and visual artists to conceive of the figure of the mulatta as an imaginative alternative to the dominant racial discourses of the time" (Sherrard-Johnson, *Portraits of the New Negro Woman: Visual and Literary Culture in the Harlem Renaissance* [New Brunswick, N.J.: Rutgers University Press, 2007], 7). For more criticism on the Tragic Mulatta, see also Hortense J. Spillers's "Mama's Baby, Papa's Maybe: An American Grammar Book," *Diacritics* 17, no. 2 (1987): 64–81. For scholarship on the Jewess in British literature, see Michael Ragussis, *Figures of Conversion: "The Jewish Question" and English National Identity* (Durham, N.C.: Duke University Press, 1995); and Nadia Valman, *The Jewess*

*in Nineteenth-Century British Literature* (Cambridge and New York: Cambridge University Press, 2007).

20. Eve Allegra Raimon, *The Tragic Mulatta Revisited: Race and Nationalism in Nineteenth-Century Antislavery Fiction* (New Brunswick, N.J.: Rutgers University Press, 2004), 25, 12.

21. Alphonse de Lamartine, *Toussaint Louverture* in *Oeuvres poétiques completes,* 1263–1401 (Paris: Gallimard, 1963), 1270.

22. Michael Rogin, Eric Lott, and, most recently, Lori Harrison-Kahan have examined connections between African American and Jewish identity in twentieth-century American culture. In addition to Rogin's *Blackface, White Noise: Jewish Immigrants in the Hollywood Melting Pot* (Berkeley and Los Angeles: University of California Press, 1996); Eric Lott's *Love and Theft: Blackface Minstrelsy and the American Working Class* (New York: Oxford University Press, 1993); and Lori Harrison-Kahan's *The White Negress: Literature, Minstrelsy, and the Black-Jewish Imaginary* (New Brunswick, N.J., and London: Rutgers University Press, 2011), see Susan Gubar's *Racechanges: White Skin, Black Face in American Culture* (New York: Oxford University Press, 1997). For additional studies on connections between Jewish and African American identity, see Emily Miller Budick's *Blacks and Jews in Literary Conversation* (New York: Cambridge University Press, 1998); Saul S. Friedman's *Jews and the American Slave Trade* (New Brunswick, N.J.: Transaction, 1998); Adam Zacheray Newton's *Facing Black and Jew: Literature as Public Space in Twentieth-Century America* (New York: Cambridge University Press, 1999); Ethan Goffman's *Imagining Each Other: Blacks and Jews in Contemporary American Literature* (Albany: State University of New York Press, 2000); and Eliza R. L. McGraw's *Two Covenants: Representations of Southern Jewishness* (Baton Rouge: Louisiana State University Press, 2005). While these studies focus on American culture, Jonathan Schorsch's *Jews and Blacks in the Early Modern World* (New York: Cambridge University Press, 2004) considers these connections in Europe.

23. As Shawn Michelle Smith argues in *American Archives: Gender, Race, and Class in Visual Culture* (Princeton: Princeton University Press, 1999), "middle-class privacy was violently denied to slaves and slave families. . . . [T]he horror of slavery was symbolized not only by the breakup of the slave family, as Harriet Beecher Stowe proclaimed, but also by the terrifying exposure to a threatening gaze that preceded and begot violence upon the slave body." On the auction block, the female slave "was relegated to the world of commodities and thereby denied the protection of middle-class domesticity" (46).

24. Menken, "Some Notes of Her Life," *New York Times,* September 6, 1868.

25. Adah Isaacs Menken, "Self Defence," in *Infelicia and Other Writings,* ed. Gregory Eiselein, 180–184 (Peterborough, Ontario: Broadview, 2002), 183; Menken's emphasis.

26. Sentilles, *Performing Menken,* 78.

27. Menken, "Self Defence," 181.

28. Michael McKeon, *Theory of the Novel: A Historical Approach* (Baltimore: Johns Hopkins University Press, 2000), 1.

29. See Paul Giles, *Virtual Americas: British Culture and the Formation of American Literature, 1730–1860* (Philadelphia: University of Pennsylvania Press, 2001); Meredith McGill, *The Traffic in Poems: Nineteenth-Century Poetry and Transatlantic Exchange* (New Brunswick, N.J.: Rutgers University Press, 2008); Amanda Claybaugh, *The Novel*

*of Purpose: Literature and Social Reform in the Anglo-American World* (Ithaca, N.Y.: Cornell University Press, 2006); Elisa Tamarkin, *Anglophilia: Deference, Devotion, and Antebellum America* (Chicago: University of Chicago Press, 2008); Julia Sun-Joo Lee, *The American Slave and the Victorian Novel* (New York: Oxford University Press, 2010); Daniel Hack, "Close Reading at a Distance: The African Americanization of *Bleak House*," *Critical Inquiry* 34, no. 4 (2008): 729–753; Laura Doyle, *Freedom's Empire: Race and the Rise of the Novel in Atlantic Modernity, 1640–1940* (Durham, N.C.: Duke University Press, 2008); and Anna Brickhouse, *Transamerican Literary Relations and the Nineteenth-Century Public Sphere* (Cambridge and New York: Cambridge University Press, 2004).

30. Médéric-Louis-Élie Moreau de Saint-Méry, *Description topographique, physique, civile, politique, et historique de la partie française de l'isle Saint-Domingue*, 2 vols. (Philadelphia, 1796), 1:95.

31. Menken, *Infelicia*, 68, 70. Of course, from the turn of the century through the Harlem Renaissance, mixed-race characters returned to passing in the works of such authors as Charles Chesnutt, Jessie Redmon Fauset, Edna Ferber, Fannie Hurst, and Nella Larsen.

## 1 / "Stamped and Molded by Pleasure": The Transnational Mulatta in Jamaica and Saint-Domingue

All translations are mine unless otherwise noted.

1. François Alexandre Stanislas Wimpffen, *A Voyage to Saint Domingo, in the years 1788, 1789, and 1790*, trans. J. Wright (London: T. Cadell, Junior, and W. Davies, 1817), 49.

2. Ibid., 111–113.

3. For scholarship on the West Indian woman in British literature, see Moira Ferguson, *Subject to Others: British Women Writers and Colonial Slavery, 1670–1834* (New York: Routledge, 1992); Carolyn Vellenga Berman, *Creole Crossings: Domestic Fiction and the Reform of Colonial Slavery* (Ithaca, N.Y.: Cornell University Press, 2006); and Sara Salih, *Representing Mixed Race in Jamaica and England from the Abolition Era to the Present* (New York: Routledge, 2010). For scholarship on representations of French West Indian women, see Marlene L. Daut's forthcoming *Science of Desire: A Literary History of the Haitian Revolution in the Atlantic World, 1789-1865*, as well as David Patrick Geggus, "Slave and Free Colored Women in Saint Domingue," in *More Than Chattel: Black Women and Slavery*, ed. D. Barry Gaspar and Darlene Clark Hine, 259–258 (Bloomington: Indiana University Press, 1996); Bernard Moitt, *Women and Slavery in the French Antilles, 1635-1848* (Bloomington: Indiana University Press, 2002); and John Garrigus, "Race, Gender, and Virtue in Haiti's Failed Foundational Fiction: *La mulâtre comme il y a peu de blanches*" (1803), in *The Color of Liberty: Histories of Race in France*, ed. Sue Peabody and Tyler Stovall, 73–94 (Durham: Duke University Press, 2003).

4. Médéric-Louis-Élie Moreau de Saint-Méry, *Description topographique, physique, civile, politique, et historique de la partie française de l'isle Saint-Domingue*, 2 vols. (Philadelphia, 1796), 23. I use "Creole" to refer to black, white, and mixed-race persons born in the West Indies, but as Sean X. Goudie observes, the term has a complex genealogy: "Colonists of European descent, as well as black and mulatto slaves and freedmen born and raised in the New World, were identified as 'creoles' by the British,

French, and Spanish empires. Yet the term denoted much more than the birth of a colonial subject or slave outside the 'borders' of national origin (Europe or Africa). Most significantly, the term 'creole' was used to account for admixtures . . . between Old and New World 'races' and cultures" (see Goudie, *Creole America: The West Indies and the Formation of Literature and Culture in the New Republic* [Philadelphia: University of Pennsylvania Press, 2006], 8).

5. Wimpffen, *A Voyage to Saint Domingo*, 39, 47.

6. Moreau de Saint-Méry, *Description de la partie française de l'isle Saint-Domingue*, 23.

7. Jennifer Greeson, "The Figure of the South, and the Nationalizing Imperatives of Early United States Literature," *Yale Journal of Criticism* 12, no. 2 (1999): 231.

8. Edward Long, *The History of Jamaica; or, a General Survey of the Antient and Modern State of That Island; with Reflections on Its Situation, Settlements, Inhabitants, Climate, Products, Commerce, Laws, and Government*, 3 vols. (London: T. Lowndes, 1774), 2:283–284.

9. Wimpffen, *A Voyage to Saint Domingo*, 295; Maria Nugent, *Lady Nugent's Journal of Her Residence in Jamaïca from 1801 to 1805*, ed. Philip Wright (Kingston: University of the West Indies Press, 2002), 98.

10. Quoted in Yvonne Fabella, "'An Empire Founded on Libertinage': The *Mulâtresse* and Colonial Anxiety in Saint Domingue," in *Gender, Race and Religion in the Colonization of the Americas*, ed. Nora E. Jaffary, 109–124 (Hampshire: Ashgate, 2007), 113.

11. Janet Schaw, *Journal of a Lady of Quality: Being the Narrative of a Journey from Scotland to the West Indies, North Carolina, and Portugal, in the Years 1774 to 1776* (New Haven: Yale University Press, 1921), 112–113.

12. Karen Weierman, *One Nation, One Blood: Interracial Marriage in American Fiction, Scandal and Law, 1820–1870* (Amherst: University of Massachusetts Press, 2005), 45.

13. Schaw, *Journal of a Lady of Quality*, 112–113.

14. Doris Garraway, *The Libertine Colony: Creolization in the Early French Caribbean* (Durham, N.C.: Duke University Press, 2005), 202–203.

15. Ibid., 205.

16. Quoted ibid., 206.

17. Ibid., 207.

18. Colin Dayan, *Haiti, History, and the Gods* (Berkeley and Los Angeles: University of California Press, 1995), 225.

19. Garraway, *The Libertine Colony*, 9, 29.

20. Moreau de Saint-Méry, *Description de la partie française de l'isle Saint-Domingue*, 85.

21. Ibid., 84.

22. S. J. Ducoeurjoly, *Manuel des Habitants de Saint-Domingue*, 2 vols. (Paris: Lenoir, 1802), cxxxvij.

23. Moreau de Saint-Méry, *Description de la partie française de l'isle Saint-Domingue*, 87.

24. Wimpffen, *A Voyage to Saint Domingo*, 113.

25. Nugent, *Lady Nugent's Journal of Her Residence in Jamaica*, 78.

26. Long, *The History of Jamaica*, 2:331, 335

27. Ibid.

28. Schaw, *Journal of a Lady of Quality*, 112–113.

29. Wimpffen, *A Voyage to Saint Domingo*, 112.

30. Garraway, *The Libertine Colony*, 231.

31. Moreau de Saint-Méry, *Description de la partie française de l'isle Saint-Domingue*, 82.

32. Ducoeurjoly, *Manuel des Habitants*, cxxxvij.

33. Moreau de Saint-Méry, *Description de la partie française de l'isle Saint-Domingue*, 81, 95.

34. Ibid., 85, 95.

35. Ibid., 84–85.

36. Wimpffen, *A Voyage to Saint Domingo*, 114.

37. Quoted in Fabella, "An Empire Founded on Libertinage," 121.

38. David Garrigus, "Sons of the Same Father: Gender, Race, and Citizenship in French Saint-Domingue," in *Visions and Revisions of the Eighteenth Century*, ed. Christine Adams, Jack R. Censer, and Lisa Jane Graham (University Park: Pennsylvania State University Press, 1997), 149.

39. Long, *The History of Jamaica*, 2:274.

40. Schaw, *Journal of a Lady of Quality*, 114.

41. Long, *The History of Jamaica*, 2:274.

42. Ibid., 2:331.

43. William Beckford, *A Descriptive Account of the Island of Jamaica*, 2 vols. (London: T. and J. Egerton, 1790), 1:389.

44. Wimpffen, *A Voyage to Saint Domingo*, 295.

45. Moreau de Saint-Méry, *Description de la partie française de l'isle Saint-Domingue*, 81.

46. Ibid., 87, 88–89.

47. Quoted in Dayan, *Haiti, History, and the Gods*, 179. Dayan also quotes the Marquise de Rouvray, who was writing in "exile from Le Cap, Saint-Domingue . . . to her daughter, Madame de Lostanges, August 13, 1793, Une Correspondence familiale": "Because of the inhabitants' conduct, we cannot count on the return of any prosperity for Saint-Domingue, since the terrible lesson the men have received has not been corrected. Everyone has their mulâtresses that they have brought up or just found, and with whom they are going to produce a new generation of mulattoes and quarterons destined to butcher our children. Here is what must happen: . . . prescribe the destruction or the deportation of every free man and woman of color, after branding them on their two cheeks with an 'L' which will mean Libre" (ibid., 187).

48. Leonara Sansay, *Secret History; or, The Horrors of St. Domingo* (Peterborough, Ontario: Broadview, 2007), 96.

49. Fabella, "An Empire Founded on Libertinage," 121.

50. Dayan, *Haiti, History, and the Gods*, 24–25.

51. French novels such as J. B. Piquenard's *Zoflora, ou la bonne négresse* (1800), François Vatar Jouannet's *Zorada, ou La Créole* (1801), and the anonymously published *La mulâtre comme il y a peu de blanches* (1803) also reimagined mixed-race women as figures of ideal womanhood.

52. Quoted in Dayan, *Haiti, History, and the Gods*, 161. For other firsthand accounts of the revolution and its aftermath, see Jeremy D. Popkin's *Facing Racial Revolution:*

*Eyewitness Accounts of the Haitian Insurrection* (Chicago and London: University of Chicago Press, 2007).

53. Anonymous, *The Woman of Color*, ed. Lyndon J. Dominique (Peterborough, Ontario: Broadview, 2008), 54; hereafter cited parenthetically.

54. Sansay, *Secret History*, 224.

55. Ibid., 29.

56. Ibid., 95.

57. Moreau de Saint-Méry, *Description de la partie française de l'isle Saint-Domingue*, 99; Sansay, *Secret History*, 70. See Elizabeth Maddock Dillon's "The Secret History of the Early American Novel: Leonora Sansay and the Revolution in Saint Domingue," *Novel* 40, no. 1–2 (2006): 77–103.

58. Carroll Smith-Rosenberg's "Black Gothic: The Shadowy Origins of the American Bourgeoisie," in *Possible Pasts: Becoming Colonial in Early America*, ed. Robert Blair St. George, 243–269 (Ithaca, N.Y.: Cornell University Press, 2000), examines Sansay's *Zelica* as a gothic narrative that "decenters race and gender" (261).

59. Sansay, *Zelica*, 1:46–47.

60. Ibid., 2:202.

61. Ibid., 1:25.

62. Ibid., 1:96–97.

63. Sansay, *Secret History*, 154.

64. Ibid., *Zelica*, 3:292, 293.

65. Ibid., 3:304, 303.

## 2 / "Fascinating Allurements of Gold": New Orleans's "Copper-Colored Nymphs" and the Tragic Mulatta

1. Jennifer M. Spear, *Race, Sex, and Social Order in Early New Orleans* (Baltimore: Johns Hopkins University Press, 2009), 192. Spear notes that the "immigration of free people of African ancestry had been fairly negligible until the 1790s, when a small number of French-speaking gens de couleur libre arrived from Saint-Domingue despite the cabildo's best efforts to keep them out, and fellow refugees continued to trickle into the city during the first decade of the nineteenth century. This trickle became a flood in 1809, when 3,102 gens de couleur libre arrived within a single year. . . . This influx of free, French-speaking, Catholic refugees tripled the size of New Orleans' gens de couleur libre population to almost five thousand in 1810. The gens de couleur libre population now made up just less than one-third of the city's inhabitants and almost one-half its free residents" (184). For more about New Orleans's *gens de couleur libre*, see Kimberly S. Hanger, *Bounded Lives, Bounded Places: Free Black Society in Colonial New Orleans, 1769–1803* (Durham, N.C.: Duke University Press, 1997); Judith Kelleher Schafer, *Becoming Free, Remaining Free Manumission and Enslavement in New Orleans, 1846–1862* (Baton Rouge: Louisiana State University, 2003); Nathalie Dessens, *From Saint-Domingue to New Orleans: Migration and Influences* (Gainesville: University Press of Florida, 2007); and Shirley Elizabeth Thompson's *Exiles at Home: The Struggle to Become American in Creole New Orleans* (Cambridge: Harvard University Press, 2009).

2. Spear, *Race, Sex, and Social Order*, 192.

3. Shirley Elizabeth Thompson's *Exiles at Home: The Struggle to Become American in Creole New Orleans* (Cambridge: Harvard University Press, 2009) offers a

detailed account of the intriguing court case *Anastasie Desarzant v. P. LeBlanc and E. Desmaziliere, his wife*, in which the specter of Saint-Domingue jeopardized Anastasie Desarzant's claim to whiteness in New Orleans. In 1858, Desarzant "filed a $10,000 slander suit against Pierre LeBlanc and Eglantine Desmaziliere, both of whom had referred to Desarzant as a woman of color on several public occasions." "With the suit," Thompson explains, "Desarzant hoped once and for all to secure her reputation as a white woman." Although Desarzant lived as a white woman, identifying herself as Madame Maurice Antoine Abat, her mother, who arrived in New Orleans from Saint-Domingue in 1809, was cited as evidence that Desarzant was not white but a woman of color (ibid., 1, 67–110).

4. Quoted ibid., 5; Spear, *Race, Sex, and Social Order*, 184.

5. Many free people of color from Saint-Domingue also relocated to Charleston, where free men of color were influential members of the free community. According to Michael P. Johnson and James L. Roark, the Brown Fellowship Society, which was founded in 1790, was "the preeminent mulatto organization in antebellum Charleston . . . the rules of the society limited membership to fifty and specified only free brown (mulatto) men could belong" (see Johnson and Roark, "'A Middle Ground,' Free Mulattoes and the Friendly Moralist Society in Antebellum Charleston." *Southern Studies* 21, no. 3 [1982]: 247).

6. Thompson, *Exiles at Home*, 142.

7. Harriet Martineau, *Society in America*, 3 vols. (New York: Saunders and Otley, 1837), 2:116. In William Wells Brown's retelling of this story in *Clotel*, one sister poisons herself while the other dies of grief after witnessing her master murder her lover who tried to rescue her (see Brown, *Clotel; or, The President's Daughter*, ed. Hilton Als [New York: Modern Library, 2000], 169–174).

8. Quoted in Harriet Martineau, *Retrospect of Western Travel*, 2 vols. (New York: C. Lohman, 1838), 1:254; William Faulkner, *Absalom, Absalom!* (New York: Random House, 1964), 157.

9. Digital archives may eventually offer more insight into the lives of free women of color in New Orleans. The Archdiocese of New Orleans recently created electronic archives for the baptismal records of slaves and free people of color from 1777 to 1801 (see www.archdiocese-no.org/archives/sfpc.php). Also, the Historic New Orleans Collection is currently preparing an electronic database of the "Vieux Carré Survey," which Howard Margot, who is compiling the database, describes as a "finding-aid tracing the legal, architectural, and, to some extent, anecdotal and cultural history of every piece of property in the French Quarter." For scholars interested in learning more about free women of color who owned property in the city, a search of the database, which covers the years from 1722 to 2000, can provide a list of the free people of color who owned property in the French Quarter. The database, which is still in progress, will be available on the Historic New Orleans Collection website (see www.hnoc.org).

10. Caryn Cossé Bell, *Revolution, Romanticism, and the Afro-Creole Protest Tradition in Louisiana, 1718–1868* (Baton Rouge: Louisiana State University Press, 1997), 13.

11. Quoted in Herbert Asbury, *The French Quarter: An Informal History of the New Orleans Underworld* (New York: Knopf, 1936), 129.

12. Paul Alliot, *Louisiana under the Rule of Spain, France, and the United States 1785–1807*, trans. James Alexander Robertson, 2 vols. (Cleveland: Arthur H. Clark, 1911), 85, 87.

13. Asbury, *The French Quarter,* 129.

14. Quoted in Henry N. Kmen, *Music in New Orleans: The Formative Years, 1791–1841* (Baton Rouge: Louisiana State University Press, 1966), 43, 44.

15. Christian Schultz, *Travels on an Inland Voyage,* 2 vols. (New York: Isaac Riley, 1810), 2:195.

16. J. S. Buckingham, *The Slave States of America,* 2 vols. (New York: Negro Universities Press, 1968), 1:358.

17. H. Didimus, *New Orleans As I Found It* (New York: Harper and Brothers, 1845), 29.

18. Bernhard, Duke of Saxe-Weimar-Eisenach, *Travels through North America, During the Years 1825 and 1826,* 2 vols. (Philadelphia: Carey, Lea and Carey, 1828), 1:62.

19. Ibid., 1:64, 71.

20. Frances Trollope, *Domestic Manners of the Americans* (London: Century, 1984), 10.

21. Schultz, *Travels on an Inland Voyage,* 2:193.

22. Bernhard, *Travels through North America,* 1:61.

23. Schultz, *Travels on an Inland Voyage,* 2:193.

24. Bernhard, *Travels through North America,* 1:61–62.

25. James Stuart, *Three Years in North America,* 2 vols. (Edinburgh: Robert Cadell, 1833), 2:238.

26. Schultz, *Travels on an Inland Voyage,* 2:193; Trollope, *Domestic Manners of the Americans,* 10.

27. Martineau, *Society in America,* 2:117.

28. Bernhard, *Travels through North America,* 1:61.

29. Lucinda Sparkle, editorial, *Louisiana Gazette,* September 18, 1810.

30. Bernhard, *Travels through North America,* 1:62, 58.

31. Quoted in Kmen, *Music in New Orleans,* 50–51.

32. ["Response to Lucinda Sparkle"], *Louisiana Gazette,* September 22, 1810.

33. Frederick Olmsted, *The Cotton Kingdom: A Traveler's Observations on Cotton and Slavery in the American Slave States,* ed. Arthur M. Schlesinger (New York: Knopf, 1953), 238.

34. ["Response to Lucinda Sparkle"], *Louisiana Gazette,* September 22, 1810.

35. Bernhard, *Travels through North America,* 1:61.

36. Stuart, *Three Years in North America,* 2:237–238.

37. Frederick Olmsted, *A Journey in the Seaboard Slave States* (New York: Mason Brothers, 1859), 244.

38. Gustave de Beaumont, *Marie; or, Slavery in the United States,* trans. Barbara Chapman (Stanford: Stanford University Press, 1958), 64, 65.

39. Ibid., 64.

40. Armand Lanusse, *Paroles d'honneur,* ed. Chris Michaelides (Shreveport, La.: Tintamarre, 2004), 78.

41. Armand Lanusse, *Les Cenelles: Choix de poésies indigènes* (Shreveport, La.: Tintamarre, 2003), 47.

42. Kmen, *Music in New Orleans,* 49. For more about quadroon balls, see Monique Guillory, "Under One Roof: The Sins and Sanctity of the New Orleans Quadroon Balls," in *Race Consciousness,* ed. Judith Jackson Fossett and Jeffrey A. Tucker, 67–92 (New York: New York University Press, 1997); and Joan M. Martin, "*Plaçage* and the Louisiana *Gens de Couleur Libre:* How Race and Sex Defined the Lifestyles of Free Women of Color," in *Creole: The History and Legacy*

*of Louisiana's Free People of Color,* ed. Sybil Kein, 57–70 (Baton Rouge: Louisiana State University Press, 2000).

43. Kmen, *Music in New Orleans,* 46.

44. Bertram Wallace Korn, *The Early Jews of New Orleans* (Waltham, Mass.: American Jewish Historical Society, 1969), 178.

45. Alexis de Tocqueville, *Journey to America,* ed. J. P. Mayer, trans. George Lawrence (New Haven: Yale University Press, 1959), 164.

46. John H. B. Latrobe, *Southern Travels Journal of John H. B. Latrobe 1834,* ed. Samuel Wilson Jr. (New Orleans: Historic New Orleans Collection, 1986), 78.

47. Ibid., 77.

48. *New Orleans Bee,* November 30, 1835.

49. Latrobe, *Southern Travels,* 79.

50. *New Orleans Bee,* November 30, 1835.

51. *New Orleans Times-Picayune,* October 27, 1837.

52. Latrobe, *Southern Travels,* 77.

53. Beaumont, *Marie,* 5.

54. Latrobe, *Southern Travels,* 77.

55. Frantz Fanon, *Black Skin, White Masks,* trans. Charles Lam Markmann (New York: Grove Press, 1967), 49, 57–58.

56. Latrobe, *Southern Travels,* 80.

57. Ibid., 77, 79.

58. Martineau, *Society in America,* 2:117.

59. Helen Tunnicliff Catterall, ed., *Judicial Cases Concerning American Slavery and the Negro,* 5 vols. (New York: Negro Universities Press, 1926), 3:589.

60. Eliza Potter's *A Hair-Dresser's Experience in High Life* (1859; New York: Arno Press, 1980) offers a vivid, and perhaps somewhat exaggerated, example of how a free woman of color engaged in various business ventures in New Orleans. Potter's memoir is an important document because it is one of the few personal accounts available from a free woman of color. During her visit to New Orleans, Potter encountered a mixed-race businesswoman whose interests varied from "speculating in pianos" to "buying and selling bales of cotton . . . [and] buying sacks of coffee, and speculating on them." Potter says that this woman even found ways to profit from selling slaves. Upon purchasing a slave who was a "very good hair-dresser," the businesswoman "told the girl that so soon as she would earn what she paid for her, besides fixing her two daughters' heads, she would give her her freedom." However, though the maid brought home forty dollars every month, until she had nearly paid for herself," the swindler "turned round and sold her for very near as much again as she paid for her." This avaricious entrepreneur also used a "nice free girl" to make money by striking the following deal with her: "She proposed to this girl to sell her, and divide the money between them, and then [the girl] was supposed to kick up a row and swear she was free" (151).

61. Martineau, *Society in America,* 2:115–116. Martineau's account of the three doomed sisters was repeated in William Wells Brown's *Clotel* and Matilda Houstoun's *Hesperos.* Houstoun records in her 1860 travel narrative how "those poor young girls—beautiful, delicate, and talented, as I have described them, were exposed in the slave auction at New Orleans, for *public sale.*" For Houstoun, the idea of ladies being subjected to public exposure is more traumatic than the sexual violence that inevitably

awaits them (see Houstoun, *Hesperos or, Travels in the West,* 2 vols. [London: John W. Parker, 1850], 2:76).

62. Guillory, "Under One Roof," 82.

63. Walter Johnson, *Soul by Soul: Life inside the Antebellum Slave Market* (Cambridge: Harvard University Press, 1999), 113, 114. Though most accounts focus on the participation of white men in the "fancy girl" trade, some white women also found ways to profit from the high market value of mixed-race flesh. Martineau reports that "a southern lady, of fair reputation for refinement and cultivation" once "possessed a very pretty mulatto girl, of whom she declared herself fond." When a gentlemen visitor staying at her home began pursuing the girl, the lady says, "She came to me . . . for protection; which I gave her." However, this protection was only temporary: "The young man . . . returned, saying he was so much in love with the girl that he could not live without her. I pitied the young man . . . so I sold the girl to him for 1,500 dollars" (see Martineau, *Society in America*, 2:123).

64. Johnson, *Soul by Soul*, 115. For more about "fancy" girls, see Sharony Green's article "'Mr. Ballard, I am compelled to write again': Beyond Bedrooms and Brothels, a Fancy Girl Speaks" (*Black Women, Gender & Families* 5, no. 1 [2011]: 17–40), in which she reconstructs the intriguing life of Avenia White, a former "fancy girl," by examining correspondence between White and Rice Ballard, a slave trader and her former master.

65. Ibid., 114; Catherine Clinton, *The Plantation Mistress: Woman's World in the Old South* (New York: Pantheon, 1982), 216.

66. Clinton, *The Plantation Mistress*, 217. While Johnson's critics voiced their anxiety over amalgamation, the issue was more complex than the mere mixing of the two races. After all, as Martineau observes, the southerners who accused northern abolitionists of supporting amalgamation were the very people who sold "their own offspring to fill their purses, who have such offspring for the sake of filling their purses." The anxiety of amalgamation, as voiced by Johnson's critics, was not about the existing interracial unions between white men and their mulatto slaves. The undercurrent of southern worries over amalgamation was a latent fear that white women would begin mixing with "black" men (see Martineau, *Society in America*, 2:118).

67. Jean Fagan Yellin, *Women and Sisters: The Antislavery Feminists in American Culture* (New Haven: Yale University Press, 1989), 71.

68. Lydia Maria Child, "The Quadroons," *Liberty Bell*, 1842, in *American Periodicals Series: 1839–1858*, 141, Proquest Direct, http://proquest.umi.com/pdqweb.

69. Thomas Moore, *Lalla Rookh*, in *The Poetical Works of Thomas Moore*, ed. A. D. Godley (New York: Oxford University Press, 1910), 344.

70. Ruth Bernard Yeazell, *Harems of the Mind: Passages of Western Art and Literature* (New Haven: Yale University Press, 2000), 8, 27.

71. Ibid., 8.

72. Martineau, *Society in America*, 2:112, 218.

73. Ibid., 2:118, 127.

74. Deborah Anna Logan, *Fallenness in Victorian Women's Writing: Marry, Stitch, Die, or Do Worse* (Columbia: University of Missouri Press, 1998), 174.

75. Martineau, *Society in America*, 2:117; Harriet Martineau, *Eastern Life, Present and Past* (Philadelphia: Lea and Blanchard, 1848), 263.

76. Logan, *Fallenness in Victorian Women's Writing*, 174.

77. Joseph Hold Ingraham, *The Quadroone; or, St. Michael's Day,* 3 vols. (London: Richard Bentley, 1840), 2:187, 188.

78. Ibid., 2:208.

79. Ibid., 2:124.

80. Child, "The Quadroons," 118.

81. Ibid.

82. Mayne Reid, *The Quadroon; or, A Lover's Adventures in Louisiana* (New York: Robert M. Dewitt, 1856), 89.

83. Ingraham, *The Quadroone*, 1: ix, 80–81.

84. Ibid., 1:152, 2:124.

85. Ibid., 1:160–161, 149.

86. Ibid., 2:100.

87. Ibid., 2:66, 207.

88. Walter Scott, *Ivanhoe* (London: Penguin, 1986), 320; Ingraham, *The Quadroone*, 1:79.

89. Ingraham, *The Quadroone*, 1:81–82.

90. Ibid., 1:84. The narrator in Beaumont's *Marie* describes a similar temptation as he watches over the sleeping mixed-race heroine: "Intoxicated by the breath of Marie who lay against my heart, by the perfume of her hair over which I bowed, possessed by the irresistible enchantment of this solitude where everything lived to love, I leaned over Marie, and my lips met her sweet lips, and I clung to that chalice of honey and delight. Silent joy! ravishing ecstasy! heavenly voluptuousness, yet incomplete! . . . Confident in my love, the pure virgin had no thought of resisting me. Then began a terrible struggle in the depths of my heart. A thousand flames consumed it, and my blood leaped boiling in my veins. Oh, my beloved! Your beauty itself, which inspired these transports, and your innocence, which would render my victory so easy, saved me from weakness and remorse. . . . I shuddered to think that I had been about to stain that white flower, to rob it of its innocent sweetness, to pollute with vice and bitterness the pure well of delight!" (see Beaumont, *Marie*, 149).

91. Barbarina Dacre, *Xarifa*, 2 vols. (London: John Murray, 1821), 5.3.91, http://lion.chadwyck.com. Dacre's drama tells the story of how the Moorish maiden Xarifa is pursued by the king of Granada and is eventually forced to marry him to protect the life of her true love, Hamad.

92. Quoted in Yeazell, *Harems of the Mind*, 70.

93. Also see Sidonie de la Houssaye's *Les Quarteronnes de la Nouvelle Orléans* (Bonnet Carré, La.: Imprimerie de Meschacébé, 1894), and Pauline Hopkins's *Hagar's Daughter: A Story of Southern Caste Prejudice,* in *The Magazine Novels of Pauline Hopkins,* ed. Hazel Carby, 1–284 (New York: Oxford University Press, 1988). In a letter to George Washington Cable, Houssaye gave the following description of *Les Quarteronnes*, a series composed of four intricately plotted novels: "It is licentious, immoral, demimondaine, but it is magnificent!" For example, in *Octavia*, the first novel in the series, the eponymous heroine is rejected by Alfred, her white lover, who seeks a proper white wife after becoming a judge. To avenge herself, Octavia kidnaps her former lover's white daughter and raises her as a quadroon *placée*. She sends her former lover a letter informing him that his missing daughter and his son have become lovers. Upon discovering his children in bed together, Alfred shoots his daughter then kills himself, leaving his son to go mad. As Houssaye explains in the conclusion to

the collection: "And now, reader, my task is finished. I have put before your eyes the different types of quadroons. When a voice is raised to condemn women like Octavia, Violetta, and Adoreah, be indulgent to those sweet creatures Gothe, Gina, and Dahlia, pushed by fate into the path of evil, and more worthy of pity than scorn" (quoted in J. John Perret, "S. de la Houssaye's Quadroon Tetralogy: 'Les Quarteronnes de la Nouvelle-Orléans,'" *Louisiana Literature: A Review of Literature and Humanities* 11, no. 2 (1994): 41, 38.

94. Ingraham, *The Quadroone*, 2:65, 1:160.

## 3 / "Oh Heavens! What Am I?": The Tragic Mulatta as Sensation Heroine

1. Mary Elizabeth Braddon, *The Octoroon; or, The Lily of Louisiana*, ed. Jennifer Carnell (Hastings, U.K.: Sensation Press, 1999), 4; Braddon's emphasis. Critics typically cite Mayne Reid's and Dion Boucicault's texts as the sources for Braddon's novel. However, she plagiarized Jules Barbier's five-act drama *Cora, ou l'esclavage* (1861), which premiered in Paris on August 21, 1861, three months before Braddon's novel began its serial run in *Halfpenny Journal* in November of that year. Barbier was a French librettist and dramatist who, like Reid and Boucicault, was inspired by the "octoroon fever" generated by *Uncle Tom's Cabin* (see Barbier, *Cora, ou l'esclavage*, ed. Barbara T. Cooper [Paris: L'Harmattan, 2006]).

2. Ibid., 61.

3. Few critics have linked American abolitionist fiction to the rise of British sensation fiction. Andrew King notes the "immense influence" of *Uncle Tom's Cabin*, "not only on American but also on British fiction" (see King, *The "London Journal," 1845–83: Periodicals, Production and Gender* [Hampshire, U.K.: Ashgate, 2004], 203). Citing Margaret Oliphant's infamous review of sensation fiction in an 1862 issue of *Blackwood's* in which Oliphant remarks, "It is only natural that art and literature should, in an age which has turned out to be one of events, attempt a kindred depth of effect and shock of incident," Susan Balée links the American Civil War to the rise of British sensation fiction (Balée, "English Critics, American Crisis, and the Sensation Novel," *Nineteenth-Century Contexts* 17, no. 2 [1993]: 125).

4. "America," *English Woman's Journal* 13, no. 74 (1864): 91.

5. See Margaret Oliphant's articles "Sensation Novels" and "Novels," published in the May 1862 and September 1867 issues of *Blackwood's*, as well as H. L. Mansels's "Sensation Novels," which was published in the April 1863 issue of the *Quarterly Review*. The *Sixpenny Journal*, which also serialized sensation novels, began publishing installments of *Lady Audley's Secret* in January 1862.

6. Quoted in Norman Page, ed., *Wilkie Collins: The Critical Heritage* (London: Routledge and Kegan Paul, 1974), 109. A review in an 1864 issue of the *New Monthly Magazine* also describes *Uncle Tom's Cabin* as "Mrs. Stowe's great-sensation novel" (see Francis Jacox, "Brutish Affinities of the Human Face Divine," *New Monthly Magazine* 132 [1864]: 37).

7. Harriet Beecher Stowe, *Uncle Tom's Cabin*, ed. Jean Fagan Yellin (New York: Oxford University Press, 1998), 409.

8. Ibid., 407. For works of literary scholarship that examine Stowe's novel as a work of gothic fiction, see Karen Halttunen's "The Haunted House of Lyman Beecher, Henry Ward Beecher, and Harriet Beecher Stowe," in *New Essays on Uncle Tom's Cabin*, ed. Eric J. Sundquist, 107–134 (New York: Cambridge University Press, 1986); and Jeanne

Elders Dewaard's "'The Shadow of Law': Sentimental Interiority, Gothic Terror, and the Legal Subject," *Arizona Quarterly* 62, no. 4 (2006): 1–30.

9. Audrey Fisch, *American Slaves in Victorian England Abolitionist Politics in Popular Literature and Culture* (New York: Cambridge University Press, 2000), 13–14, 16.

10. Quoted ibid., 12, 23–24.

11. Ibid., 21.

12. Shelley Streeby, *American Sensations: Class, Empire, and the Production of Popular Culture* (Berkeley and Los Angeles: University of California Press, 2002), 11.

13. "Sense v. Sensation," *Punch* 41 (1861): 31.

14. Ibid.; Michael Diamond, *Victorian Sensation: or, The Spectacular, the Shocking and the Scandalous in Nineteenth-Century Britain* (London: Anthem, 2003), 3.

15. Fisch, *American Slaves in Victorian England*, 70.

16. In his introduction to *The Organisation of Knowledge in Victorian Britain*, Martin J. Daunton notes that scientific lectures, for example, "might shade into entertainment. The leading scientists were themselves showmen, using dramatic presentations to win an audience and hold their attention. Equally, showmen used the marvels of science and nature to attract paying customers. *The Origins of Species* sold many copies for a serious work of science; even so, its major themes were popularized by less cerebral means, such as touring shows of gorillas and *Punch* cartoons about the 'missing link'" (see Daunton, *The Organisation of Knowledge in Victorian Britain* [Oxford: Oxford University Press, 2005], 3). See also Bernard V. Lightman's *Victorian Popularizers of Science: Designing Nature for New Audiences* (Chicago: University of Chicago Press, 2007).

17. Quoted in Fisch, *American Slaves in Victorian England*, 75.

18. Ibid., 76.

19. Ibid., 77.

20. Ibid., 120; Estlin's emphasis.

21. Quoted in Margaret McCaskill, "'Yours Very Truly': Ellen Craft—The Fugitive as Text and Artifact," *African American Review* 28, no. 4 (1994): 521.

22. Ibid., 523.

23. Quoted in Teresa C. Zackodnik, *The Mulatta and the Politics of Race* (Jackson: University Press of Mississippi, 2004), 48–49.

24. Quoted in William Still, *The Underground Railroad* (New York: Arno Press, 1968), 375, 376.

25. Kate Flint, "Exhibiting America: The Native American and the Crystal Palace," in *Victorian Prism: Refractions of the Crystal Palace*, ed. James Buzard, Joseph W. Childers, and Eileen Gillooly, 171–185 (Charlottesville: University of Virginia Press, 2007), 172.

26. Quoted in Fisch, *American Slaves in Victorian England*, 71. In 1855, the American author Elizabeth D. Livermore published *Zoe; or, The Quadroon's Triumph: A Tale for the Times*, while in Britain, America's mixed-race slaves became the subjects of serialized novels, such as Percy B. St. John's *Quadroona; or the Slave Mother* (1856–57); popular songs, such as Carl Veley's "Quadroon Dance for the Pianoforte" (1867); as well as the heroines of such plays as *Quadroona, or, The Blot upon Humanity* (1857) and *The Quadroon, the Slave Bride, or, the Tree Cavern* (1857).

27. Patrick Dunae, "(Thomas) Mayne Reid," in *Victorian Novelists before 1885*, ed. Ira Bruce Nadel and William E. Fredeman, vol. 21 of *Dictionary of*

*Literary Biography* (Detroit: Gale Research, 1983), http://go.galegroup.com/ps/start.do?p=LitRC&u=clemson_itweb.

28. Elizabeth Reid, *Captain Mayne Reid: His Life and Adventures* (London: Greening, 1900), 214–215.

29. Mayne Reid, *The Quadroon; or, A Lover's Adventures in Louisiana* (New York: Robert M. Dewitt, 1856), v.

30. When *The Octoroon* debuted in London, Reid wrote a letter to the *Athenaeum* to address similarities between his novel and Boucicault's drama: "With regard to the 'Quadroon' and the Adelphi drama, the resemblance is just that which must ever exist between a melodrama and a romance from which it is taken; and when the 'Octoroon' was first produced in New York—January, 1860—its scenes and characters were at once identified by the newspaper critics of that city as being transcripts from the pages of the 'Quadroon.' . . . It might be . . . in good taste if the clever dramatist were to come out before the public with a frank avowal of the source whence his drama has been drawn" (E. Reid, *Captain Mayne Reid*, 138–139).

31. For more about Hannah Crafts's novel, particularly the connections between American slavery and British sensation fiction, see Daniel Hack's "Close Reading at a Distance: The African Americanization of *Bleak House*," *Critical Inquiry* 34, no. 4 (2008): 729–753. See also Henry Louis Gates Jr. and Hollis Robbins's edited collection *Hannah Crafts: Critical Essays on "The Bondwoman's Narrative"* (New York: Basic Civitas, 2004).

32. Braddon, *The Octoroon*, 374.

33. Reid, *The Quadroon*, 70, 89.

34. Dion Boucicault, *The Octoroon*, in *Selected Plays of Dion Boucicault*, ed. Andrew Parkin, 135–190 (Washington, D.C.: Catholic University of America Press, 1987), 153.

35. Quoted in Werner Sollors, *Neither Black nor White Yet Both: Thematic Explorations of Interracial Literature* (New York: Oxford University Press, 1997), 155–156. For an extensive discussion of this motif, see the chapter in Sollors's work titled "The Bluish Tinge in the Halfmoon; or, Fingernails as a Racial Sign."

36. Boucicault, *The Octoroon*, 153, 154.

37. Lyn Pykett, *The 'Improper' Feminine: The Women's Sensation Novel and the New Woman Writing* (London: Routledge, 1992), 82.

38. Braddon, *The Octoroon*, 236.

39. Boucicault, *The Octoroon*, 145, 146.

40. For other examples of fiction in which the heroine does not know her race, see Grace King's "The Little Convent Girl"; Kate Chopin's "Désirée's Baby"; and Pauline Hopkins's *Hagar's Daughter.*

41. Van Buren Denslow, *Owned and Disowned; or, The Chattel Child: Tale of Southern Life* (New York: H. Dayton, 1857), 43.

42. Ibid., 64–65.

43. Ibid., 56, 57–58. In Pauline Hopkins's *Hagar's Daughter*, Hagar, "her name gone, her pride of birth shattered at one blow," has a similar moment of reflection in front of the mirror during which she tries to puzzle out her identity: "Her education, beauty, refinement, what did they profit her now if—horrible thought—Ellis, her husband, repudiated her? . . . She examined her features in the mirror, but even to her prejudiced eyes there was not a trace of the despised chattel. One blow with her open hand shattered its shining surface and the pieces flew about in a thousand tiny particles; she

did not notice in her frenzy that the hand was torn and bleeding. Then she laughed a dreadful laugh: first, silently; then in a whisper; then a peal that clashed through the quiet house and reached the sorrow-stricken man in the silent library." Unlike Denslow's Julia and Kingsley's Marie, Hagar breaks the mirror, disavowing the slave identity but also acknowledging her now fractured identity (see Hopkins, *Hagar's Daughter: A Story of Southern Caste Prejudice,* in *The Magazine Novels of Pauline Hopkins,* ed. Hazel Carby, 1–284 (New York: Oxford University Press, 1988), 57–58.

44. Denslow, *Owned and Disowned*, 43.

45. Ibid., 59.

46. Franny Nudelman, "Harriet Jacobs and the Sentimental Politics of Female Suffering," *English Literary History* 59, no. 4 (1992): 947.

47. Braddon, *The Octoroon*, 53.

48. Ibid., 55, 56.

49. Ibid., 59.

50. Ibid., 7, 59.

51. Reid, *The Quadroon*, 377.

52. Boucicault, *The Octoroon*, 151–152, 166.

53. Ibid., 169, 183.

54. Braddon, *The Octoroon*, 97, 98.

55. Ibid., 5.

56. Joseph Roach, *Cities of the Dead: Circum-Atlantic Performance* (New York: Columbia University Press, 1996), 217.

57. Saidiya V. Hartman, *Scenes of Subjection: Terror, Slavery, and Self-Making in Nineteenth-Century America* (New York: Oxford University Press, 1997), 16.

58. Stowe, *Uncle Tom's Cabin*, 343.

59. P. Gabrielle Foreman, "Who's Your Mama?: 'White' Mulatta Genealogies, Early Photography, and Anti-Passing Narratives of Slavery and Freedom," *American Literary History* 14, no. 3 (2002): 515.

60. Reid, *The Quadroon*, 304, 308.

61. Ibid., 305. Although New Orleans law required quadroons to wear the toque to distinguish themselves from white Creole women, there are no references to Aurore wearing this headdress while residing on Eugénie's plantation.

62. Denslow, *Owned and Disowned*, 285.

63. Ibid., 286.

64. Ibid., 287, 288; Charles Kingsley, *Two Years Ago,* 2 vols. (Leipzig: Bernhard Tauchnitz, 1857), 1:125.

65. Braddon, *The Octoroon*, 161, 173.

66. Ibid., 175.

67. Pamela Gilbert, *Disease, Desire, and the Body in Victorian Women's Popular Novels* (New York: Cambridge University Press, 1997), 3.

68. Reid, *The Quadroon*, 378–379.

69. Boucicault, *The Octoroon*, 154, 183.

70. E. Reid, *Captain Mayne Reid*, 139.

71. Quoted in Sollors, *Neither Black nor White Yet Both*, 356–357.

72. With Bertha Rochester's wild mane and "giant propensities" (Charlotte Brontë, *Jane Eyre*, ed. Richard J. Dunn [New York: Norton, 1987], 302), and Miss Rhoda Swartz's "big rolling eyes" and "woolly hair" (William Makepeace Thackeray, *Vanity*

*Fair*, ed. Peter L. Shillingsburg [New York: Norton, 1995], 4), the mixed-race West Indian woman is constructed as a grotesque and dangerous presence that reflected British anxieties about racial mixing.

73. Braddon, *The Octoroon*, 210.

74. Denslow, *Owned and Disowned*, 296.

75. Kimberly Harrison, "Political Persuasion in Mary Braddon's *The Octoroon; or The Lily of Louisiana*," in *Victorian Sensations: Essays on a Scandalous Genre*, ed. Harrison and Richard Fantina, 212–224 (Columbus: Ohio State University Press, 2006), 213.

76. Cora's racial passing isn't so much a treacherous secret, but a sign that the text has finally recognized and rewarded her embodiment of domestic womanhood. Subsequent British sensation fiction, however, reflected deep anxiety about women's ability to pass for something they were not. The sensation novels of Braddon, Collins, and Wood depicted ideal womanhood as a construction or a role that a clever and devious woman could perform. In such texts as Wood's *East Lynne* (1860), Braddon's *Lady Audley's Secret* (1862), and Collins's *Armadale* (1866), dangerous femmes fatales—women with a compromised character—passed into the domestic sphere and threatened the social order there until their true identities were exposed.

77. Henry James, "Miss Braddon," *Nation* 9 (1865): 593–595, in *Wilkie Collins: The Critical Heritage*, ed. Norman Page, 119–120 (London: Routledge and Kegan Paul, 1974), 122.

## 4 / "I Wonder What Market He Means That Daughter For": The Beautiful Jewess and the Tragic Muse

1. Robyn Asleson, ed., *Notorious Muse: The Actress in British Art and Culture 1776–1812* (New Haven: Yale University Press, 2003), 5, 4.

2. Jonathan Bate, "Shakespeare and the Rival Muses: Siddons versus Jordan," in *Notorious Muse*, ed. Asleson, 82.

3. Quoted in Rachel M. Brownstein, *Tragic Muse: Rachel of the Comédie-Française* (Durham, N.C.: Duke University Press, 1995), 66.

4. Ibid., 51.

5. Livia E. Bitton, "The Jewess as a Fictional Sex Symbol," *Bucknell Review* 21, no. 1 (1973): 65.

6. Quoted ibid., 63.

7. Quoted in Michael Ragussis, *Figures of Conversion: "The Jewish Question" and English National Identity* (Durham, N.C.: Duke University Press, 1995), 203.

8. Christopher Marlowe, *The Jew of Malta*, ed. James R. Siemon (London: A & C Black, 1994), 1.2.289.

9. Ibid., 2.2.48–55; William Shakespeare, *Merchant of Venice*, in *William Shakespeare: The Complete Works*, ed. Alfred Harbage (New York: Viking Penguin, 1969), 2.8.15–17.

10. Marlowe, *The Jew of Malta*, 1.2.363–370.

11. Ibid., 2.3.49, 34, 57–59.

12. Ibid., 2.3.226–229, 236–238.

13. Bitton, "The Jewess as a Fictional Sex Symbol," 69.

14. Marlowe, *The Jew of Malta*, 2.3.240–241, 3.3.34–35, 3.4.29–30.

15. Shakespeare, *The Merchant of Venice*, 2.3.10–11, 16–21.

16. *The Merchant of Venice* is one of the few Beautiful Jewess narratives in which the daughter survives conversion and marriage to her Christian suitor. Michael Ragussis discusses how conversion is typically followed by the Jewish heroine's demise: "In her illness, which is the path to her spiritual transformation, the 'beautiful daughter of Israel' is robbed of all physical beauty, all erotic allure, so that her conversion, instead of making her available for Christian marriage, simply equips her to die peacefully after fulfilling her role as spectator at the marriage she herself wanted with" the Christian hero (see Ragussis, *Figures of Conversion*, 42).

17. Jean Racine, *Berenice*, in *Mid-Career Tragedies*, trans. Lacy Lockert (Princeton: Princeton University Press, 1958), 42, 68.

18. Ibid., 81.

19. Ragussis, *Figures of Conversion*, 242.

20. Harriet Martineau, *Society in America*, 3 vols. (New York: Saunders and Otley, 1837), 2:310.

21. The American sensation author George Lippard, whose *The Quaker City; or, The Monks of Monk Hall* was a best seller, knew Bulwer-Lytton's work. As Carl Ostrowski notes, "Bulwer's *Zanoni* initially appeared in the U.S. in two mammoth weeklies, the *New World* and *Brother Jonathan*, shortly after British publication in 1842. Harper and Brothers (and smaller reprint firms) soon came out with book versions, and a stage adaptation was performed in the Chestnut Street Theater of Philadelphia within months of publication, in the summer of 1842. Set in late-eighteenth-century Europe, *Zanoni* is the story of an ancient supernatural being who gives up his powers in order to marry a Neapolitan opera singer and eventually sacrifices himself to save her from the guillotine during the French Revolution. Lippard may have hoped to capitalize on *Zanoni*'s popularity by devising a character with a similarly mystical appeal" (see Ostrowski, "Inside the Temple of Ravoni: George Lippard's Anti-Exposé," *ESQ: A Journal of the American Renaissance* 55, no. 1 [2009]: 6).

22. Maria Edgeworth, *Harrington*, ed. Susan Manly (Peterborough, Ontario: Broadview Press, 2004), 67.

23. For more about this correspondence, see Edgar E. MacDonald, ed., *The Education of the Heart: The Correspondence of Rachel Mordecai Lazarus and Maria Edgeworth* (Chapel Hill: University of North Carolina Press, 1977).

24. Maria Edgeworth, *Castle Rackrent* (Oxford: Oxford University Press, 1995), 31; Edgeworth's emphasis.

25. Quoted in Edgeworth, *Harrington*, 298; Mordecai's emphasis.

26. Ibid., 299.

27. Edgeworth, *Harrington*, 70, 72, 75.

28. Ibid., 108, 142.

29. Ibid., 135, 136.

30. Ibid., 136, 139.

31. Ibid., 141, 200.

32. Ibid., 207, 208.

33. Ibid., 290.

34. Edgeworth, *Harrington*, 203.

35. Quoted ibid., 300, 301.

36. Quoted ibid., 303. In the second edition of the novel, Edgeworth, at her father's urging, removed any trace of the courtship between Belinda and the West Indian Mr.

Vincent, as well as the interracial marriage of Mr. Vincent's black servant Juba to the daughter of an English farmer. Although Mr. Vincent is a white West Indian gentleman, the controversy surrounding his relationship with Belinda reflects the ways in which his colonial status was racialized by British readers.

37. Quoted in Valman, *The Jewess*, 24. In *Ivanhoe*, Rebecca's father, Isaac of York, embodies the greed of Barabas and Shylock. However, unlike the Jewish father in Marlowe's and Shakespeare's Renaissance dramas, Isaac is a figure of ridicule who is politically and socially powerless in Scott's novel.

38. Walter Scott, *Ivanhoe* (London: Penguin, 1986), 80, 82.

39. Ibid., 83.

40. Ibid., 88, 89.

41. Ibid., 398, 400.

42. Ibid., 442–443.

43. Ibid., 494, 495.

44. Ibid., 499, 506.

45. Ibid., 510, 519. William Makepeace Thackeray was so dissatisfied with this ending of the novel that he composed *Rebecca and Rowena*, in which he "resolves the religious dilemma of the lovers by causing Rowena's death in a Norman prison and by marrying the Saxon knight to the Jewish maiden, who . . . had previously converted to the true faith." Bitton argues that Thackeray's revision of *Ivanhoe* "slighted the Jewess image by naively substituting the superior aspect of the Jewess pattern—the tragic virgin—with its inferior alternative, the happy convert" (see Bitton, "The Jewess as a Fictional Sex Symbol," 77).

46. Edward Bulwer-Lytton, *Leila; or, The Siege of Granada* (Philadelphia: Lippincott, 1888), 56, 57.

47. Ibid., 33.

48. Ibid., 32, 33–34.

49. Ibid., 30.

50. Ibid., 101, 106–107.

51. Ibid., 101, 107, 118.

52. Ibid., 230, 231.

53. Anna Cora Mowatt, *Autobiography of an Actress: or, Eight Years on the Stage* (Boston: Ticknor, Reed and Fields, 1854), 426; Geraldine Jewsbury, *The Half Sisters* (Oxford: Oxford University Press, 1994), 254.

54. Adam Badeau, *The Vagabond* (New York: Rudd and Carleton, 1859), 267–268.

55. Kerry Powell, *Women and Victorian Theatre* (Cambridge: Cambridge University Press, 1997), 66.

56. Brownstein, *Tragic Muse*, 130, 129.

57. Nina Auerbach, *Private Theatricals: The Lives of the Victorians* (Cambridge: Harvard University Press, 1990), 80; Faye E. Dudden, *Women in American Theatre: Actresses and Audiences 1790–1870* (New Haven: Yale University Press, 1994), 2.

58. Quoted in Brownstein, *Tragic Muse*, 209; Brownstein's translation.

59. Quoted in Georges d'Heylli, *Rachel D'après sa correspondence* (Paris: Librairie des Bibliophiles, 1882), 208.

60. Quoted in Brownstein, *Tragic Muse*, 204.

61. "Rachel," *New York Times*, September 7, 1855.

62. Ibid., 206.

63. Ibid., 208.

64. Ibid., 151, 16.

65. Benjamin Disraeli, *Tancred; or, The New Crusade,* vols. 15–16, *The Works of Benjamin Disraeli* (New York: AMS Press, 1976), 16:195, 215.

66. Benjamin Disraeli, *Coningsby; or, The New Generation,* vols. 12–13, *The Works of Benjamin Disraeli* (New York: AMS Press, 1976), 12:336.

67. Walter Benjamin, *Reflections: Essays, Aphorisms, Autobiographical Writings,* trans. Edmund Jephcott (New York: Schocken, 1986), 157.

68. Mary Jean Dudden, *Women in American Theatre: Middle-Class Subjectivity in Victorian and Edwardian Women's Autobiographies* (New York: Oxford University Press, 1992), 2.

69. Corbett, *Representing Femininity* 14; Dudden, *Women in American Theatre*, 64.

70. Balzac's *Illusions perdues* (1837) also features a Jewish actress and courtesan. Coralie "was one of the most charming and captivating actresses in Paris. . . . Coralie was a woman of a type that exerts at will a power of fascination over men. With an oval face of deep ivory tint, a mouth red as a pomegranate . . . Coralie was a Jewess of the sublime type" (*Lost Illusions,* trans. Herbert J. Hunt [New York: Penguin, 1971], 295). Her love affair with Lucien results in her dying in poverty; she converts to Christianity on her deathbed. Esther Gobseck, the Jewish courtesan in Balzac's sequel to *Lost Illusions, Splendeurs et misères des courtisanes* (1844), is briefly mentioned in *Cousin Bette* as a warning to Baron Hulot. Known as La Torpille (or the Torpedo), Esther falls in love with Lucien, the man who rescued her from prostitution and transformed her into a courtesan. She eventually kills herself when the villain, Vautrin, tries to force her to become the mistress of a banker.

71. Honoré de Balzac, *Cousin Bette*, trans. Marion Ayton Crawford (New York: Penguin, 1965), 22, 158.

72. Ibid., 147, 366.

73. Ibid., 85, 86, 366.

74. George Henry Lewes, *On Actors and the Art of Acting* (London: Smith, Elder, 1875), 23–24.

75. Quoted in Brownstein, *Tragic Muse*, 224–225.

76. Charlotte Brontë, *Villette* (New York: Bantam, 1986), 247.

77. Ibid.

78. Susan A. Glenn, *Female Spectacle: The Theatrical Roots of Modern Feminism* (Cambridge: Harvard University Press, 2000), 3.

79. Brontë, *Villette*, 247.

80. Ibid., 248.

81. Lynn M. Voskuil, "Acting Naturally: Brontë, Lewes, and the Problem of Gender Performance," *English Literary History* 62, no. 2 (1995): 436.

82. Brontë, *Villette*, 191, 192; Brontë's emphasis.

83. Ibid., 195, 196, 197.

84. Ibid., 249.

85. Mary Elizabeth Braddon, *Rupert Godwin*, 2 vols. (Leipzig: Bernhard Tauchnitz, 1867), 1:200.

86. Ibid., 1:201, 202. While the Jewish actress in E.O.S.'s *Isolina, or, the Actor's Daughter* (Philadelphia: Lippincott, 1873) is not a femme fatale like Braddon's Esther Vanberg, she is a spectacle of beauty and desire. Although Isolina Camelli is

identified as Italian, she is also compared to Scott's Rebecca. When a suitor compares her to Rebecca, Lady Emmeline responds, "The same has occurred to me; but there is nothing of the Jewess in Miss Camelli's classical line of features." Isolina is socially marked because she is the daughter of an actor and holds a "doubtful position . . . in society, which prevents her marrying" (415). Lady Emmeline believes that Isolina would have been better suited as a "shop-girl at Woodford, or school-mistress" (415), but the young heroine has decided to become a singer. Lady Emmeline's description of Isolina reflects an anxious distaste for the social interloper, characterizing the girl as a seductress who knows the power of her charms and has tried to entrap Captain Mowbray after she failed to marry his brother. Eventually, Isolina's health fails and she dies.

87. Brontë, *Villette*, 245, 249, 254.

88. Braddon, *Rupert Godwin*, 1:200, 2:99.

89. Powell, *Women and Victorian Theatre*, 34–35. Powell provides an array of examples of narratives that discipline their actress heroines, such as *A Leading Lady* (1891), in which Sybil Collier is scarred in a theater fire, and *Teresa Marlowe, Actress and Dancer* (1884), in which the heroine rejects a proposal of marriage from the man she loves because she believes that she is too tainted by the theater and public life to be a wife. She chooses instead to become a deaconess.

90. Anna Cora Mowatt, *Mimic Life, or, Before and Behind the Curtain* (Boston: Ticknor and Fields, 1856), 21.

91. Ibid., 184, 185, 250.

92. Jewsbury, *The Half Sisters*, 233.

93. Bianca's character is contrasted to the singer La Fornasari, who does not seek a profession, but the money and fame the profession will bring: "Music, singing, acting, all seemed nothing but so many vehicles for glorification of *herself*." Though Jewsbury does not make explicit reference to La Fornasari's race, the opera singer refers to herself as a "gilded Ishmaelite." The brief subplot involving La Fornasari reveals that she has abandoned her son, leaving him with an Italian peasant family to pursue her career, a plot that is echoed in *Daniel Deronda* (see Jewsbury, *The Half Sisters*, 340, 346).

94. Margaret Harris and Judith Johnston, eds., *The Journals of George Eliot* (Cambridge: Cambridge University Press, 1998), 146.

95. George Saintsbury, review of *Daniel Deronda*, by George Eliot, *Academy*, September 9, 1876, in *George Eliot: The Critical Heritage*, ed. David Carroll, 371–175. London: Routledge, 1971; *Saturday Review*, September 16, 1876. Disappointment in the novel's ending led the American reader Anna Clay Beecher to pen a sequel, *Gwendolen; or, Reclaimed: A Sequel to Daniel Deronda by George Eliot* (1878), in which Deronda converts and returns to England, where he eventually marries Gwendolen after Mirah dies in childbirth in Palestine. For more about this sequel, see John M. Picker, "George Eliot and the Sequel Question," *New Literary History* 37, no. 2 (2006): 361–388.

96. R. E. Francillon, review of *Daniel Deronda*, by George Eliot, *Gentleman's Magazine* (October 1876): 411–427, in *George Eliot: The Critical Heritage*, ed. David Carroll, 382–398 (London: Routledge, 1971); Henry James, "Daniel Deronda: A Conversation," *Atlantic Monthly*, December 1876, 684–694, in *George Eliot: The Critical Heritage*, ed. David Carroll, 417–433 (London: Routledge, 1971).

97. Eliot to John Blackwood, September 11, 1866.

98. For more about *Daniel Deronda* as a work of "sensational realism," see Marlene

Tromp, *The Private Rod: Marital Violence, Sensation, and the Law in Victorian Britain* (Charlottesville: University Press of Virginia, 2000).

99. George Eliot, *Daniel Deronda* (Oxford: Oxford University Press, 1988), 102.

100. Ibid., 113.

101. For more about the connections between Eliot and Stowe's works, see Monika Mueller, *George Eliot U.S.: Transatlantic Literary and Cultural Perspectives* (Madison, N.J.: Fairleigh Dickinson University Press, 2005); Jennifer Cognard-Black, *Narrative in the Professional Age: Transatlantic Readings of Harriet Beecher Stowe, George Eliot, and Elizabeth Stuart Phelps* (New York: Routledge, 2004); and Clare Cutogno, "Stowe, Eliot, and the Reform Aesthetic," in *Transatlantic Stowe: Harriet Beecher Stowe and European Culture*, ed. Denise Kohn, Sarah Meer, and Emily Bishop Todd, 111–130 (Iowa City: University of Iowa Press, 2006).

102. Brownstein, *Tragic Muse*, 83.

103. Eliot, *Daniel Deronda*, 183, 186.

104. Eliot, "To Harriet Beecher Stowe," October 29 1876, in *The George Eliot Letters*, ed. Gordon S. Haight, 6:301–302 (New Haven: Yale University Press, 1955). In her response, Stowe declared, "This last work of yours is to be your best," and compared her brother, Henry Ward Beecher, who had been publicly accused and tried for adultery with a married woman to Eliot's Daniel Deronda. After providing a detailed biography of Henry, emphasizing in particular his use of Plymouth Church's pulpit to encourage members of the congregation to donate money to purchase the freedom of slaves in the community, Stowe quotes from Eliot's novel, explaining: "In your portrait of Deronda, you speak of him as one of those rare natures in whom a private wrong bred no bitterness. 'The sense of injury breeds, not the will to inflict injuries, but a hatred of all injury;' and I must say, through all this conflict my brother has been always in the spirit of Him who touched and healed the ear of Malchus when he himself was attacked" (see Charles Edward Stowe, *Life of Harriet Beecher Stowe Compiled from Her Letters and Journals* [Boston: Houghton, Mifflin, 1890], 482, 481).

105. Eliot, *Daniel Deronda*, 160.

106. Ibid., 375, 477.

107. Ibid., 694, 688.

108. Stowe, *Uncle Tom's Cabin*, 440. Stowe's emphasis.

109. Quoted in Brownstein, *Tragic Muse*, 241.

110. Gallagher, "George Eliot and *Daniel Deronda*," 46.

111. Eliot, *Daniel Deronda*, 537, 546.

112. Catherine Gallagher, "George Eliot and *Daniel Deronda*: The Prostitute and the Jewish Question," in *Sex, Politics, and Science in the Nineteenth-Century Novel*, ed. Ruth Bernard Yeazell, 39–62 (Baltimore: Johns Hopkins University Press, 1986), 46, 40.

113. Eliot, *Daniel Deronda*, 548.

114. Before she began writing *Daniel Deronda*, Eliot explored the figure of the female artist betrayed by her body in the dramatic poem *Armgart* (1870). When the opera-singer heroine loses her voice, she must decide how to live as an ordinary woman: "my song / Was consecration, lifted me apart / From the crowd chiselled like me, sister forms, / But empty of divineness." Refusing to marry because she believes her talent would be wasted on a husband ("sing in the chimney corner to inspire / My husband reading news?"), she is eventually disciplined by the narrative for desiring

to distinguish herself from other women (see George Eliot, *Armgart,* in *George Eliot: Collected Poems,* ed. Lucien Jenkins, 115–151 [Suffolk, U.K.: Skoob Books, 1989], http://lion.chadwyck.com. For more about *Armgart,* see Rebecca A. Pope's "The Diva Doesn't Die: George Eliot's Armgart," in *Embodied Voices: Representing Female Vocality in Western Culture,* ed. Leslie C. Dunn and Nancy A. Jones, 139–151 (Cambridge: Cambridge University Press, 1994); Kathleen Blake's "Armgart: George Eliot on the Woman Artist," *Victorian Poetry* 18 (1980): 75–80; and Gail Marshall's *Actresses on the Victorian Stage: Feminine Performance and the Galathea Myth* (Cambridge: Cambridge University Press, 1998).

## 5 / "After All, Living Is but to Play a Part": The Tragic Mulatta Plays the Tragic Muse

1. Kingsley, *Two Years Ago,* 2 vols. (Leipzig: Bernhard Tauchnitz, 1857), 1:122; hereafter cited parenthetically.

2. Susan A. Glenn, *Female Spectacle: The Theatrical Roots of Modern Feminism* (Cambridge: Harvard University Press, 2000), 3.

3. Catherine Gallagher, "George Eliot and *Daniel Deronda*: The Prostitute and the Jewish," in *Sex, Politics, and Science in the Nineteenth-Century Novel,* ed. Ruth Bernard Yeazell, 39–62. Baltimore: Johns Hopkins University Press, 1986.

4. Amanda Anderson, *Tainted Souls and Painted Faces: The Rhetoric of Fallenness in Victorian Culture* (Ithaca, N.Y.: Cornell University Press, 1993), 57.

5. With the onset of the Civil War, Kingsley's attitude toward abolitionism changed when he saw that the Union threatened to "exterminate" the southern aristocracy. He became increasingly disdainful of American slaves and black West Indians. See Robert Bernard Martin's *The Dust of Combat: A Life of Charles Kingsley* (London: Faber and Faber, 1959), 258–259; Susan Chitty's *The Beast and the Monk: A Life of Charles Kingsley* (London: Hodder and Stoughton, 1974), 285; and James Eli Adams's *Dandies and Desert Saints: Styles of Victorian Masculinity* (Ithaca, N.Y.: Cornell University Press, 1995), 112–147.

6. Adams, *Dandies and Desert Saints,* 136. Indeed, a review in *Putnam's Magazine* surmises: "As a *type,* [Marie] is wonderfully well drawn—the idiosyncrasies of the mixed blood being seized with an insight quite amazing, and painted with a minuteness and reality worthy of Balzac. Whatever may be the probability of Marie's theatrical history, every man at all familiar with the character and temperament of the mixed races will recognize the hand of a master in Marie's intercourse with her lover, and with Sabina Mellot. You need not look for the pink-purple of the fingernails after listening to the confession which the poor, proud, passionate girl pours out to her sweet and sagacious friend while the small white hand of the artist's wife plays with her glossy black curls" (unsigned review of *Two Years Ago* by Charles Kingsley, *Putnam's Magazine,* no. 53 [May 1857]: 513). While the reviewer from *Putnam's* viewed the presence of Marie in the novel as a "trifle too vivid and melo-dramatic to consist with the tone of the rest of the work," other critics found Marie and her success on the stage "simply repulsive." A reviewer from *Mrs. Stephen's Illustrated New Monthly* declares: "Marie is an impossible character; and one is vexed to see Mr. Kingsley descend to the machinery of the cheap romances, in the extravagant and impossible successes upon the stage which he causes her to achieve. Transcendent geniuses, in novels, have

become a bore" (unsigned review of *Two Years Ago*, by Charles Kingsley, *Mrs. Stephen's Illustrated New Monthly*, June 1857, 288).

7. Adams, *Dandies and Desert Saints*, 137.

8. Kerry Powell, *Women and Victorian Theatre* (Cambridge: Cambridge University Press, 1997), 31.

9. According to George Henry Lewes, Rachel had a similar ability to mold her physiognomy. She molds hers in the opposite direction, making "a common Jewish physiognomy lovely by mere force of expression" (see Lewes, *On Actors and the Art of Acting* [London: Smith, Elder, 1875], 170).

10. Kingsley employs what Karen Tracey describes as a double-proposal plot, a narrative device that explores "questions and problems about courtship and marriage in the rejected proposal(s) and then partially answer those questions or solves those problems with the accepted proposal" (see Tracey, *Plots and Proposals: American Women's Fiction, 1850–90* [Urbana: University of Illinois Press, 2000], 7).

11. Anderson, *Tainted Souls and Painted Faces*, 10.

12. As Claudia Tate argues, "a woman had to be white to have access to the ideologies of true womanhood" (see Tate, *Domestic Allegories of Political Desire: The Black Heroine's Text at the Turn of the Century* [New York: Oxford University Press, 1992], 24). Indeed, Hazel Carby asserts that although black women existed "outside the definition of true womanhood, black female sexuality was nevertheless used to define what those qualities were" (see Carby, *Reconstructing Womanhood: The Emergence of the Afro-American Woman Novelist* [New York: Oxford University Press, 1987], 30).

13. Thomas Hood, "The Bridge of Sighs," in *Selected Poems of Thomas Hood*, ed. John Clubbe, 317–120 (Cambridge: Harvard University Press, 1970), lines 16–20.

14. Kingsley's novel is one of the first Tragic Mulatta stories to allow a mixed-race woman to marry her white lover legally. Van Buren Denslow's *Owned and Disowned; or, The Chattel Child: Tale of Southern Life* (1857) and Mary Elizabeth Braddon's serial *The Octoroon; or, the Lily of Louisiana* (1861) follow this trend, but it seems that Kingsley was the progenitor of this theme.

15. Quoted in Amy Dru Stanley, *From Bondage to Contract: Wage Labor, Marriage, and the Market in the Age of Slave Emancipation* (Cambridge: Cambridge University Press, 1998), 177.

16. Lord Scoutbush's sister, Valencia, for example, though vivacious and flirtatious—traits attributed to her Irish heritage, or as Kingsley describes it, her "tinge of southern blood"—nonetheless detests being pressured to marry: "Men . . . admire—not me, for they do not know me, and never will—but what in me—I hate them!—will give them pleasure" (see Kingsley, *Two Years Ago*, 1:290, 2:181). Her aunt, Lady Knockdown, who is eager "to get the wild Irish girl off her hands," compares arranging a marriage for Valencia to "those men who carry about little dogs in the Quadrant. I always pity the poor men so, and think how happy they must be when they have sold one" (ibid., 1:291). Valencia's experience resonates with some earlier gossip recounting how a girl whom Scoutbush remembers singing in "Cavendish Square, as innocent as a nestling thrush," was sold to ruin by her parents. Scoutbush and his friends worry that the girl, who subsequently jilted her attorney husband for a cavalry officer, could be robbed of the independent income she brought to her second marriage: "Poor child . . . sold at first—perhaps sold again now. The plunger has bills out, and she has ready money. I know her settlements" (ibid., 2:64–65).

17. Deborah Pickman Clifford, *Crusader for Freedom: A Life of Lydia Maria Child* (Boston: Beacon Press, 1992), 96.

18. Carolyn L. Karcher, *The First Woman of the Republic: A Cultural Biography of Lydia Maria Child* (Durham, N.C.: Duke University Press, 1994), 523.

19. Quoted ibid., 590.

20. Lydia Maria Child, "A Chat with the Editor of the Standard," *National Anti-Slavery Standard*, January 14, 1865, in *The Collected Correspondence of Lydia Maria Child, 1817–1880*, ed. Patricia G. Holland, Milton Meltzer, and Francine Krasno (Millwood, N.Y.: Kraus Microform, 1980), fiche 61, letter 1616.

21. Lydia Maria Child, *A Romance of the Republic* (Lexington: University Press of Kentucky, 1997), 173; hereafter cited parenthetically.

22. Aileen Ribeiro, "Costuming the Part: A Discourse of Fashion and Fiction in the Images of the Actress in England, 1776–1812," in *Notorious Muse: The Actress in British Art and Culture 1776–1812*, ed. Robyn Asleson (New Haven: Yale University Press, 2003), 114.

23. For more about Child's use of the half brothers to critique the construction of racial identity, see the chapter "The Identity of Slavery," in Shirley Samuels's, *Romances of the Republic: Women, the Family, and Violence in the Literature of the Early American Nation* (New York: Oxford University Press, 1996).

24. Nathaniel Hawthorne, *The Marble Faun* (London: Everyman, 1995), 17; hereafter cited parenthetically.

25. Arthur Riss traces connections between Hawthorne's representation of Donatello as a faun and his comparison of fauns and slaves in the essay "Chiefly about War Matters" (1862). Riss quotes the following description of fugitive slaves in Hawthorne's essay: "They seem a kind of creature by themselves, not altogether human, but perhaps quite as good, and akin to the fauns and rustic deities of olden times" (Riss, "The Art of Discrimination," *English Literary History* 71, no. 1 [2004]: 251). For additional connections between *The Marble Faun* and slavery, see Nancy Bentley's "Slaves and Fauns: Hawthorne and the Uses of Primitivism," *English Literary History* 57, no. 4 (1991): 907–937.

26. In the obscure sensation novel *The Beautiful Jewess: Rachel Mendoza* (Philadelphia: E. E. Barclay, 1853), written by B. T., murder codes for the loss of sexual innocence in the young male hero, who is corrupted by the dark crime that threatens the Jewish heroine. When Charles kills the man who tried to strangle Rachel Mendoza, she cries, "'O, he *is* dead!' . . . in an accent, not of horror, but of intense and quivering joy—and her eyes flashed, and her colour went and came, and her bosom dilated—she was the picture of frenzied joy" (14; B.T.'s emphasis). When he visits her the evening after the murder, he says that "hours passed away in a delirious intoxication. . . . [W]e both forgot the dead man, who lay in his rude grave, in the cellar of the house, in which was also our bridal bed" (18). Charles's murder of a man, who turns out to be his half brother, leads to a downward spiral of adultery and crime.

27. Alexandre Dumas *fils*, *L'Étrangère*, trans. Frederick A. Schwab (Paris: C. Lévy, 1880), 17.

28. Ibid., 31.

29. Sarah Bernhardt, *Memories of My Life: Being My Personal, Professional, and Social Recollections as Woman and Artist* (New York: D. Appleton, 1907), 283–284; Bernhardt's emphasis.

30. Henry James, *The Scenic Art: Notes on Acting and the Drama, 1872–1901,* ed. Allan Wade (New Brunswick, N.J.: Rutgers University Press, 1948), 57, 58. Though James wasn't enamored with Dumas's play, it did provide the source for his first novel, *Roderick Hudson* (1875).

31. Ibid., 101.

32. Ibid., 103.

33. Ibid., 105.

34. Ibid., 107.

35. Though she died in 1861, Lola Montez is a persistent specter in Mary Elizabeth Braddon's *Aurora Floyd* (1862–63; Peterborough, Ontario: Broadview, 1998) and Louisa May Alcott's *Moods* (1864). Both authors use references to Lola Montez to exoticize their female characters. For example, in Braddon's *Aurora Floyd,* the eponymous heroine is compared to both Cleopatra and Montez: "She is like Cleopatra sailing down the Cydnus . . . she is like Lola Montez giving battle to the Bavarian students . . . she is everything that is beautiful, and strange, and wicked, and unwomanly, and bewitching, and she is just the sort of creature that many a fool would fall in love with" (93). Like Montez, Aurora's ancestry is ambiguous. Though we are told that her father is a Scottish banker, Braddon ascribes no specific race to Aurora's mother, Eliza Floyd, who had a "dark complexion, and great flashing black eyes that lit up a face . . . into the splendour of absolute beauty" (46).

36. Florence Marryat, *Daughter of the Tropics,* 2 vols. (Leipzig: B. Tauchnitz, 1888), 1:49; hereafter cited parenthetically

37. Marryat's emphasis.

38. Marryat's emphasis.

39. Dumas, *L'Étrangère,* 67.

40. Marryat's emphasis.

41. Dumas, *L'Étrangère,* 173.

42. Ibid., 87.

## Conclusion: "I Know What I Am": Race and the Triumphant "New Woman"

1. Fran Luther Mott, *Golden Multitudes: The Story of Best Sellers in the United States* (New York: Bowker, 1947), 181–182.

2. American figures also contributed to the cultural construction of the New Woman. Elizabeth Robins, for example, has been described as a "species" of the New Woman (see Sally Ledger, "Ibsen, the New Woman and the Actress," in *The New Woman in Fiction and in Fact: Fin-de-siècle Feminisms,* ed. Angelique Richardson and Chris Willis, 79–93 [New York: Palgrave, 2001], 89). Like many of her contemporaries, Robins, who became a sensation in Britain for bringing to life Ibsen's Hedda Gabler, was caught between her professional career and a husband who wanted her to retire from the stage to be a full-time wife. When she refused to retire, her husband, who was also an actor, "hurled himself into the Charles River, weighed down by a suit of armor from the Boston Museum acting company" (Kerry Powell, *Women and Victorian Theatre* [Cambridge: Cambridge University Press, 1997], 19). Robins achieved success on the British stage and eventually produced her own plays, including *Alan's Wife* (1893), about a mother who is executed for killing her crippled baby. In *Theatre and Friendship* (1932), she claims that Henry James responded with "'a start, and a look of horror'" when she mentioned that she might write a play (quoted in Gail Marshall,

*Actresses on the Victorian Stage: Feminine Performance and the Galathea Myth* [Cambridge: Cambridge University Press, 1998], 145). The New Woman writing evidently was as threatening as her fictional representations.

3. Lyn Pykett, *The 'Improper' Feminine: The Women's Sensation Novel and the New Woman Writing* (London: Routledge, 1992), 142. See, for example, Kristina Brooks, "New Woman, Fallen Woman: The Crisis of Reputation in Turn-of-Century Novels by Pauline Hopkins and Edith Wharton," *Legacy: A Journal of American Women Writers* 13, no. 2 (1996): 91–112; Martha Helen Patterson, "'Survival of the Best Fitted: The Trope of the New Woman in Margaret Murray Washington, Pauline Hopkins, Sui Sin Far, Edith Wharton, and Mary Johnston" (Ph.D. diss., University of Iowa, 1996); and Charlotte J. Rich, *Transcending the New Woman: Multiethnic Narratives in the Progressive Era* (Columbia: University of Missouri Press, 2009), which consider nonwhite heroines in the works of such authors as Hopkins and Sui Sin Far.

4. Rebecca Stott, "'Scaping the Body: Of Cannibal Mothers and Colonial Landscapes," in *The New Woman in Fiction and in Fact: Fin-de-siècle Feminisms,* 150–166 (New York: Palgrave, 2001), 158.

5. Angelique Richardson, *Love and Eugenics in the Late Nineteenth Century: Rational Reproduction and the New Woman* (Oxford: Oxford University Press, 2003), 9.

6. Ouida, who saw herself writing against the New Woman, as defined by Sarah Grand, was one of the few writers who featured raced heroines in her texts. As Pamela Gilbert explains, Ouida's heroines "tend to be racial hybrids, culturally displaced, of uncertain class origins, fated by their circumstances and 'the doom of sex' to tragic ends, yet honored for their reliance on self-generated codes of behavior which preserve their integrity in situations wherein traditional gender roles lose their explanatory power." Although Ouida did not see her heroines as New Women, the protagonists in *Under Two Flags* (1867) and *Folle-Farine* (1871) do act outside the bounds of true womanhood. Folle-Farine, "the bastard child of a French peasant girl seduced by a very Africanized Spanish gypsy," is sold by her father as a "street performer and later as a courtesan" (see Pamela Gilbert, "Ouida and the Other New Woman," in *Victorian Women Writers and the Woman Question*, ed. Nicola Diane Thompson, 170–188 [New York: Cambridge University Press, 1999], 173, 178, 179). The father's commodification of his daughter echoes narratives about the mixed-race daughters of planters on the auction block and stories (as in *Daniel Deronda*) of the Jew who sells his daughter for financial gain. Not only is Folle-Farine an object of exchange, but like the Tragic Mulatta and the Beautiful Jewess, her raced body also represents questions about inheritance and origins, as it is believed to embody the best and worst features of two distinct races.

7. Nadia Valman, *The Jewess in Nineteenth-Century British Literature* (Cambridge and New York: Cambridge University Press, 2007), 160.

8. Emily Marion Harris, *Estelle*, 2 vols. (London: George Bell and Sons, 1878), 1:124, 245; hereafter cited parenthetically.

9. Valman, *The Jewess*, 160. Harris's contemporary, Amy Levy, offers a different version of the Jewish New Woman's narrative in *Reuben Sachs* (1888) than we see in *Estelle* and James's *The Tragic Muse*. Valman asserts, "Although Deborah Epstein Nord locates Levy as part of 'a generation of women who imagined, and for a time lived out, the possibility of social and economic independence,' *Reuben Sachs* does not project such a possibility for its heroine, despite her 'strong, slow-growing passions, her

strong, slow-growing intellect.' Instead, like later New Woman writing, the narrative serves only to 'awaken' Judith from her habit of passivity to a bitter consciousness of her oppression, to feel 'hatred of the position into which she had been forced.' . . . self-consciousness itself is her reward" (Valman, *The Jewess*, 187).

10. Valman suggests that Estelle "unconsciously turns to Christian art for a more worshipful valuation of the female: 'she copied every fold of the drapery, every limb and soft curve of her photographed Madonnas, acquiring gradually a firmness and delicacy of touch' (1:9). Her own name, Estelle Mary, evoking *stella maris*, also suggests a secret affinity with the Virgin" (Valman, *The Jewess*, 163).

11. Unlike Amy Levy's *Reuben Sachs*, Estelle and Lexie are not at the mercy of the marriage market. Quoting Levy's article, "'Middle Class Jewish Women of To-Day," in which she asserts that the "shadow of the harem" informs gender roles in Jewish society, Valman explains that Levy "laments the fate of the middle-class Jewess, who is taught to suppress 'her healthy, objective activities . . . her natural employment of young faculties' and 'to look upon marriage as the only satisfactory termination to her career.' In this, she is governed by mercenary concerns, since Jews 'have not been educated to a high ideal of marriage.'" The "mercenary concerns" that Valman cites here are not part of Harris's representation of marriage. In fact, although reuniting with Philip would alleviate the financial strain placed on the family after Dr. Hofer's death, this is not presented as an option (Valman, *The Jewess*, 186).

12. Henry James, *The Tragic Muse* (London: Penguin, 1995); 235, 236; hereafter cited parenthetically.

13. Henry James, *The Portrait of a Lady* (New York: Signet, 1995), 362.

14. George Eliot, *Daniel Deronda* (Oxford: Oxford University Press, 1988), 44.

15. Henry James, *The Bostonians* (New York: Penguin, 1986), 93, 96.

16. Ibid., 125, 130.

17. Ibid., 77.

18. Ibid., 82. James makes a similar move in *The Golden Bowl* (1905), in which he describes Fanny Assingham's "richness of hue, her generous nose, her eyebrows marked like those of an actress—these things, with an added amplitude of person on which middle age had set its seal, seemed to present her insistently as a daughter of the South, or still more of the East, a creature formed by hammocks and divans, fed upon sherberts and waited upon by slaves. . . . She was in fact, however, neither a pampered Jewess nor a lazy Creole." He even describes her clothing as being like the Queen of Sheba (Henry James, *The Golden Bowl* [New York: Oxford University Press, 1999], 26).

19. James, *The Bostonians* 83.

20. Ibid., 104, 176.

21. Though they are romantic rivals, Julia, like Miriam, is also an ambitious "public" woman in *The Tragic Muse* who arouses the uneasiness of men. But as a wealthy widow, Julia is able to interact in the public world of politics in a way that Miriam never could. As Nick says of his cousin, "Julia's a real English lady and at the same time a very political woman" (193). Nick even believes that when he won his seat, the people were voting for Julia. The novel suggests that she was a more effective politician than her husband, who would rather collect things of beauty. In the same way that Peter finds Miriam's public life off-putting, Nick refers to Julia's "horrible ambition" (173), asking her, "Must you *always* live in public, Julia?" (175; James's emphasis). This question comes after Julia has told him that she is inviting guests to

dinner. Just as Miriam asks Peter whether he is willing to share in her glory, Julia tells Nick, "You've got to be a very great man, you know. . . . I *am* ambitious" (179; James's emphasis). Lady Agnes recognizes in Julia the "perfect companion" for a "public man": "She's made for public life—she's made to shine, to be concerned in great things, to occupy a high position and to help him on" (162). Much like Oliphant's heroine in *Phoebe Junior* (1876), who engages in politics by writing her husband's speeches, Julia would operate as the politician, guiding her husband through the tricky realm of politics. (Oliphant, who detested New Woman fiction, wrote novels in which her heroines, who are often the epitome of ideal Victorian womanhood, use their roles as wives to create opportunities for involvement in or contributions to the public sphere. In both *Miss Marjoribanks* (1866) and *Phoebe Junior* (1876), as Valerie Sanders explains, Oliphant presents strong-willed heroines who "reform marriage from within, rejecting the life of childbearing and submission that their mothers suffered, and subtly adjusting the balance of power, so that the estate management or parliamentary speech-writing fall to their lot, while their husbands provide the public façade" (Sanders, "Marriage and the Antifeminist Woman Novelist," in *Victorian Women Writers and the Woman Question*, ed. Nicola Diane Thompson, 24–41 [Cambridge: Cambridge University Press, 1999], 34). When their relationship ends because of the presence of another "public" woman in Nick's studio, Lady Agnes correctly surmises, "Julia would have got over the other woman, but she would never get over his becoming a nobody" (344).

22. James, *The Bostonians*, 328.

23. Ibid., 315, 342, 390.

24. Ibid., 382.

25. Ibid., 433.

26. See Sigmund Freud's "Medusa's Head," which reads this as a myth capturing castration anxiety (see Freud, *The Complete Works of Sigmund Freud*, ed. James Strachey, 24 vols. [London: Hogarth Press, 1955], 28:273–274).

27. Frances Harper, *Iola Leroy* (New York: Oxford University Press, 1988), 205, 208; hereafter cited parenthetically,

28. Pauline Hopkins, *Contending Forces* (New York: Oxford University Press, 1988), 115, 128; hereafter cited parenthetically.

29. Hopkins's emphasis.

30. Hopkins takes up the issue of racial passing in *Hagar's Daughter* (1901–2) and in *Of One Blood* (1902–3).

31. For more about Harper's and Hopkins's representations of true womanhood, see Hazel Carby, *Reconstructing Womanhood: The Emergence of the Afro-American Woman Novelist* (New York: Oxford University Press, 1987); Claudia Tate, *Domestic Allegories of Political Desire: The Black Heroine's Text at the Turn of the Century* (New York: Oxford University Press, 1992); and Teresa Zackodnik, *The Mulatta and the Politics of Race* (Jackson: University Press of Mississippi, 2004).

32. As Claudia Tate observes, the domestic novels of such African American authors as Harper and Hopkins depict "love . . . however, it is not passionate ardor but rather compassionate duty, spiritualized affection, and sentimental attachment. By resorting to the mid-nineteenth-century ideology of love, the authors of the post-Reconstruction domestic novels . . . wed sentimental love to racial uplift, producing a marriage of mutual harmonious satisfaction in which the fictive spouses dedicate

themselves to the progress of self, family, community, and race" (Tate, *Domestic Allegories of Political Desire*, 167–168).

33. Menken, *Infelicia*, 121.

34. In "Of Queen's Gardens," Ruskin declares: "And wherever the true wife comes, this home is always around her. The stars only may be over her head; the glow-worm in the night-cold grass may be the only fire at her foot: but home is yet wherever she is; and for a noble woman it stretches far round her" (Ruskin, *Sesame and Lilies*, ed. C. R. Rounds, 81–113 [New York: American Book Company, 1916], 93).

# Index

# About the Author

**Kimberly Snyder Manganelli** is an assistant professor of English at Clemson University, where she teaches nineteenth-century British and American literature.